Inflation

INTERNATIONAL STUDIES IN ECONOMIC MODELLING

Series Editor

Homa Motamen-Scobie

Executive Director
European Economics and Financial Centre
P.O. Box 2498
London W2 4LE
Tel: (071)229-0402
Fax: (071)221-5118

Inflation

Penelope A. Rowlatt

National Economic Research Associates

London, UK

CHAPMAN & HALL

London · Glasgow · New York · Tokyo · Melbourne · Madras

Published by Chapman & Hall, 2-6 Boundary Row, London SE1 8HN

Chapman & Hall, 2-6 Boundary Row, London SE1 8HN, UK

Blackie Academic & Professional, Wester Cleddens Road, Bishopbriggs, Glasgow G64 2NZ, UK

Chapman & Hall Inc., 29 West 35th Street, New York NY 10001, USA

Chapman & Hall Japan, Thomson Publishing Japan, Hirakawacho Nemoto Building, 6F, 1-7-11 Hirakawa-cho, Chiyoda-ku, Tokyo 102, Japan

Chapman & Hall Australia, Thomas Nelson Australia, 102 Dodds Street, South Melbourne, Victoria 3205, Australia

Chapman & Hall India, R. Seshadri, 32 Second Main Road, CIT East, Madras 600 035, India

First edition 1992

© 1992 Penelope A. Rowlatt

Typeset in 10/12 pt Sabon by Thomson Press (India) Ltd, New Delhi
Printed in Great Britain by T. J. Press, Padstow, Cornwall

ISBN   0 412 35870 0

A catalogue record for this book is available from the British Library

Library of Congress Cataloging-in-Publication data

Rowlatt, Penelope A.
    Inflation: From modelling to policy/Penelope A. Rowlatt.—1st ed.
      P.   cm.—(International studies in economic modelling; 14)
    Includes bibliographical references and index.
    ISBN   0-412-35870-0
    1. Inflation (Finance)—Great Britain—Mathematical models.
    2. Monetary policy—Great Britain. I. Title. II. Series.
    HG939.5.R69   1993   92–33585
    332.4'1'0151—dc20   CIP

♾ Printed on permanent acid-free text paper, manufactured in accordance with the proposed ANSI/NISO Z 39.48-199X and ANSI Z 39.48-1984

Contents

Acknowledgements

The book has grown out of work that I did in HM Treasury in the mid-1980s. This being so, it draws on the thoughts and ideas of the many economists who were there at the time or had been there previously and influenced our thinking. It has benefited from countless discussions with colleagues, and of these, John Odling-Smee was particularly helpful. It has also profited from the comments and criticisms of those on the Academic Panel to the Treasury at the time. I am particularly indebted to David Hendry, Marcus Miller, Patrick Minford and Stephen Nickell who read the papers on which this work is based and passed on their suggestions.

While writing the book I have received help, encouragement, criticism and advice from a number of people who have read and commented on drafts of all or part of the text. These include Peter Bird, Huw Evans, Dermot Glynn, Amanda Rowlatt, Roger Salmon, Honor Stamler and David Walton. Edith Penrose read the entire draft and gave me extensive comments; she has substantially improved the quality of the work. I am very grateful to David Slijper who acted as research assistant for part of the period during which I was writing the book. In particular, he produced the first draft of most of the part that deals with the literature in Chapters 2, 3 and 4, clarified the argument in Chapters 5 and 6 and contributed to the first draft of Chapter 8. Errors and misjudgements that remain are, of course, entirely my own responsibility.

Finally, I am heavily indebted to Dermot Glynn and colleagues at National Economic Research Associates, in particular Judith Aitken, Warwick Hood and Paul Plummer, who made it possible for me to complete the work in spite of my commitments there. My husband has given me encouragement and support throughout, and has improved the quality of the drafting; he and my children have suffered in the way people do if they are close to someone who is writing a book.

Introduction to the Series

There has been a growing dependence in the past two decades on modelling as a tool for better understanding of the behaviour of economic systems, and as an aid in policy and decision making. Given the current state of the art globally, the introduction of a series such as this can be seen as a timely development. This series will provide a forum for volumes on both the theoretical and applied aspects of the subject.

International Studies in Economic Modelling is designed to present comprehensive volumes on modelling work in various areas of the economic discipline. In this respect one of the fundamental objectives is to provide a medium for ongoing review of the progression of the field.

There is no doubt that economic modelling will figure prominently in the affairs of government and in the running of the private sector, in efforts to achieve a more rational and efficient handling of economic affairs. By formally structuring an economic system, it is possible to simulate and investigate the effect of changes on the system. This in turn leads to a growing appreciation of the relevance of modelling techniques. Our aim is to provide sufficient space for authors to write authoritative handbooks, giving basic facts with an overview of the current economic models in specific areas and publish a useful series which will be consulted and used as an accessible source of reference.

The question may arise in some reader's minds as to the role of this series *vis-à-vis* other existing publications. At present, no other book series possesses the characteristics of *International Studies in Economic Modelling* and as such cannot fill the gap that will be bridged by it. Those journals which focus in this area do not present an exhaustive and comprehensive overview of a particular subject and all the developments in the field. Other journals which may contain economic modelling papers are not sufficiently broad to publish volumes on all aspects of modelling in a specific area which this series is designed to cover.

A variety of topics will be included encompassing areas of both micro and macroeconomics, as well as the methodological aspects of model construction. Naturally, we are open to suggestions from all readers of, and contributors to, the series reading its approach and content.

Finally, I would like to thank all those who have helped the launch of this series. The encouraging response received from authors who have contributed the forthcoming volumes and from the subscribers to the series has indicated the need for such a publication.

Homa Motamen-Scobie
European Economics and Financial Centre
London, 1992

Preface

This book describes the way the inflation process works in the UK. The questions that stimulated it arose when I was working in HM Treasury in the mid-1980s and price inflation was falling. What was the cause? Was it due to government policy or to factors external to the UK? Was it related to the dynamics with which inflation passes from the past into the future?

In attempting to answer these questions the first task was to define the inflation sector (Chapter 1). This leads to the identification of the decision processes that contribute to the inflation spiral. From that starting point, I have simply aimed to deduce the consequences for the inflation process of plausible assumptions relating to individual motivation in the relevant markets.

A fair proportion of the book is concerned with modelling and with numbers. This does not mean that the book is solely about modelling. It is not intended as a handbook on how to model the inflation sector of the UK economy; nor is it merely an analysis of the causes of UK inflation in the recent past. In order to evaluate hypotheses it is necessary to examine them against data (the UK is used as a testing ground); to assess their implications for the future it is helpful to discover the interpretation that they would give to the past.

I have endeavoured to produce an account of the way in which the inflation spiral works which gives the reader an insight into the key features and which clarifies the assessment of policy options.

1

Introduction

1.1 THE NATURE OF INFLATION

During the past twenty years we have witnessed large variations in the rate of inflation, both in the UK between one year and another, and between different parts of the world. Further, it is generally agreed that a high or volatile inflation rate is one of the major economic ills. What is it that determines its path? What are the policy options available for controlling it? These are the questions that are addressed in this book.

In economics the term 'inflation' generally describes the prevailing annual rate at which the prices of goods and services are increasing. However, it is a commonplace that all prices tend to rise at broadly the same rate: thus, when prices of domestic goods and services are rising fast this will generally be true also of wages, of the prices of imported goods, of the money supply and of the prices of assets. This is because inflation in one sector of the economy permeates rapidly into other sectors. The phrase 'a high rate of inflation' therefore usually describes a situation in which the money values of all goods in an economy are rising at a fast rate.

The view commonly taken is that inflation should be kept close to zero: prices should rise at no more than about 2 to 3 per cent a year on average. This is because high inflation affects the economy adversely in a number of ways. For example, it distorts the income distribution: because of the difficulty and risk associated with the complete index-linking of pensions, those on pensions tend to suffer (although, in the UK, less now than previously). Also, it biases investment decisions: the cost of borrowing money rises making debt finance expensive in the early years of a project and reducing the incentive to invest. In theory inflation accounting could correct for this, but in practice this has proved difficult to implement. Further, because different prices are set at different times of year, high price inflation is associated with a volatility of relative prices. This can lead to an inefficient allocation of resources: it is difficult for decision takers to interpret price signals correctly when relative prices are volatile. Thus, when inflation is high decisions may not be taken in a way that is consistent with the efficient allocation of scarce resources.

The control of inflation is therefore an issue of primary concern in designing macroeconomic policy. In order to use policy instruments to prevent inflation from rising, or to reduce it when there has been an increase, it is necessary to understand as fully as possible the processes that create it, the way in which it perpetuates itself, and the circumstances in which it declines.

However, it is not an easy matter to discover the cause of a rise in inflation. It is a familiar fact that prices influence each other: wages follow prices of goods and services, prices follow wages; the currency tends to depreciate when domestic inflation is higher than that abroad, and to rise when it is lower, influencing the domestic currency price of imports. Import prices, in their turn, affect domestic prices. The 'inflation spiral' has a dynamic structure that results from the interaction of these markets. The factors that tend to increase or reduce domestic inflation rather than just allowing it to continue at its own rate are numerous and may originate in any of these markets. But it is not usually at all obvious which of the possible causes has been the initiating factor of any particular rise or fall in inflation. Indeed it is usually unclear in which market an inflationary pressure originates; for as soon as an inflationary shock impinges on any one market, its influence is spread across a wide range of other markets by the feed-backs in the inflation spiral and its origin becomes difficult to detect.

A proper understanding of the inflation process requires the construction of a model that separates the internal dynamics of the domestic inflation spiral from the factors that impinge upon it from outside. This will permit an analysis of the influence of the external factors that affect inflation and of their importance in the recent past.

Here we develop a model of price-setting behaviour in each market that is relevant to the inflation process. For each market the price-setting equation is derived from a hypothesis relating to individual behaviour in a specific market situation and fitted to the data using econometric estimation methods. Our final model consists of one equation which is derived from these by substitution. It is a reduced form equation which describes the inflation spiral and, for convenience, I have called it the 'Inflation Spiral Equation' or ISE. Its track of the data is presented. Our analysis of the dynamic properties of the ISE leads to some interesting propositions regarding the response of inflation in various situations and we note the assumptions upon which these are predicated. The ISE is used to analyse the path of inflation in the recent past and to assess the anti-inflation policy options which are available.

1.2 DEVELOPMENTS IN THE MODELLING OF INFLATION

The two main strands of empirical work on modelling inflation relate to the Phillips curve (the relation between inflation and unemployment) and the money supply (the role of the monetary authorities in determining nominal values).

In 1958 Phillips reported an apparent empirical trade-off between inflation and the rate of unemployment, subsequently known as the 'Phillips curve', with its implication that the level of unemployment could, in principle, be used as if it were a policy instrument to control the rate of inflation. In this version of the Phillips curve there is an inflation/unemployment trade-off. In the late 1960s this equation was criticized for implying that it is the nominal wage rather than the real wage that responds to excess supply or demand in the labour market. The Phillips curve equation was re-written by Phelps (1967) and by Friedman (1968) in terms of the (expected) real wage to give the Expectations Augmented Phillips Curve (EAPC). With simple assumptions about price-setting and expectations formation this has the implication that there is only one rate of unemployment at which inflation will not accelerate or decelerate (this was later christened the non-accelerating inflation rate of unemployment, or NAIRU).

In his 1968 paper Milton Friedman stressed the role the money authority might play in the determination of the price level. If the money supply were within the authority's control, if money velocity were constant and if there were a natural, built-in tendency for a return to full employment, then the statement that 'the money authority controls nominal quantities' (ibid., p. 11) would be an obvious consequence. A great deal of work on reduced form models of the relation between money and prices followed, because of the power of this simple proposition.

Since the late 1960s the world economy has been subject to a series of inflationary shocks. There have been massive changes in real oil prices and large swings in the real prices of other commodities. Shifts in policy have involved substantial alterations to tax rates; various forms of price control and incomes policy have been fed into the inflation process. There have also been changes in the institutional structure within which the labour market works, while both institutional change and technological developments have affected the operation of foreign exchange markets.

This has resulted in a number of papers and books reporting work in this area that has an empirical bias, relating the profile of the inflation rate to the various inflationary events that have taken place. In an interesting series of papers Gordon (1977, 1982, 1985, for example) has developed an estimated model of US inflation. He has used it to illuminate the possible roles of alternative sources of inflationary pressure and to identify the factors that may have contributed to the change in the US rate of inflation over specified periods. Argy (1981), in his analysis of the post-war period, examined a number of hypotheses concerning causes of inflation. He also attempted an assessment of the importance of various factors in influencing inflation rates around the world. Tylecote (1981) has provided another view of this.

As a result, a more sophisticated view of the inflation process than that embodied in either the one-equation, labour market orientated Phillips curve or the money/ price reduced form has been developing. The contribution of the goods market to the inflation process has been made explicit. This has encouraged an appreciation of the way in which factors other than unemployment come to influence inflation. For example, Gordon (1985) estimated the reduced form equation obtained by substituting a Phillips curve type of wage equation into a constant mark-up price equation. The resulting reduced form contains considerably more explanatory variables than the conventional Phillips curve. This developing appreciation of the role the goods market plays in the inflation process has brought with it an increasing awareness of the likely influence of inflation in other countries. In particular, there has been an increasing awareness of the importance of changes in primary commodity prices (e.g., Beckerman and Jenkinson, 1986 and Rowlatt, 1987). This raises further questions; in particular we address those that concern the role of the foreign exchange market in the inflation process.

1.3 THE ANALYSIS OF INFLATION

One objective of our analysis is to develop a framework within which the factors causing inflation can be identified, insofar as the data permit, and then to use this to distinguish which of the available policy options may prevent inflation rising and which are likely to bring it down once it has risen.

(a) Definition of the inflation spiral

We treat the inflation process as being a spiral that involves feed-backs and interactions between the four markets that are directly involved in the generation of price inflation. It is this that we call the 'inflation spiral'. Thus, a structural approach to the setting of prices for consumer goods and services explains those prices in terms of current costs combined with a model of the margin for profits and overheads. The costs include labour costs and the cost of fuel and raw materials; the margin may be affected by the prices of competing goods and services. The four markets directly involved in the inflation process are, therefore: the domestic goods and services market (setting the mark-up on costs to reflect the level of demand, competitors' prices and so on); the labour market (setting the price of labour); the foreign exchange market (affecting the domestic currency cost of imported inputs and foreign competitors' prices for given world prices); and, the world market for primary commodities (setting the price of materials and fuel in world currencies). Foreign finished goods and labour markets will influence the prices of manufactured goods and services that are imported from them and so have an effect on domestic price-setting. It is implicitly assumed that these markets work in a similar way to their domestic counterparts.

Given this approach it is clear that if the dynamic feed-backs in the spiral are to be modelled correctly, the exchange rate needs to be treated as an integral part of the inflation spiral. An explicit model of the foreign exchange market is therefore incorporated in our model of the inflation spiral, as well as models of price-setting and wage-setting. This enables us to investigate the effect on domestic price inflation of policy initiatives that influence the path of the exchange rate, and to examine the effect of the path of world commodity prices in world currencies.

(b) Some methodological issues

The approach taken to the modelling exercise is to start from individual behavioural hypotheses in specified market structures. Thus entrepreneurs are assumed to be maximizing profits in imperfectly competitive markets, and the price equation is derived from this assumption. The validity of this assumption is discussed in Chapter 2. Wages are taken to be set in a process of bargaining between profit-maximizing firms and unions who aim to maximize the real wage accruing to their members (Chapter 3). The exchange rate is set in a continuously clearing market; it ensures that the volatile, speculative flows of currency equal the underlying demand on trade, invisible and capital account (Chapter 4). In each case the price-setting process is modelled by an equation which is derived from the behavioural assumption and tested against the data.[1] These equations explain how price-setting in one market is affected by price-setting in each of the other markets.

The result is a set of equations for price changes which include a number of other explanatory factors besides (lagged) price change variables. These other variables are treated as exogenous for the purposes of our analysis; that is, it is assumed that they are determined outside the sector that is being modelled.

The limits of this modelling exercise are thus determined by the following criterion. Consider first the structural equation for price inflation. Any explanatory variable included in this equation which 'trends' with the level of price inflation (wage inflation, or the increase in the price of some other input) is treated as being endogenous to the inflation spiral; a structural equation explaining its path is derived and estimated. Further, any explanatory variable included in the resulting set of equations that also trends with the level of price inflation (the rise in consumer prices that influences wage rises, for example) is treated in the same way: a structural equation explaining its path is derived and estimated. This process is continued until the system is closed: that is, until all the explanatory variables that qualify as endogenous, given this criterion, in all the equations already have equations included in the system. The result is that the model includes equations for all the variables that both trend with price inflation and play a role in the feed-back of the inflation spiral. Not surprisingly, given the variability of inflation, the endogenous variables included in the model tend to be those which are most highly significant in explaining each others' paths.

Given this process of determining endogeneity, the factors that end up being treated as exogenous are all expressed in 'real' terms. Put another way, their influence on the inflation spiral is independent of the rate of inflation and of the price level.

The resulting equations are tested against the data. The empirical work consists of hypothesis testing rather than the estimation of coefficient values for use in forecasting. We are concerned with hypotheses relating to prior constraints on the values taken by sets of coefficients, and on whether or not individual coefficients are significantly different from prior values. Do a set of coefficients sum to a number significantly different from unity? Is a coefficient estimate significantly different from zero? The presumption is that the result of our hypothesis testing will remain valid for data from periods other than that which was used for estimation (although the precise specification of any individual equation in terms of coefficient values may change) so long as there has been no obvious structural change in the market in question since. The equations reported were mostly estimated in the mid-1980s using the techniques current at that time over data from the late 1960s to the earlier part of the 1980s.

The set of estimated equations is then combined into our model of the inflation spiral, the ISE. The track of this equation, which is used to analyse the inflation process, is shown in Figure 7.1.

(c) Questions relating to the structure of the spiral

One set of questions the model can elucidate relates to the degree of inertia in the inflation spiral. To what extent is inflation high this year simply because it was high last year? This property of inertia results from the feed-through of inflationary pressure from one market to another. Thus, the increase in wages this year will be higher if prices have risen substantially since the last wage settlement. Prices will rise by more next year if there have been large increases in labour costs this year. If domestic prices are rising faster than overseas prices this year then the exchange rate is likely to fall causing import prices to rise by more next year. All these factors mean that a high rate of inflation last year will lead to high inflation this year too. What are the assumptions relating to individual market behaviour on which this inertia rests? How compelling are they? Do they imply that the markets work in such a way that there is automatically complete inflation indexation in equilibrium, so that the inflation rate remains constant from one period to the next unless some external influence affects the spiral? To what extent are they supported by the data? Indeed, what light does this throw on the possible role for policy to reduce this property of inertia to which the inflation spiral is subject?

The structure of the inflation spiral is such that the rate of inflation this year reflects a number of 'real' pressures, as well as depending on the rate of inflation last year. These are the factors that cause inflation this year to be greater or less than it would have been given the influence of last year's inflation alone. They include excess demand or supply in any of the markets, direct effects of policy measures such as changes in tax rates or incomes policies, the rate of increase of primary commodity prices in world currencies and the effect of market imperfections such as the possibility of an aspirations gap in the labour market (Baxter, 1973). Another set of questions for the model relate to these. In which markets do the most important of these factors originate? Which of these have mattered most for inflation in the past? Are the data such that an unambiguous answer can be given to this question?

Given this approach to the inflation spiral, the rate of inflation at any point in time results from the cumulation of the effects of all the upward and downward pressures that have operated on the spiral in the past. Some of these are exogenous, random events totally independent of domestic economic policy such as a world oil price rise, or a war; the inflationary pressure associated with events such as these cannot be avoided. Some are the indirect result of government action or lack of action, possibly easier to explain *ex post* than to forecast *ex ante*. Some represent the effect of deliberate government policy initiatives, possibly designed with the intention of influencing the inflation rate.

This analysis of the inflation spiral leads to a better understanding of the factors that determine its structure and an evaluation of the degree of certainty with which the data support the various relevant aspects of it. It is then possible to address the main purpose of this work: to describe the dynamic structure of the inflation spiral and, in the light of this, to examine the likely benefits and costs of the policy initiatives used in the 1970s and 1980s to prevent or to cure inflation, and to search for other policy prescriptions.

(d) Effect of exogeneity assumptions

The model developed is confined to the inflation spiral rather than covering the whole economy. This means that it relates inflation only to the proximate influences on price rises, that is, those that are included in structural equations describing price-setting in the relevant markets; for example, the excess demand in the labour market that impinges on wage setting. For the analysis of the inflation spiral most of these proximate influences are treated as exogenous, determined by factors external to the spiral. Generally, because they are influenced by the policy decisions taken by the authorities, this is a valid assumption. It is beyond the scope of this analysis to look behind them and explain their paths in terms of the factors, including policy decisions, that determine their paths. However, where the feed-back from one of the variables that forms part of the inflation spiral is crucial, as in the case of the trade balance, an analysis of its effect is presented.

An important implication of this approach to the modelling of the inflation spiral concerns the role of money. There would only be a role for a direct effect of the growth in the money supply on price inflation if the money supply occurs in one of the structural equations of the inflation spiral. And, according to the model developed, money does not enter directly into any of the equations; it has no direct structural effect on the inflation spiral. Instead, the activity variables (excess demands and supplies) that impinge on the inflation spiral, treated here as exogenous, will be affected by fiscal and monetary policy. This should not be interpreted as implying that monetary policy is not important to the path of price inflation. Indeed, as is apparent in Chapter 8, since it lies behind some of the most important proximate causes of inflation identified and discussed, it can be of considerable importance.

1.4 THE RECENT PATH OF INFLATION

Throughout the 1950s and 1960s price inflation in the UK barely exceeded 5 per cent; by 1970 prices generally were about twice the level they had been in 1950. In the early 1970s, however, following the oil and commodity price boom of 1973/74, prices rose steeply in the UK with retail price inflation reaching a peak of just under 27 per cent in August 1975 (Figure 1.1).

By the end of 1975 the price level was about twice that of 1970. Price inflation in the UK subsided slowly through the following years only to rise again at the turn of the decade, following the second oil price rise, and reaching around 20 per cent in mid-1980. It then declined to a rate of about 5 per cent at the end of 1982 and remained at around that level for nearly six years before finishing the decade on an upward trend, rising towards the 10 per cent level.

This profile broadly mirrors the path of inflation in the OECD taken as a whole although, as the chart shows, inflation in the UK has tended to be higher than that in the rest of the OECD. However, the profile of the peaks in UK inflation broadly match those in average OECD inflation in both relative magnitude and in timing.

Figure 1.2 shows price inflation in two countries prone to hyperinflation, Israel and Brazil, during the same period.

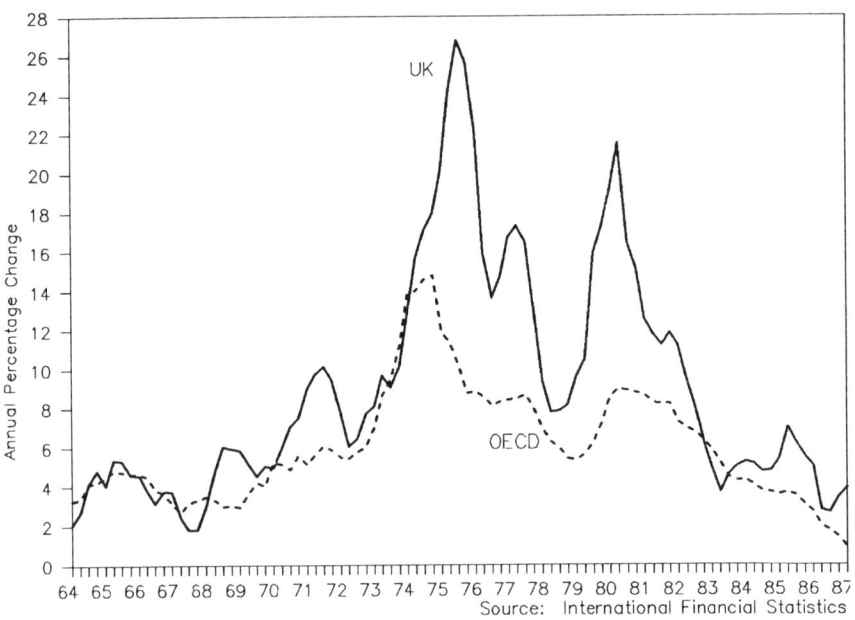

Source: International Financial Statistics

Fig. 1.1 Consumer price inflation in OECD and UK.

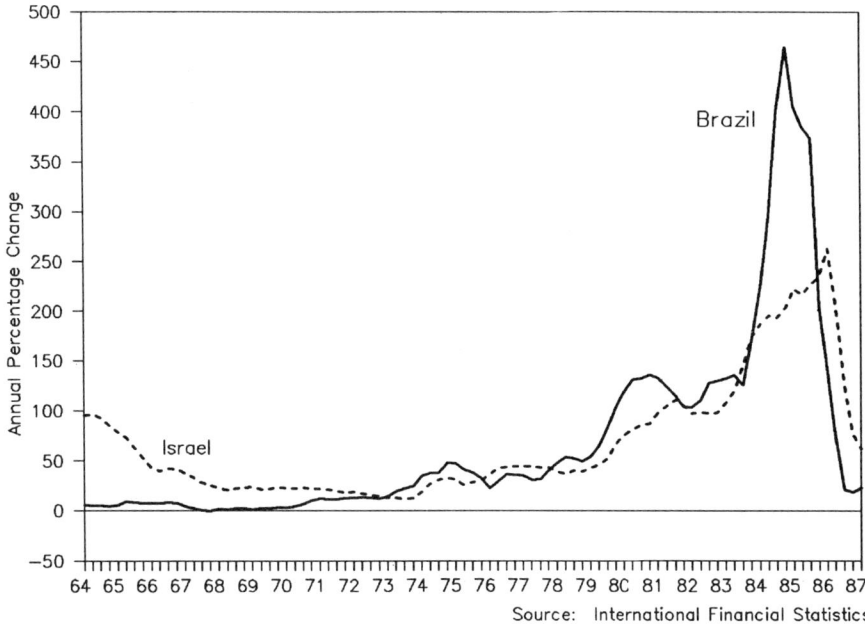

Fig. 1.2 Inflation in Brazil and Israel.

It is clear from these charts that inflation in different countries does not always move in line. Very wide disparities can arise; in particular, inflation can become very high and very volatile.

1.5 OUTLINE OF ARGUMENT

Our objective is to describe the way the inflation spiral works in the UK. The approach involves developing the consequences of simple, acceptable assumptions concerning individual behaviour in relevant markets. The assumptions are transformed into propositions that can be tested against the data. The consequences are interesting and in some cases quite alarming. Policy options that may alleviate the unacceptable consequences are examined.

The process by which prices are set is somewhat different in each of the markets that is relevant to the inflation spiral. These processes are examined in the early chapters of the book. Chapters 2, 3 and 4 examine price-setting in the domestic goods and services market, the labour market and the foreign exchange market respectively. They look at the likely motivation of the decision-taker and examine the market structure. In each case the different approaches taken to modelling price-setting in the academic literature are summarized, and the existing empirical evidence noted. The equation that is to be used in the later chapters of the book is derived from a theoretical approach chosen in the light of the earlier discussion and is tested against the data. Any properties that are particularly important to the explanation of the inflation process are noted.

Chapters 5 and 6 are the core chapters of the book, examining the dynamic structure of inflation and its implications. Readers not interested in the specification of the individual equations but interested in the consequences of the assumptions for inflation should start here. In each of the equations derived in Chapters 2, 3 and 4, the explanatory variables are split into two classes: those which are themselves an integral part of the inflation spiral (prices, wages and the exchange rate) and those (such as unemployment, excess demand or changes in tax rates) which impinge upon the spiral causing inflation to accelerate or decelerate. In Chapter 5 the equations are combined into the reduced form equation for the inflation spiral (the ISE) by substitution into the prices equation and the broad implications of this for the properties of the inflation spiral are summarized.

The equations are dynamic functions and are founded on the assumption of no money illusion. This means that the nominal price level is irrelevant to the inflation process and, indeed, that all the terms impinging on the domestic inflation spiral (apart from world price rises) are 'real' variables. Many of the properties of the spiral that are of interest in the development of our story depend on the dynamic properties of these equations. Chapter 6 looks in more depth at the theoretical implications this has for the long-run determination of inflation.

In Chapter 7 the Inflation Spiral Equation is used to analyse the path of inflation in the UK over a recent period of fifteen years. The contributions of the individual domestic markets are estimated and, insofar as the data permit, changes in inflation are allocated to the separate factors that have been included in the models of each market. The contribution of movements in foreign prices, such as those of primary commodities, is also estimated. The reliability of the results is assessed. This analysis is updated, using the latest data, in Appendix 7A.

The policy implications of the analysis are presented in Chapter 8. This covers the policy options for both the prevention and the cure of inflation. It looks at the potential for macroeconomic policies, operating mainly through the demand side, and examines the conditions under which demand management is likely to be successful in creating a lasting reduction in the rate of inflation. It raises the question of whether the effects of such a policy are merely temporary, being reversed when the economy expands out of a recession, and identifies the possibility that such a strategy may, in fact, increase the likelihood of inflation arising in the future. The evidence supporting a role for price expectations in the determination of the inflation rate is examined. The potential for influencing the inflation rate through manipulation of the exchange rate is investigated.

Chapter 8 also looks at the role of supply side policies and microeconomic restructuring in the tackling of inflation. It includes, for example, the case for intervention to improve the operation of the labour market and a discussion of the likely benefit from restructuring some aspects of the goods market.

Chapter 9 collects together the assumptions, the conclusions regarding the dynamic structure of the spiral, the likely causes of inflation and the policy prescriptions for both preventing and curing inflation. It thus contains a summary of the main points of interest.

REFERENCES

Argy, V. (1981) *The Postwar International Money Crisis*, George Allen and Unwin, London.

Baxter, J. L. (1973) Inflation in the context of relative social deprivation and social justice, *Scottish Journal of Political Economy*, 20, 263–82.

Beckerman, W. and Jenkinson, T. (1986) What stopped the inflation? Unemployment or commodity prices? *The Economic Journal*, 96, 39–54.

Friedman, M. (1968) The role of monetary policy, *The American Economic Review*, 58, 1–17.

Gordon, R. J. (1977) Can the inflation of the 1970s be explained? *Brookings Papers on Economic Activity*, 1, 253–77.

Gordon, R. J. (1982) Inflation, flexible exchange rates, and the natural rate of unemployment, in Bailey, M. N. (ed.) *Workers, Jobs and Inflation*, Brookings Institution, Washington, D.C.

Gordon, R. J. (1985) Understanding inflation in the 1980s, *Brookings Papers on Economic Activity*, 1, 263–99.

Phelps, E. S. (1967) Phillips curves, expectations of inflation and optimal unemployment over time, *Economica*, 34, 254–81.

Phillips, A. W. (1958) The relation between unemployment and the rate of change of money wage rates in the United Kingdom, 1861–1957, *Economica*, 25, 283–99.

Rowlatt, P. A. (1987) Analysis of the Inflation Process, *Government Economic Service Working Paper No. 99*, HM Treasury, London.

Tylecote, A. (1981) *The Causes of the Present Inflation*, The Macmillan Press Ltd, London and Basingstoke.

ENDNOTE

1. We make the usual assumption that the equation relevant to individual behaviour can be estimated using aggregate data.

2

The domestic market for goods and services

2.1 INTRODUCTION

Our object is to use a model of the inflation spiral to examine the inflation process in the UK. The equation which explains price-setting is central to this. We start by presenting the theoretical and empirical underpinning for this equation and identifying the features that are important in the context of understanding the working of the inflation spiral.

Initially, we need to decide on the precise definition of the price index whose path is to be explained. There are a number of different indicators of price inflation. While each one moves slightly differently from the others at any point in time, they all move in broadly the same way over any substantial period (Figure 2.1).

Since we are concerned with the determinants of the general rate at which prices are rising, not with the precise timing with which inflationary pressures affect any particular price indicator, this choice is not of great strategic importance.

The behavioural equation that is developed for domestic price-setting is designed to explain the path of factory gate prices (before value added tax) that are set in the UK manufacturing sector. The dependent variable is therefore the Producer Price Index (Output), or PPIO. The version that omits the food, drink and tobacco sectors has been chosen because variations in these prices are particularly heavily influenced by temporary factors such as weather, seasonal variations and detailed changes in government policy. The Producer Price Index is chosen rather than the conventional indicator of price inflation, the Retail Prices Index (RPI), because the latter includes special factors such as mortgage interest rates (which move in a very different manner from prices generally), and nationalized industry prices and local authority rents (which are set in the public sector and influenced by different factors from those that determine private sector price-setting behaviour). It is also preferred to the GDP deflator which, being constructed from an identity that adds net exports on to domestic demand, responds in a rather unusual way to changes in import prices: a rise in import prices leads, initially, to smaller increases (or larger falls) in the GDP deflator than would otherwise have been the case.

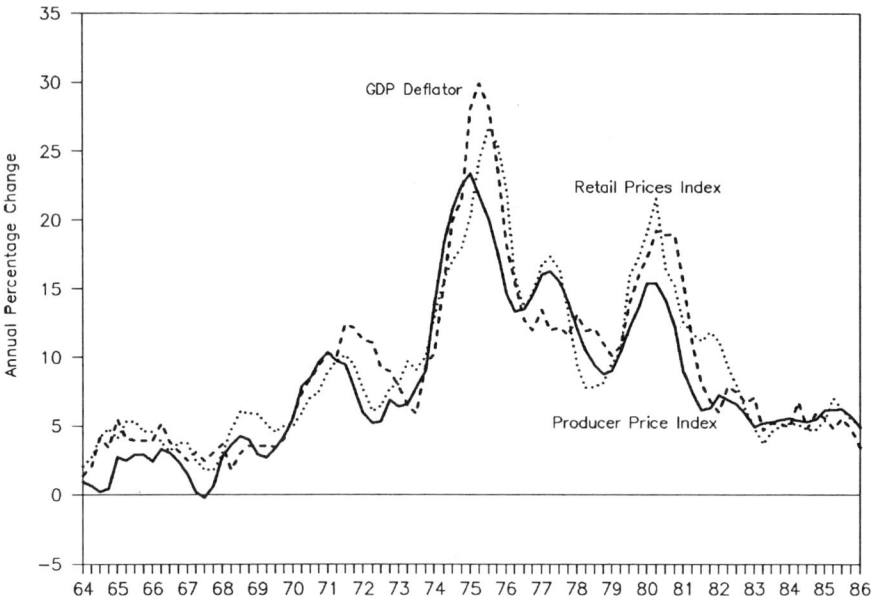

Fig. 2.1 Price inflation indicators.

However, the RPI cannot be ignored in this work. It is the conventional measure of price inflation in the UK and, as such, includes the prices most relevant to the wage-setting process (the prices of the services and commodities bought by consumers as well as the prices of manufactured goods). It is therefore an essential part of any model of the inflation process. An equation relating the path of the RPI to that of the Producer Price Index, along with other relevant factors, is described in Appendix 2A.

In section 2.2 the theoretical approach to the modelling of price-setting is examined. Section 2.3 summarizes the existing empirical results concerning price-setting. The derivation of our equation for price-setting takes account of these, and is presented in section 2.4. Section 2.5 reports the results of estimating this equation. It also identifies the aspects of the equation that matter for the analysis of the inflation process and includes an assessment of the support given to these by the data. Finally, section 2.6 notes some specific policy implications which will follow from the model if this equation is incorporated into the model of the inflation spiral.

Some of the explanatory variables in the equation for domestic price-setting relate to the path of the sterling prices of imported goods and services. Thus, in addition to constructing a model of price-setting for goods and services produced within the domestic economy, an explanation of how the foreign currency prices of imported goods and services are converted into prices in domestic currency is needed. Without this we cannot complete the model of the inflation spiral.

Appendix 2B reports equations which model the domestic currency prices of imported finished goods and services, and of primary commodities, in terms of their foreign currency prices given the path of the exchange rate. The question of the determinants of the path of the exchange rate is addressed in Chapter 4.

2.2 THEORETICAL APPROACHES

2.2.1 Introduction

In order to establish a sound theoretical basis for a model of price-setting in any final market for goods or services we need to address three issues. One concerns motivation. It may be that decision-takers, setting prices and choosing the level of output, are attempting to maximize some indicator of profits over some time horizon. However, there may be a principal-agent problem: if the decision-takers do not themselves benefit by increasing profits they may, in fact, have some other objective. The theoretical discussion below (section 2.2.2) considers whether distinctions such as these are likely to be significant for the modelling and understanding of the inflation process.

The second main area where assumptions are needed concerns the nature of the market. Do the producers sell at the price that is operating in the market or is their product differentiated from that of other producers, allowing them to set their own price and take the consequences on the demand for their product? This issue is discussed in section 2.2.3.

Third, it may be difficult to obtain the information needed to implement an optimizing policy with a reasonable expectation of success. One issue concerns the likely effect of uncertainty about the level of demand on the outcome for price and output; this is discussed in section 2.2.4. However, if there is not adequate information, then the firm's approach may change more radically: it could be that a rule of thumb is more cost-effective than any explicit attempt at optimization in achieving the desired objective. Section 2.2.5 examines the case for this.

Our conclusions on the theoretical underpinning for the estimated price equation are summarized in section 2.2.6.

2.2.2 The corporate objective

(a) Profit maximization and price-setting

The assumption that profit maximization is the principal corporate objective has been much criticized by academic economists for being oversimplistic and not representative of behaviour.[1] Yet it is the cornerstone on which a great and complex array of theories has been built. Conditional upon the assumption that decision-takers are seeking to maximize profits, economists are able to predict how investment, pricing and output decisions would be taken in the presence of any number of different market conditions. But how valuable can these results be if they are based on an unrealistic abstraction of behaviour?

Before addressing this question we note the form this assumption takes when it is to be used in an equation to describe aggregate price-setting behaviour. Price and output decisions are taken on a short-run basis. That is, they are constrained by the amount of capacity that is available, and reflect a view of the current level of demand and of competitors' current price behaviour. The financial variable that is being maximized when this decision is taken, given that the decision-taker is interested in maximizing profits in the long run, is therefore operating cash-flow (total revenue less operating costs). The investment decision, along with the method of financing (given taxation), is taken with a view to maximizing profits (profits after interest and taxation), and this has implications for both output and prices if the paths of the relevant variables turn out as expected.

(b) The relevance of dynamic issues

A criticism of this short-run characterization of the profit maximization assumption is that it ignores the dynamic nature of pricing behaviour. For example, if high prices charged in an industry in the short run enable unusually large profits to be made, this is likely to attract an influx of new competitors into the area.[2] This could lead to a situation in which a lower price needs to be set in some future period, possibly so low that revenue at that time is insufficient to cover long term costs. To what extent are feed-backs such as this predictable? If they are, then this suggests that it might be more realistic to assume that prices are set to maximize the present value of the expected stream of future operating cash-flow, discounted at some appropriate rate.

Of course, ideas such as these are more relevant to the setting of individual prices than to the path of a price index. The effect of dynamic feed-backs such as this, which may result in prices higher or lower than they would otherwise have been, will tend to cancel out when we look at the path of an index constructed from a great number of individual prices. However, to the extent that this is not the case, two factors are relevant. First, the implication may be that the mark-up on costs is smoothed over the cycle and is therefore independent of the path of demand. This we can test against the data (section 2.5). Second, any attempt to take on board the implications of these dynamic considerations will run into the problems involved in modelling expectations of the future values of variables. Again, an attempt can be made to assess the relevance of expectations (section 2.5) but the significance of the outcome of this test will inevitably depend on the extent to which a good proxy for expectations is obtained.

(c) Alternative objectives

The other main criticism of the assumption that prices are set with a view to maximizing operating cash-flow in the short term is simply that it may, in fact, be the case that other objectives matter more to the decision-taker. There has been a number of proposals for other aspects of corporate success which could be relevant. We examine the two most popular of these.

Baumol (1959) suggested that firms might attempt to maximize **revenue** subject to a constraint on the minimum acceptable level of profits. Under profit maximization output will be increased until the revenue from selling an additional unit is less than the cost of producing it. If instead output is increased until profits fall to the minimum level acceptable, then firms will produce a greater output and charge a lower price at the margin than would have been the case under profit maximization. Indeed, if revenue is being maximized, firms will aim to earn a rate of profit equal to the minimum that is acceptable whenever that is feasible. Baumol argued that whenever profits are greater than the minimum acceptable level the firm will spend the excess on advertising aimed to increase total sales given the price level. If profits seem likely to be less than this minimum, the firm may cut back the demand for its output (increase the price). The modelling issue that arises with Baumol's approach concerns the requirement for a model of the level of profit that is considered acceptable: both output and price decisions are very sensitive to this.

Marris' (1964) suggestion is quite similar to that of Baumol: it is that managers seek to maximize the **rate of growth** of the firm subject to an adequate degree of security (from the possibility of takeover). Growth is financed by means of a capital market and through this the security requirement imposes a constraint on the speed at which a firm can expand. As with Baumol's hypothesis, the price and output decisions predicted by Marris' growth model depend on the assumptions made about the operation of the constraint. Again, this is related to the amount of profits earned.

Empirical evidence lends some support both to the profit maximization assumption and to Baumol's revenue maximizing hypothesis. Survey results (section 2.3) find that firms usually report profit as being an important factor in their objective functions, although this is rarely viewed as being the sole corporate objective.

It is clear that the level of profits will be of crucial concern in every objective function suggested; if it were not the firm would be unlikely to survive. The variables relevant to profit maximization are therefore likely to be those that will be included in a decision function deriving from any plausible objective function; the values of the parameters may vary. In this study the values of the parameters are to be informed by the data, so the question of the precise specification of the price-setter's objective is of little importance so long as the coefficient estimates are plausible in the light of the likely objective. In the absence of a consensus for some alternative behavioural assumption, we therefore take our starting point for the motivation underlying price-setting to be that price-setters aim to maximize short-run operating cash-flow.

2.2.3 Effect of market structure

Two main types of market for goods and services are explored in the academic literature. One is the perfectly competitive market, in which the demand elasticity facing each participant is infinite and the price is always such as to clear the market (demand and supply are always equal). We note, with Arrow (1959), that in this perfectly competitive market all firms are price takers: none has the market power to set its own price level, it can only choose the output. This means that, effectively, the prices have to be treated as if they were set in the tâtonnement process described by Arrow and Hahn (1971); the result is as if a 'super-auctioneer' sets prices with the objective of clearing the market.

In the second type of market, entrepreneurs set the prices at which their goods or services will be marketed; they choose the quantity of the output they expect to sell given the prices of competing goods and their view of the level and response of demand, taking into account the prices of the inputs and the production process. Demand is not necessarily equal to supply. Mistakes in estimating the level of demand or in assessing its reaction to relative price differentials result in a build-up (or run-down) of stocks, rationing, queuing, price rises (or cuts) and/or an increase (or decrease) in imports. The effects of these mistakes concerning demand levels will feed back onto future output and price behaviour.

The second type of market is of interest in the context of price-setting in the domestic goods and services market. If prices are set in a market in which goods are heterogeneous and entrepreneurs can choose their own price, then they can usefully be viewed as being set as a mark-up on costs. However, given profit maximization, the size of the mark-up will vary with the level of demand and other producers' prices (apart from in the special case explored by Lerner (1944) in which the elasticity of demand is constant).

The literature relating to price-setting in this market has been concerned mainly with four aspects of the price equation. First, there is the measure of costs to be included: should it be actual costs, or should it be assumed that entrepreneurs will price with respect to some smoothed or trend measure of costs, known as 'normal' costs? This is largely a matter for the data to resolve, and the published evidence is summarized in section 2.3. Second, is the question of uncertainty; to what extent and in what way does uncertainty concerning the current or future level of relevant variables, such as demand, affect the level of prices implied by profit maximization? This is addressed in section 2.2.4. Third, and related to the uncertainty issue, there is the rule of thumb question. Given the problems with obtaining information, is the optimal decision-taking strategy the use of a rule of thumb? We examine this issue in section 2.2.5. Finally, given all of the above, will the mark-up vary with the level of demand? This is of obvious importance to our analysis of the inflation spiral and, again, it is the data that will give us the answer, see section 2.3.

2.2.4 Profit maximizing under uncertainty

There is a substantial body of literature[3] which compares the pricing and output decisions of a profit maximizing firm facing uncertain demand with the decision that would be made under the standard, unrealistic assumption that the firm faces no uncertainty. Does this have any contribution to make to the specification of the price equation?

In fact, the results of this work seem to have little relevance to the understanding of the inflation process. The conclusions that can be drawn from the studies are inconclusive and depend critically on five issues:

- the precise functional form in which uncertainty is entered into the demand function;
- the choice of behavioural mode under which the firm is assumed to operate;
- the firm's assumed attitude towards risk;
- aspects of the costs faced by the firm;
- the time horizon considered.

Further, the conclusions relate mainly to whether or not prices and output will be higher or lower in the face of uncertainty than would have been the case with certainty. They suggest that various of the parameters in the price equation may take different values depending on the existence and extent of uncertainty and on the precise form it takes. They also imply that uncertainty will only affect the rate of inflation if the degree of uncertainty were suddenly to change substantially.

We conclude that no changes to the basic specification of the equation are needed because the firm is operating in an uncertain environment, since the values of the coefficients are to be derived from the data.

2.2.5 Rules of thumb

In the face of uncertainty, it may be rational for the firm to abandon the explicit attempt to maximize profits and, instead, to use a 'rule of thumb' to set prices.

The role of rules of thumb in the context of price-setting has been treated in the classic paper by Baumol and Quandt (1964). Where information is imperfect and costly to obtain Baumol and Quandt suggest that truly rational management will only acquire information up to the point where the incremental cost of additional information is equal to its expected yield. The optimal amount of information may not be sufficient to perform any sort of maximization with sufficient accuracy. In this case it will be optimal for firms to use cruder, but more efficient rules of thumb. In a simulation experiment Baumol and Quandt found these 'optimally imperfect decision rules' could produce profit rates remarkably close to the maximum obtainable with perfect information.

This issue is crucial to our thesis. We aim to identify those factors that impinge on the inflation cycle, causing it to speed up or slow down; and a price equation that takes the form of a constant mark-up on costs will contribute very little to the story. The decision to include a role for demand in the mark-up on costs has implications both for the causes of inflation and for the policy prescriptions for controlling inflation.

2.2.6 Conclusion

We conclude that a reasonable starting point for the modelling of price-setting behaviour is the assumption that decision-takers are attempting to maximize operating cash-flow and are setting prices for differentiated goods in a market in which the demand for them is price elastic. The empirical analysis should reveal whether the variables that this approach suggests are relevant to setting the mark-up have a significant effect or whether, instead, a fixed mark-up on costs is to be preferred.

2.3 RESULTS OF EMPIRICAL WORK

2.3.1 Introduction

Econometric investigations into price setting have attempted to deal principally with the questions raised in section 2.2.3. First, given that prices are viewed as responding to costs: do they react to changes in actual costs, or do they respond instead to changes in 'normal' or trend costs? The answer to this question may be relevant to the degree of inertia in the inflation spiral; it may affect the feed-through of inflationary pressures into the longer term rate at which prices rise. Second, excess demand appears to influence prices: does it exert a direct and independent effect on prices through the mark-up, or is its effect confined to its influence on unit costs, operating through factor prices and, in particular, through unit labour costs? The answer to this is relevant to the policy issue of the effect on inflation of measures to control the level of aggregate demand.

The literature has concentrated on the hypothesis that prices are a constant mark-up on trend costs. Tests of this against the hypothesis of a demand dependent mark-up are difficult to devise. Advocates of the normal cost hypothesis define normal costs in such a way that the main determinant of the difference between them and actual costs is the difference between trend and actual productivity. Obviously, this is correlated with the deviation of demand from trend. This means that the discrepancy between actual and normal costs automatically mops up a substantial portion of any demand dependence of the profit margin. This being so, it may not be possible to reject the normal cost hypothesis even if it were invalid.

Section 2.3.2 briefly reviews some of the attempts over the past few decades to use econometrics to elucidate the answers to these questions. Section 2.3.3 contains a summary of the evidence on pricing in practice that can be derived from surveys of price-setters.

2.3.2 Econometric results

The first econometric investigations of price-setting concentrated mainly on the reaction of prices to changes in costs. Indeed, early empirical work on price equations supported the hypothesis that prices were a simple mark-up on unit costs. The controversial issues at that time concerned whether the labour cost variable should contain trend or actual productivity variables, the existence of lags between changes in costs and the resulting changes in prices, the role of expectations and the possibility of effects relating to demand pressure, capacity use and the build-up or run-down of stocks.

Neild (1963) made one of the first econometric attempts to test the normal cost hypothesis, that is, that prices are generally set in relation to long-run considerations and consist of a conventional mark-up on the costs that would pertain if the firm were operating at 'normal' capacity with the real wage per employee growing at the trend productivity rate. In this case, they would be invariant to changes in demand or to variations in unit costs which are perceived as temporary. Neild's methodology was to specify and estimate a simple price equation containing a term proportional to the direct cost per unit of output, constructed as a linear combination of the wage rate and a price index for materials (including fuel). He tested the normal cost hypothesis by incorporating a productivity variable into the regressions. He found that normal costs gave a better result than actual costs, that his productivity trend was superior to the estimated trend, and that the demand variable he included was not significant. He therefore concluded that the normal cost hypothesis could not be refuted and that prices are not sensitive to fluctuations in either productivity or demand.

Neild's interpretation of these results was re-examined by Rushdy and Lund (1967) who argued that the level of demand and output per man hour are positively correlated over the cycle, so using the productivity trend series implicitly introduces the level of demand into the equation. They showed that the demand variables are significant in regressions that use changes in actual cost indices as explanatory variables.[4]

Numerous studies were then performed, which found positive and statistically significant coefficients on a number of different excess demand variables. Rushdy and Lund (1967) and McCallum (1970) both used the Dow–Dicks-Mireaux index (Dow and Dicks-Mireaux, 1958). A study by Solow (1969) included an excess demand index calculated by Paish (1962), while Brechling (1972) used the difference between real national product and a quadratic trend.

In 1972, Nordhaus and Godley published the results of further tests of the normal cost hypothesis. They specified this hypothesis to be the assertion that: 'the mark-up of price over normal historical current average cost is independent of the conditions of demand in the factor and product markets and is independent of the deviations of actual cost from normal cost' (p. 869). They concluded that for the non-food, drink and tobacco manufacturing industry, at least, the normal price hypothesis was consistent with the data. A subsequent study of seven individual industries by Coutts, Godley and Nordhaus (1978), using the same model as in their 1972 study, supported these findings.

However, a study by Smith (1982) again refuted the normal cost hypothesis finding significant coefficients on various demand variables. Further, econometric studies from outside the UK have obtained similar results. McFetridge (1973), for example, tests for the effect of demand on the pricing behaviour of the Canadian textile industry at the disaggregated industry level and rejects the normal price hypothesis for this industry.

In conclusion, it seems that, although the results are mixed, the balance of the econometric evidence rejects the normal cost hypothesis that prices are set according to a fixed mark-up on long-run, trend or 'normal' costs. Further, this conclusion is supported by the results of the work described in section 2.5. Demand factors do seem to play an independent role in price-setting behaviour although it is difficult to isolate the demand effect sufficiently well to estimate its importance in determining prices. These findings are supported by the results of the survey and questionnaire studies into pricing behaviour noted in the next section.

2.3.3 Survey results

An early survey of pricing behaviour, conducted by Hall and Hitch (1939), gives some insight into the firm's view of its own behaviour. A total of 38 firms, mainly in manufacturing, were investigated. Twelve of them claimed to adhere strictly to a full-cost pricing policy, while another 18 said they attempted to practise it in principle or in normal market conditions. This is a substantial majority appearing to be in favour of the full cost approach as opposed to the notion of profit maximization by equating marginal cost with expected marginal revenue.

However, the 30 firms which claimed to adopt some form of full-cost pricing strategy were then asked under what circumstances they would deviate from this rule and charge a lower price. Of these, 12 responded that they would reduce prices in the face of depressed demand and a further nine that they would reduce prices in order to match competitors' price adjustments.

Further, the firms were also asked for reasons and circumstances under which they would not be prepared to charge a price different from full cost. Twenty-four responses were given explaining why a higher price would not be charged, of which 17 were due to the existence of competition. Thirty-five responses were given as to why a lower price would not be charged of which nine related to demand being unresponsive to price changes and 11 to competitors matching price cuts.

These results were interpreted by Hall and Hitch as evidence in support of the full-cost hypothesis and against 'marginalism'. However, others have interpreted them as being supportive of the economists' conventional marginalist, profit maximizing approach to pricing. It has been suggested that the reasons given for not departing from the full-cost price, along with the importance of the demand situation are suggestive of marginal revenue considerations. Indeed, it has been concluded by some, on the basis of this survey, that firms' pricing policies seem, in fact, to be closer to 'implicit marginalism' than to the full-cost approach (in this context, see Machlup, 1946).

More recent surveys of pricing behaviour have found broadly similar results. Skinner (1970) collected 172 questionnaire responses of which some 70 per cent claimed to be using a mark-up on average costs as the basis for their pricing decisions. However, 68 per cent of these had a range of different mark-ups which were applied according to the product or the particular order under consideration. The mark-up was varied either according to competitive pressures or in response to demand conditions. Thus it seemed that cost was used only as a broad basis for price setting and that actual prices were varied according to a number of non-cost considerations.

Hague, in 1971, reported the results of an investigation of the pricing decisions of 13 firms, studied in some depth during the period 1964 to 1968. He also found the pricing decision was based on a variety of strategies. Of the 13 firms studied he labelled five 'profit maximizers' and eight 'satisficers'. The profit maximizers were interested in profit as a simple sum of money, not always calculating it in the way that would be used in published accounts. He found little interest in profit as a return on sales or as a return on capital, although both measures featured among those monitored. All the firms, satisficers as well as maximizers, had profit objectives.

A survey by Atkin and Skinner (1975), addressed to the marketing managers of a large number of manufacturing firms, received 220 responses. Of the firms which use some form of cost-based pricing technique 63 per cent seemed to adhere to full cost pricing while 35 per cent appeared to use a marginal cost pricing rule. In all, 40 per cent of firms reported that they usually adjusted the price to take into account some form of non-cost consideration, such as the level of demand, regardless of the type of product sold or the market in which it was being sold. Only 14 per cent claimed always to base their price on cost factors alone.

Shipley, in 1981, reported similar results from his study of 728 British firms. He found that the vast majority pursued profit-related objectives in one form or another.

Much of this survey evidence suggests that other factors in addition to costs are important in determining output prices. A cost base appears to be the foundation on which prices are usually set. The existence of different margins for different products and at different points in the trade cycle, price discounts which vary according to customer class, and various other non-cost factors suggest that the full-cost price theory does not do justice to all the factors actually involved in a price decision.

We should not necessarily conclude from these results that firms choose prices according to the marginalist principle in which marginal revenue is set equal to marginal costs, in spite of the case made by Machlup. Entrepreneurs do not often have the detailed cost information which is required and, in a world of uncertain demand, will anyway be unable to calculate revenue curves with any degree of accuracy. However, the predominant pricing strategy seems to be one in which costs form the basis for a mark-up that depends on non-cost considerations such as demand and competitors' prices, the objective being to arrive at a price likely to ensure that the entrepreneur makes a reasonable amount of money.

2.4 DERIVATION OF MODEL EQUATION

2.4.1 Behavioural hypothesis

The theory discussed in section 2.2 suggested that a case could be made for modelling firms' aggregate price-setting behaviour either by assuming that they maximize the current level of operating cash-flow, or by assuming they use a 'rule of thumb' type of approach such as a constant mark-up on normal costs. The empirical work summarized in section 2.3 is ambivalent about the role of excess demand in price-setting. The results of the surveys are slightly more supportive of a role for demand and also for competitors' prices.

We favour starting out with the operating cash-flow maximization hypothesis. This theoretical approach, combined with the assumption that the firms are operating in an imperfectly competitive market, predicts that demand and competitors' prices will both have a role in determining the size of the mark-up. Starting here, we can test this hypothesis against the null that these terms have no role to play.

It is therefore assumed that firms take decisions concerning their price, output and variable inputs with the object of maximizing current period operating cash-flow and that they sell their output in an imperfectly competitive market (that is, that the demand for it is price-elastic). For simplicity, the treatment in the following section omits taxes and abstracts from any dynamics. Both are included in the equation derived in sections 2.4.3 and 2.4.4 and used for the empirical work reported in section 2.5.

2.4.2 Derivation of basic equation

Given the outcome on the wage, W, and the cost of material inputs and fuel, P_i, and given the existing productive capacity,[5] $\bar{Y}$, the firm is assumed to choose the current levels of output, Y, price, P, employment, E, and material and fuel inputs, M, to maximize operating cash-flow in the current period:

$$\max_{Y,P,E,M} \Pi = PY - WE - P_iM \tag{2.1}$$

The maximization is subject to two constraints. One is a price elastic demand function:

$$Y = f(Z, P/P_f^*) \tag{2.2}$$

where P_f^* represents competitors' prices and Z represents the other variables affecting demand. The other is a short-term production function in which the output, Y, achieved by employing labour and material inputs E and M depends on the capacity available, K:

$$Y = g(E, M|K). \tag{2.3}$$

As demand, Y, reaches full capacity output, $\bar{Y}$, a further constraint (the capacity constraint $Y \leq \bar{Y}$) becomes relevant. Our simple model suggests that at full capacity the price, P, will be set in such a way as to set demand equal to full capacity output, that is, it will be determined by the inverse of equation 2.2 with Y replaced by $\bar{Y}$.

When the capacity constraint does not bite the marginal conditions to the problem set out in equations 2.1 to 2.3 are:

$$Y + \lambda_1 f_2/P_f^* = 0 \tag{2.4}$$

$$P - \lambda_1 - \lambda_2 = 0 \tag{2.5}$$

$$-W + \lambda_2 g_1 = 0 \tag{2.6}$$

$$-P_i + \lambda_2 g_2 = 0 \tag{2.7}$$

where λ_1 and λ_2 are the Lagrange multipliers attributed to the constraints in equations 2.2 and 2.3; g_1 is $\partial g / \partial E$, the marginal product of labour; g_2 is $\partial g / \partial M$, the marginal product of the material inputs; while f_2, or $\partial f / \partial (P/P_f^*)$, is the relative price elasticity of demand $(f_2 < 0)$.

These equations can be combined with the constraints to give a set of equations for the decision variables. The equation for the price is obtained by substituting for the λ's in equation 2.5 using 2.4, 2.6, and 2.7. It takes a linear form:

$$P = \mu \frac{W}{g_1} + (1 - \mu) \frac{P_i}{g_2} + \frac{P_f^* Y}{|f_2|} \tag{2.8}$$

where μ can be chosen at will since in the case of flexible substitution between variable inputs:

$$\frac{W}{g_1} = \frac{P_i}{g_2} \tag{2.9}$$

Equation 2.8 demonstrates clearly that, given our hypothesis of profit maximizing entrepreneurs selling heterogeneous goods in an imperfectly competitive market, we would expect to find a mark-up that varies with the level of demand and with competitors' prices.[6]

In order to transform equation 2.8 into one suitable for estimation using aggregate data it is assumed that the marginal product g_1 (equal to $\partial Y / \partial E$) varies with the average productivity for the sector PR (equal to Y/E) and that variations in the marginal product of material and fuel inputs can be ignored (that is, that g_2 is constant). The dependence of the coefficients in equation 2.8 on economic factors such as the level of activity, the price elasticity of demand or technical change are assumed to be of secondary importance compared to the effect of the economic factors that are explicitly included. The data correspond to a great variety of productive processes and a large number of firms; it is assumed that the results of estimating using aggregate data are meaningful and remain stable over differing time periods.

With price indices appropriately scaled at a time when $Y = \bar{Y}$, equation 2.8 can be written:

$$P = (1 - \beta)C + \beta P_f^* Y / \bar{Y} \tag{2.10}$$

where β indicates the weight attributed to the determinants of the profit margin, and C represents the cost per unit of output. It is implied by this equation that the effect of output on the margin depends on the full capacity level of output. The effect of any given level of demand on price-setting thus depends on the productive potential in the economy. It is through this term that the effect of bottlenecks on inflation is modelled.

2.4.3 Specification of unit costs

The specification of the cost per unit of output, C, for the empirical work is rather more complicated than in the above example. The relevant costs fall into four categories. **Unit labour costs** are given by:

$$ULC = W \cdot LT/PR \qquad (2.11)$$

where LT is the labour tax ratio and PR is an appropriate weighted average of productivity in the whole economy and in manufacturing. The **sterling cost of imported inputs** P_{im} is a combination of primary commodities' prices and the prices of foreign finished goods in sterling (equation 2.22). The foreign currency prices of these are set in world markets (Appendix 2B). The **cost of other inputs,** P_a, includes, for example, the price of electricity (over the estimation period this was influenced by the UK authorities). **Taxes** incurred by the firm, TX, include industrial rates, vehicle excise duty etc. (VAT is not included as the price variable used is the Producer Price Index (Output) which indicates the level of prices at the factory gate.)

It follows that C can be written:

$$C = \alpha_1 ULC + \alpha_2 P_{im} + \alpha_3 P_a + \alpha_4 TX \qquad (2.12)$$

where the α_1 ($i = 1, \ldots, 4$) are parameters. If the price indices ULC, P_{im}, P_a, TX and C are all normalized to take the same numerical value (e.g., 100) in some year, then obviously:

$$\alpha_1 + \alpha_2 + \alpha_3 + \alpha_4 = 1 \qquad (2.13)$$

in that year. This relation will then also hold, to a reasonable approximation, in the other years of the sample.

2.4.4 The equation to be estimated

For estimation purposes equation 2.10, with equation 2.12 substituted into it, has been approximated by a log-linear[7] form. In order to allow for costs of adjustment it has been estimated as a dynamic process of the error correction type:

$$\Delta p = \alpha_1' \Delta ulc + \alpha_2' \Delta p_{im} + \alpha_3' \Delta p_a + \alpha_4' \Delta tx + \alpha_5' \Delta p_f^* + \alpha_6' (\Delta y - \Delta \bar{y})$$
$$- \phi(L)(p - \beta_1 ulc - \beta_2 p_{im} - \beta_3 p_a - \beta_4 tx - \beta_5 p_f^* - \beta_6 (y - \bar{y})) \qquad (2.14)$$

where $\alpha_1' = (1 - \beta)\alpha_1$, $i = 1, \ldots 4$, and $\alpha_5' = \beta$.

This formulation has been derived from equation 2.10 by differencing it (combined with equation 2.12), dividing by the lagged price level and using the approximation:

$$\Delta \ln X = \Delta X/X_{-1}$$

Given this, the linear form of equation 2.12, from which equation 2.14 is derived, carries with it the implication that the coefficients α_1' to α_5' sum to unity. The small variation in the individual coefficients in equation 2.14, which depend on the ratios of relative prices and so may vary slightly over time, is assumed to be unimportant to the exercise under consideration. The lagged log-levels term is included to allow for a possible effect on price-setting from the deviation of the (real) profit margin from its long-run equilibrium level, entailing the prior constraint that the coefficients β_1 to β_5 sum to unity.

(a) Money illusion and homogeneity

The prior constraints on the coefficients in equation 2.14 are important to the dynamic properties of the inflation spiral, see Chapters 5 and 6, so it is worth considering them carefully at this point.

They arise because an absence of money illusion has been built into the decision function (equations 2.1 to 2.3) and this leads directly to a linear form for equations 2.10 and 2.12. The linear form of these equations then implies the constraints that have been imposed on the estimated coefficients in equation 2.14.

In terms of equation 2.14 itself, the economic justification for the constraints is as follows. If all prices were stable (so $\Delta p = 0$ and all the input costs are constant in nominal terms) an absence of money illusion suggests that the profit margin should be independent of the level of prices generally. This implies static homogeneity, that is:

$$\beta_1 + \beta_2 + \beta_3 + \beta_4 + \beta_5 = 1 \qquad (2.15)$$

Further, if all input costs and the competitors' prices were rising at the same rate, output were at full capacity and the feed-back levels term in equation 2.14 were zero, then the principle of no money illusion implies that the profit margin will remain constant so the price rises at the same rate as the costs. This implies that the equation should have dynamic homogeneity, that is:

$$\alpha'_1 + \alpha'_2 + \alpha'_3 + \alpha'_4 + \alpha'_5 = 1 \qquad (2.16)$$

The result of estimating equation 2.14 with these constraints imposed is reported in section 2.5. These constraints, which are important to our story about the dynamics of the inflation spiral, were not rejected by the data. It is the estimated version of this equation that is used in the empirical work reported in Chapter 7.

(b) Effect of constrained capacity

Our theory[8] suggests that if demand is expanded beyond the level that can be met from existing capacity, and there is insufficient time to construct or otherwise acquire the needed capacity, then the price will rise by more than it would otherwise have done.

If this extra large price rise leads to a rise in wages, say, and therefore in costs, that is larger than would otherwise have been the case, then the price rise will remain in the system, travelling round the inflation spiral. The rationale for the rise in price that initiates this process is illustrated in Figure 2.2.

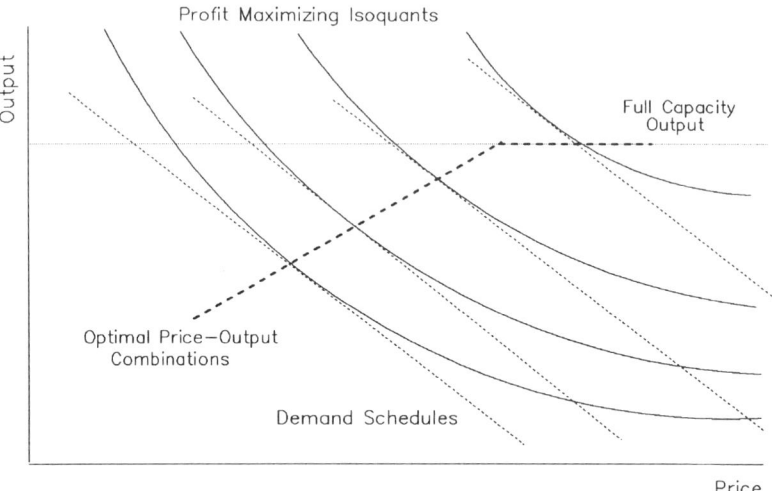

Fig. 2.2 Constrained capacity.

This shows the path of price and output as the demand schedule is shifted outwards (perhaps as a result of an expansionary fiscal policy creating higher real disposable incomes, or following a fall in the savings ratio).

Tests of the hypothesis that this phenomenon explains the path of price-setting were not included in the specification of the price equation. Further, examination of the residuals on the estimated equation does not reveal any evidence that this effect has influenced the inflation spiral during the period investigated (Figure 2.3 in section 2.5.8).

2.4.5 Implications for inflation spiral

(a) Separation of endogenous from exogenous terms

To facilitate the theoretical consideration of the inflation process (in Chapters 5 and 6) it is helpful to split the terms of this equation into two classes, those which are part of the feed-back that makes up the domestic inflation spiral and those which are not. We have allocated changes in real administered prices ($\Delta p_a - \Delta p$) and in the tax ratio (real taxes per unit of output, $\Delta tx - \Delta p$) to those variables that are not part of the inflation spiral but impinge upon it. This introduces terms in (lagged) domestic inflation into the right-hand side of the equation.

The imported input prices, P_{im}, have been split into those for primary commodities, P_c, and those for imported finished goods used as inputs, P'_f. The two series for prices of imported finished goods, one corresponding to imported inputs (P'_f) and the other to competing imported finished goods (P^*_f), have been combined into the series labelled P_f.

Given these adjustments, equation 2.14 can be written:[9]

$$\Delta p = a(L)(\Delta w - \Delta pr) + b(L)\Delta p_f + c(L)\Delta p_c + d(L)\Delta p + X_1 \qquad (2.17)$$

The term X_1 then encompasses all the factors that are not part of the spiral, and the equation has the property:

$$a(1) + b(1) + c(1) + d(1) = 1 \qquad (2.18)$$

that is, the coefficients on explanatory price inflation variables sum to unity.

In the reduced form equation for the inflation spiral, derived in Chapter 5, wages, W, and the exchange rate, RX, (which influences the paths of P_f and P_c) are treated as being part of the domestic inflation spiral. As a result, behavioural equations are substituted for these variables in equation 2.17. The variables impinging on inflation as a result of this model of price-setting behaviour in the goods market are therefore world price rises in world currencies and the variables incorporated into X_1, namely:

- the rate of increase of material and fuel prices in world currencies Δp_c^w
- the rate of increase of imported finished goods' prices in world currencies Δp_f^w
- the deviation of demand growth from the increase in full capacity output $(\Delta y - \Delta \bar{y})$
- the level of capacity utilization $(y - \bar{y})$
- the difference between the price level and the level of unit costs $(p - ulc)$, $(p - p_{im})$, $(p - p_a)$ and $(p - tx)$
- the difference between the price and the competitors' price level $(p - p_f^*)$
- the rate of growth of productivity Δpr
- changes in the relevant tax rates Δlt and $(\Delta tx - \Delta p)$
- changes in the real value of administered prices $(\Delta p_a - \Delta p)$.

(b) Features likely to be important to spiral

The role that capacity utilization plays in this equation is analogous to that which labour market disequilibrium plays in a conventional Expectations Augmented Phillips Curve. It can be viewed as a measure of the disequilibrium in the goods market. A disequilibrium of this sort may persist for a considerable length of time and, since this can have a cumulative effect on inflation, it could be of considerable importance in determining the rate of inflation. Indeed, it plays an important part in our story. The coefficients on this term (or other proxies for the same economic concept) and on the term in demand growth, were the subject of the controversy in the literature in the 1970s reported in section 2.3.2.

A change in the real value of administered prices (or in the tax rate) will cause only a once-off shock to the inflation spiral, since such a change will involve administered prices growing at a different rate from other prices only for the period during which the change is taking place. The effects of a deviation of output growth or of productivity growth from their trend rates are also likely to be short lived.

Finally, because we find that commodity prices can play an important role in the inflation spiral, it is worth noting that changes in the relative weights on the margin and on costs will have little effect on the weights given to commodity price rises in this equation. This is because the margin depends on competitors' prices and their dependence on commodity prices will be broadly similar to that of the prices of domestically produced goods.

2.5 AN EQUATION FOR PRICES

2.5.1 Introduction

This section reports the results of estimating the equation for the change in the Producer Price Index (Output). The objective is to test the hypotheses relating to the characteristics of the equation that were identified as being relevant to the inflation spiral.

Since this is the purpose, the important features of the estimation are not the precise values taken by the coefficients, nor the timing with which changes in the explanatory variables affect the price inflation variable. Instead we are concerned to discover whether the coefficient constraints that have been identified as being important to the dynamic structure of the inflation spiral (homogeneity constraints), or to the efficacy of policy to influence inflation (a significant demand effect), are supported by the data.

With this in mind, the period over which the hypotheses are tested is of no great relevance providing there is no reason to suppose that changes in institutional arrangements since then have been so great as to render the information incorporated in the data irrelevant. It is important, however, to specify the variables in such a way as to minimize the likelihood of measurement error or bias. The equations reported here were estimated in HM Treasury in the mid-1980s using data covering most of the 1970s and the earlier part of the 1980s. The work done at that time included a careful consideration of the definition of the data series included (Rowlatt 1986 and 1987). Although the precise estimates of the coefficients will obviously be different, as they will include new data, there is no reason to suppose that these aspects of price-setting behaviour have undergone a sea-change, so the fact that they were estimated a few years ago should not invalidate the results that rest on them.

2.5.2 The chosen equation

The equation estimated for price-setting is equation 2.14, reproduced here:

$$\Delta p = \alpha'_1 \Delta ulc + \alpha'_2 \Delta p_{im} + \alpha'_3 \Delta p_a + \alpha'_4 \Delta tx + \alpha'_5 \Delta p^*_f + \alpha'_6 (\Delta y - \Delta \bar{y})$$
$$- \phi(L) [p - \beta_1 ulc - \beta_2 p_{im} - \beta_3 p_a - \beta_4 tx - \beta_5 p^*_f - \beta_6 (y - \bar{y})] \quad (2.19)$$

The estimated version of this equation that is used in the analysis in the later chapters of this book is listed below (and shown in column XVI of Table 2.3):

$$\Delta p = 0.315\Delta ulc(-1) + 0.117\Delta ulc(-2) + 0.098\Delta ulc(-3) + 0.114\Delta p_{im}$$
$$\quad\text{(i)}\qquad\qquad\quad\text{(2.5)}\qquad\qquad\quad\text{(2.2)}\qquad\qquad\quad\text{(1.6)}$$
$$+\ 0.134\Delta p_{im}(-2) + 0.083\Delta p_a(-1) + 0.039\Delta tx(-1)$$
$$\quad\text{(1.9)}\qquad\qquad\text{(iii)}\qquad\qquad\text{(iii)}$$
$$+\ 0.092\Delta p_f^*(-1) + 0.008\Delta p_f^*(-2) + 0.19\Delta y(-1)$$
$$\quad\text{(iv)}\qquad\qquad\text{(1.0)}\qquad\qquad\text{(3.4)}$$
$$-\ 0.144[p(-1) - \bar{p}(-1)] + \text{intercept} + \text{residual} \qquad\qquad (2.20)$$
$$\quad\text{(3.0)}$$

with:

$$ulc = w + lt - pr \qquad\qquad (2.21)$$

$$P_{im} = \ln[0.184P_{fm} + 0.527P_s + 0.174P_{fu} + 0.115P_b] \qquad\qquad (2.22)$$

$$P_f^* = 0.544P_{fm} + 0.456P_s \qquad\qquad (2.23)$$

$$\bar{p} = 0.375ulc(-3) + 0.181p_{im}(-2) + 0.083p_a + 0.039tx$$
$$\quad\text{(i)}\qquad\qquad\quad\text{(ii)}\qquad\qquad\quad\text{(iii)}\qquad\quad\text{(iii)}$$
$$\quad + 0.437p_f^*(-2) + 0.146cu(-1) \qquad\qquad (2.24)$$
$$\quad\text{(3.6)}\qquad\qquad\quad\text{(v)}$$

period 1971Q1 to 1983Q3 $R^2 = 0.92$ $SEE = 0.70$ $DW = 2.0$
degrees of freedom $= 38$ Box-Pierce $\chi^2 = 7.5$ (9 df)

The data series for the logarithms of P_{im} and P_f^* in equations 2.22 and 2.23 are constructed from series for imported finished manufactures, P_{fm}, semi-manu-factures, P_s, fuel (including North Sea oil as well as imported oil), P_{fu}, and basic materials, P_b, using input–output coefficients and trade shares. The variable cu is a measure of capacity utilization derived from survey data (by the CBI) and used as a proxy for the term $(y - \bar{y})$ in equation 2.19. There is some evidence suggesting the price-setting may depend on this in a non-linear fashion.

2.5.3 The homogeneity constraint

In equations 2.20 to 2.24, the coefficients marked (i) have been constrained to maintain dynamic and static homogeneity. Table 2.1 shows the results of testing these constraints. Column I lists the result of estimating an initial version of the equation with the coefficients on the dynamic price terms constrained to sum to unity;[10] Column II shows the same equation estimated without this constraint. Various other coefficients are constrained at initial values in both of these

Table 2.1 Tests of homogeneity constraints and input–output weights

Independent variables	initial constr equ'n I	dynamic homog II	test of static homog III	test of long-run I-O constr IV	stat & dynamic homog V	joint test of stat hom & I-O constr VI	joint test of stat & dyn hom & I-O constr VII
$\Delta ulc(-1)$	0.230^1	0.221^* (2.8)	0.228^1	0.230^1	0.193^* (1.0)	0.229^1	0.174^* (1.2)
$\Delta ulc(-2)$	0.162 (3.1)	0.152 (2.5)	0.159 (3.1)	0.161 (3.0)	0.127 (2.0)	0.161 (3.0)	0.111 (1.3)
$\Delta ulc(-3)$	0.136 (2.7)	0.124 (1.9)	0.138 (2.8)	0.137 (2.7)	0.098 (1.4)	0.136 (2.7)	0.083 (1.0)
$\Delta p_{im}(-1)$	0.059 (1.1)	0.058 (1.1)	0.064 (1.2)	0.061 (1.1)	0.061 (1.1)	0.058 (1.0)	0.067 (1.2)
$\Delta p_{im}(-2)$	0.091 (1.9)	0.087 (1.7)	0.089 (1.8)	0.089 (1.8)	0.074 (1.4)	0.094 (1.9)	0.062 (1.0)
Δp_a	0.083^1	0.083^1	0.083^1	0.083^1	0.083^1	0.083^1	0.083^1
Δtx	0.039^1	0.039^1	0.039^1	0.039^1	0.039^1	0.039^1	0.039^1
$\Delta p_f^*(-1)$	0.100^1	0.100^1	0.100^1	0.100^1	0.100^1	0.100^1	0.100^1
$\Delta p_f^*(-2)$	0.100^1	0.100^1	0.100^1	0.100^1	0.100^1	0.100^1	0.100^1
$\Delta y(-1)$	0.22 (3.6)	0.21 (2.9)	0.23 (3.7)	0.22 (3.4)	0.21 (2.9)	0.23 (3.4)	0.20 (2.8)
$p'(-1)^2$	−0.142 (3.1)	−0.132 (1.8)	−0.131 (1.0)	−0.141 (3.0)	−0.087 (1.3)	−0.099 (1.1)	−0.102 (1.1)
$ulc(-4)$	0.067^1	0.060^1	0.061^* (2.7)	0.066^1	0.032^* (0.8)	0.029^* (0.4)	0.019^* (0.3)
$p_{im}(-3)$	0.033^1	0.030^1	0.030^1	0.037^* (1.3)	0.016^1	0.014^* (0.4)	0.026^* (0.7)
$p_f^*(-3)$	0.042 (2.0)	0.042 (2.0)	0.044 (2.1)	0.038 (1.1)	0.044 (2.1)	0.060 (1.5)	0.027 (0.5)
$cu(-2)$	−0.085 (3.6)	−0.047 (2.8)	−0.085 (3.7)	−0.051 (3.2)	−0.061 (3.1)	−0.061 (3.3)	−0.596 (3.1)
$\bar{R}^2$	0.76	0.75	0.76	0.75	0.76	0.75	0.75
SEE (%)	0.78	0.79	0.78	0.79	0.78	0.79	0.79
DW	2.0	2.0	2.1	2.0	2.1	2.1	2.0
DF	39	38	38	38	37	37	36
B-P(df)	12.5(9)	12.6(9)	13.6(9)	12.4(9)	14.5(9)	14.1(9)	14.7(9)
$\chi^2(df)^3$		0.1(1)	1.5(1)	0.1(1)	2.3(2)	1.6(2)	1.8(3)
Period	711–833	711–833	711–833	711–833	711–833	711–833	711–833

[1] Coefficient value constrained.
[2] Lagged dependent variable with constrained effect from p_a and tx, that is, $p' = p - 0.083p_a - 0.039tx$.
[3] Test of constraint imposed; equation of comparison in column I.

Note: The coefficient(s) being tested in each equation are marked *.

equations. (These initial constraints include the imposition of static homogeneity and the constraint that the coefficients on the prices of inputs in the long-run equilibrium term of the equation conform with the values implied by input–output analysis). It is clear from the two equations that imposing the dynamic homogeneity constraint makes very little difference to the estimated values of the coefficients. Further, the χ^2 statistic at the foot of column II indicates that the constraint is easily accepted by the data.

Column III of Table 2.1 tests the static homogeneity constraint, and column V tests the two homogeneity constraints jointly, by freeing both at the same time. Again the χ^2 statistics at the foot of the columns indicate that these constraints are easily accepted by the data.

The rationale for imposing the homogeneity constraints in this equation has been explained in section 2.4.4. If they were not imposed – and the coefficients on explanatory price and cost variables would then sum to slightly less than unity (bottom line of Table 2.1) – the reduced form equation for the inflation spiral would not have unit homogeneity. The implications of this for the dynamics of the inflation spiral are an important element in our story and are noted in Chapter 5.

2.5.4 The input–output coefficient constraint

Column IV of Table 2.1 tests the constraint that the coefficients on the input prices in the model of the long-run equilibrium price level contained within our equation conform to input–output ratios (the relevant coefficient is marked (ii) in equation 2.24). A comparison of the coefficient values with those in Column I again indicates that the constraint is easily accepted, and again, this is confirmed by the χ^2 test at the bottom of the column. Columns VI and VII of Table 2.1 report joint tests of the three constraints considered in this table. In each case the constraints are easily consistent with the data at the 5 per cent level.

The input–output coefficient constraint is, perhaps, less important than the homogeneity constraints in determining the properties of the inflation spiral. It affects the influence of the exchange rate on inflation in the model. The view taken was that the estimated coefficients are not well defined and the input–output values are likely to be closer to the 'true' values.

The constraints marked (iii) in equations 2.20 and 2.24 are designed to ensure that the coefficients on the administered price and tax terms in the dynamic part of the equation and in the long-run model will be consistent with input–output coefficients. A comparison of Column I and the columns labelled IX and X in Table 2.2 show the results of freeing these constraints. The coefficient estimates show that the freely estimated values are quite different from the values implied by input–output analysis and the χ^2 statistics at the bottom of the table show that the chosen values are rejected by the data at the 5 per cent level. It was decided that the input–output values should be imposed in spite of the fact that they were rejected by the data in order to investigate the properties of the inflation spiral.

Table 2.2 Tests of competitors' price, administered price and tax terms

Independent variables	initial constr equ'n I	dynamic compet price VIII	test of Nat Ind price IX	tax v'ble X	joint test of compet price & NI price XI	compet price & tax vbl XII	all 6 constr XIII
$\Delta ulc(-1)$	0.230^1	0.209^1	0.214^1	0.236^1	0.200^1	0.208^1	0.046*
							(0.5)
$\Delta ulc(-2)$	0.162	0.125	0.167	0.138	0.140	0.103	0.108
	(3.1)	(2.4)	(3.5)	(3.2)	(2.8)	(2.5)	(1.9)
$\Delta ulc(-3)$	0.136	0.086	0.115	0.154	0.082	0.097	0.105
	(2.7)	(1.6)	(2.5)	(3.8)	(1.7)	(2.4)	(1.8)
$\Delta p_{im}(-1)$	0.059	0.118	0.088	0.062	0.126	0.130	0.232
	(1.1)	(2.1)	(1.8)	(1.4)	(2.4)	(3.0)	(4.0)
$\Delta p_{im}(-2)$	0.091	0.140	0.094	0.088	0.130	0.140	0.187
	(1.9)	(2.8)	(2.1)	(2.3)	(2.7)	(3.6)	(3.6)
Δp_a	0.083^1	0.083^1	-0.083^*	0.083^1	-0.015^*	0.049*	-0.001^*
			(1.6)		(0.4)	(1.3)	(0.0)
Δtx	0.039^1	0.039^1	0.039^1	-0.006^*	0.039^1	0.004*	-0.006^*
				(0.6)		(0.4)	(0.5)
$\Delta p_f^*(-1)$	0.100^1	-0.001	0.100^1	0.100^1	0.026	0.003	-0.103
$\Delta p_f^*(-2)$	0.100^1	-0.001^*	0.100^1	0.100^1	0.026	0.003	-0.103
		(0.0)			(0.6)	(0.1)	(1.9)
$\Delta y(-1)$	0.22	0.20	0.16	0.14	0.15	0.10	0.17
	(3.6)	(3.4)	(2.6)	(2.6)	(2.6)	(2.0)	(3.0)
$p'(-1)^2$	-0.142	-0.109	-0.096	-0.162	-0.079	-0.114	-0.106
	(3.1)	(1.5)	(1.6)	(4.0)	(0.8)	(1.7)	(1.0)
$ulc(-4)$	0.067^1	0.038^1	0.037^1	0.072^1	0.020^1	0.034^1	0.002^*
							(1.4)
$p_{im}(-3)$	0.033^1	0.019^1	0.018^1	0.035^1	0.010^1	0.016^1	0.079^*
							(2.5)
$p_f^*(-3)$	0.042	0.052	0.041	0.055	0.049	0.064	0.002
	(2.0)	(2.6)	(2.2)	(3.2)	(2.6)	(4.0)	(0.0)
$cu(-2)$	-0.085	-0.048	-0.045	-0.070	-0.030	-0.028	-0.035
	(3.6)	(2.6)	(2.9)	(3.1)	(2.3)	(1.8)	(2.5)
$\bar{R}^2$	0.76	0.74	0.71	0.63	0.70	0.56	0.53
SEE (%)	0.78	0.78	0.80	0.84	0.81	0.87	0.89
DW	2.0	2.2	1.7	1.5	1.8	1.5	1.8
DF	39	37	38	38	36	36	32
B-P(df)	12.5(9)	10.2(9)	13.8(9)	13.5(9)	9.6(9)	14.4(9)	9.4(9)
$\chi^2(df)^3$		6.5(1)	9.8(1)	22.3(1)	13.7(2)	36.7(3)	46.8(7)
Period	711–833	711–833	711–833	711–833	711–833	711–833	711–833

[1] Coefficient value constrained.
[2] Lagged dependent variable with constrained effect from p_a and tx, that is, $p' = p - 0.083p_a - 0.039tx$.
[3] Test of constraint imposed; equation of comparison in column I.

Note: The coefficient(s) being tested in each equation are marked *.

2.5.5 The competitors' price variable

The theory from which the equation was derived suggests that the coefficient on the change in competitors' prices should be the same as that on demand growth. However, whereas the competitors' price variable in the model of the long-run price level incorporated into this equation makes a significant contribution to the explanation of the path of the price (it has a t-statistic of 2.0 in the equation in Column I), the data offered no support for the inclusion of the dynamic term in competitors' prices. This can be seen from column VIII of Table 2.2 where the coefficient on the sum of the two lags of the change in competitors' prices has been estimated freely and is found to be negative. However, estimation of a corresponding equation for import prices displayed a significant influence from dynamic terms in domestic competing prices and competitiveness effects of this sort are significant in various estimated equations for export prices.

It was decided, therefore, that a non-zero value should be imposed on the dynamic terms at a level substantially below that of the freely estimated coefficient in the implicit model of the long-run equilibrium price level. The coefficient marked (iv) in equation 2.20 was constrained in such a way that the total effect summed to 0.1 in the final version of the equation (column XVI of Table 2.3). The χ^2 statistic at the base of column VIII in Table 2.2 reveals that there is a probability of more than 95 per cent that this coefficient is less than 0.2 (the value of the estimated coefficient on the demand change term).

Columns XI and XII of Table 2.2 show the results of joint tests of the constraints on the dynamic competitors' price, the Nationalized Industry price index and the tax terms. The final column shows the effect of relaxing these six contraints at the same time.

2.5.6 Other constraints on the equation

Table 2.3 takes the initial equation shown in Column I of Tables 2.1 and 2.2 and submits it to some final adjustments. The equation included in the model is listed in the column labelled XVI in this table.

Column XIV of Table 2.3 shows the equation of Column VIII of Table 2.2 (repeated in Table 2.3) with an outlier in 1979Q3 (Figure 2.3) omitted from the data. Excluding this observation (by including a dummy variable set equal to unity in that quarter and zero elsewhere), the equation offers some slight support for the inclusion of the dynamic competitors' price terms. Further, the estimated standard error of the equation is quite strikingly improved, while the other coefficient values are little affected.

In the final equation the coefficient on the capacity utilization level term, marked (v) in equation 2.24, has been constrained to take a value about a quarter of the size of the freely estimated coefficient, see Column XVI of Table 2.3. The χ^2 statistic indicates that this value is rejected by the data at the 5 per cent level. This constraint was imposed within the Treasury following an examination of the properties of

Table 2.3 Final tests of price equation

Independent variables	initial constr equ'n I	dynamic compet price VIII	test of VIII excl 1979Q3 XIV	XIV with dyn comp price XV	XV with capac'y util'n XVI
$\Delta ulc(-1)$	0.230^1	0.209^1	0.287^1	0.319^1	0.315^1
$\Delta ulc(-2)$	0.162 (3.1)	0.125 (2.4)	0.146 (3.1)	0.136 (3.0)	0.117 (2.5)
$\Delta ulc(-3)$	0.136 (2.7)	0.086 (1.6)	0.129 (2.8)	0.029 (3.0)	0.098 (2.2)
$\Delta p_{im}(-1)$	0.059 (1.1)	0.118 (2.1)	0.124 (1.6)	0.081 (1.2)	0.114 (1.6)
$\Delta p_{im}(-2)$	0.091 (1.9)	0.140 (2.8)	0.149 (3.6)	0.152 (2.3)	0.134 (1.9)
Δp_a	0.083^1	0.083^1	0.083^1	0.083^1	0.083^1
Δtx	0.039^1	0.039^1	0.039^1	0.039^1	0.039^1
$\Delta p_f^*(-1)$	0.100^1	-0.001^1	0.022^* (0.5)	0.105^1	0.092^1
$\Delta p_f^*(-2)$	0.100^1	-0.001^* (0.0)	0.021 (0.2)	-0.005 (0.1)	0.008 (1.0)
$\Delta y(-1)$	0.22 (3.6)	0.20 (3.4)	0.22 (3.7)	0.21 (3.9)	0.19 (3.4)
$p'(-1)^2$	-0.142 (3.1)	-0.109 (1.5)	-0.162 (3.8)	-0.157 (3.9)	-0.144 (3.0)
$ulc(-4)$	0.067^1	0.038^1	0.074^1	0.073^1	0.054^1
$p_{im}(-3)$	0.033^1	0.019^1	0.036^1	0.036^1	0.026^1
$p_f^*(-3)$	0.042 (2.0)	0.052 (2.6)	0.052 (2.8)	0.048 (2.7)	0.063 (3.6)
$cu(-2)$	-0.085 (3.6)	-0.048 (2.6)	-0.083^* (3.5)	-0.083^* (3.6)	-0.021^1
$\bar{R}^2$	0.76	0.74	0.89	0.93	0.92
SEE (%)	0.78	0.78	0.67	0.67	0.70
DW	2.0	2.2	2.2	2.2	2.0
DF	39	37	36	37	38
B-P(df)	12.5(9)	10.2(9)	11.9(9)	12.6(9)	7.5(9)
$\chi^2(df)^3$		6.5(1)	8.1(2)XVI	7.1(1)XVI	
Period	711-833	711-833	711-833^4	711-833	711-833

[1]Coefficient value constrained.
[2]Lagged dependent variable with constrained effect from p_a and tx, that is, $p' = p - 083p_a - 0.039tx$.
[3]Test of constraint imposed; equation of comparison in column I unless otherwise stated.
[4]Excluding 793.

Note: The coefficient(s) being tested in each equation are marked *.

the Treasury macroeconomic model with this equation (and the larger coefficient) included: the effect was to make the implied profit margin unacceptably volatile.

In the context of the present analysis this constraint, apart from having a small influence on the magnitude of the freely estimated coefficients in the equation (which were estimated with it imposed) has two effects. It changes the allocation of the 'goods market influence on inflation' between the capacity utilization variable and the residual (see Table 7.5, in which it is demonstrated that this term offsets the 'disequilibrium' in some periods), and it suggests a smaller contribution from the price equation to the levels effect in the 'Phillips curve' than is, in fact, implied by the data (Chapter 7).

2.5.7 The significance of demand

It is clear from the equations reported in this section that the data supported a role for demand; significant coefficients were found on both the change in manufacturing output and the CBI measure of capacity utilization. When the equation was tested with the productivity variable replaced by the trend productivity series used in the next chapter, the fit of the equation was significantly worse. It was therefore concluded that the 'normal cost' hypothesis (section 2.3.2) should be rejected in favour of the actual cost specification presented here. This has a mark-up that varies with demand and with the level of competitors' prices.

In the light of the earlier work on the possible role of demand in determining the mark-up on unit costs, it is interesting to note the way in which it enters the equation for price-setting. First, there are two variables in the equation that model the effect of demand on prices: the change in the level of demand and the level of capacity utilization (the lagged level of demand itself was found not to be significant). The effect of these in policy prescriptions for reducing inflation is noted in section 2.6 and discussed in Chapter 8. Second, the plot of the residuals does not reveal any obvious effect of excess demand on price-setting not picked up by the explanatory variables in the equation. A ratchet effect when capacity limits are reached (when output is at its maximum level, in 1974 for example) is not apparent from a simple examination of these data.

2.5.8 The fit of the equation

Figure 2.3 shows the residuals of the chosen equation, reported in column XVI of Table 2.3. It indicates the magnitude of the outlier in 1979Q3.

The track of this equation is shown in Figure 2.4. This shows the estimated path of quarterly price inflation when the long-run equilibrium term is constructed using data for the lagged value of the price level. Figure 2.5 indicates the track of the annual inflation rate when the estimated value of the lagged price variable is used. This should give a better indication of the way the equation might be expected to behave in a forecasting situation in which forecasts of future price rises must be based on forecasts, rather than data, for lagged price inflation. In fact, because there is little serial correlation among the residuals, the two are very similar.

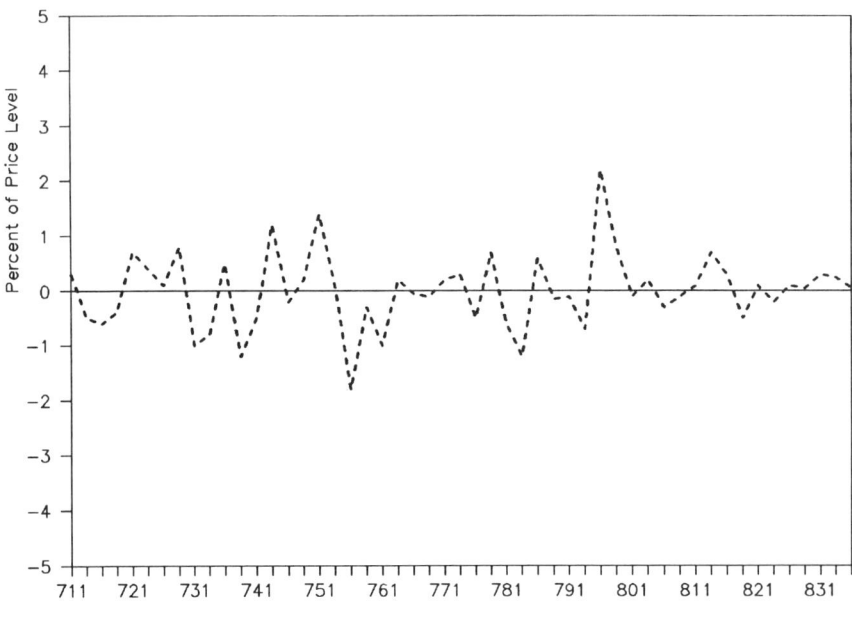

Fig. 2.3 Residuals on estimated equation.

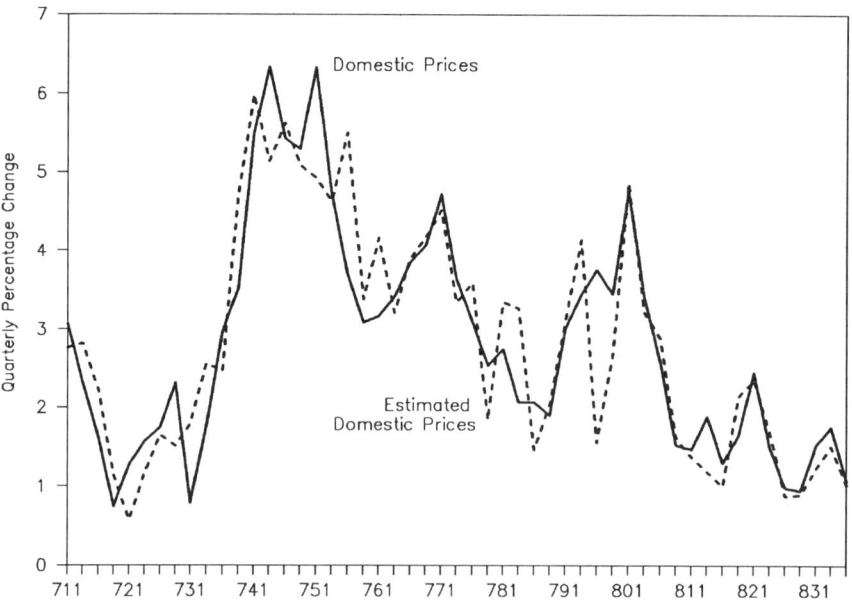

Fig. 2.4 Track of estimated equation.

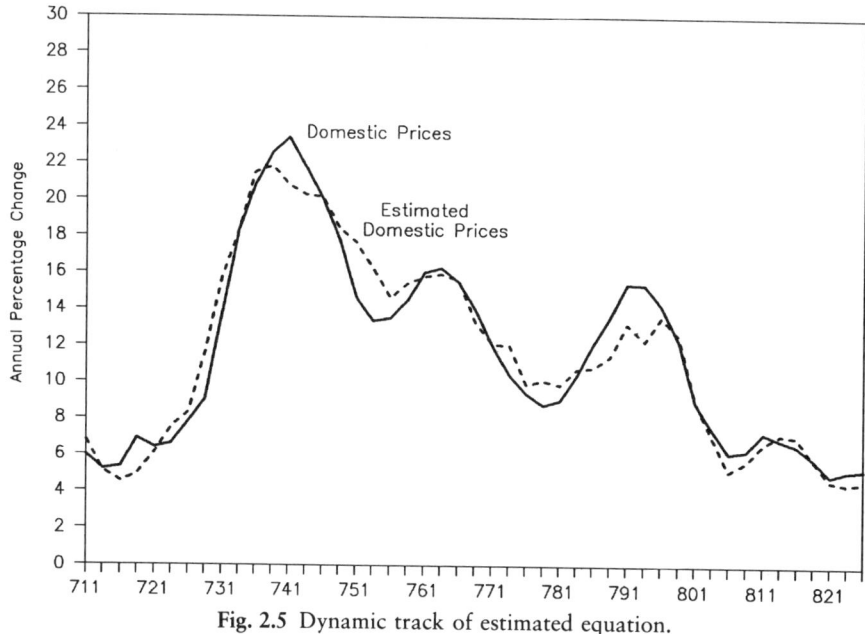

Fig. 2.5 Dynamic track of estimated equation.

2.6 IMPLICATIONS FOR POLICY

This section considers the implications of the equation presented in section 2.5 for policy initiatives to prevent or to reduce inflation. It examines this from various points of view. First, we examine the role of money; this is because the relevance of money growth to inflation has played such a prominent role in inflation policy in recent years. Second, we look at the effect on price inflation of the path of real demand; reducing the level of demand is the conventional method of dealing with inflation when it has become too high. Next, we note the magnitude of the implied influence of the exchange rate on price inflation.

We then examine the evidence for the homogeneity properties that affect the degree of inflation indexation, that is, the extent to which this equation passes inflation from one period to the next when the market is in equilibrium (the inertia of the inflation spiral). In order to design policy in this area it is helpful to have a view about whether, when the real economy is in equilibrium, the inflation rate will automatically fall back to an acceptable level or whether positive action on the part of the government is needed to get it down. Finally, we note the likely potential there is in this market for generating inflationary pressure.

(a) The role of money

One question that remains is whether there is a role for money growth in determining the rate at which prices rise. It is interesting to note that there is no direct role for the money supply in this equation for price setting. Unless there is a direct effect of money growth on wage setting or on the path of the exchange rate, any effect of monetary policy on the rate of inflation must operate through other terms in the equations, for example, those in the level of demand.

This analysis suggests that if monetary policy creates an expansion of demand, that is, an outward shift of the demand function, then this will be met by increases in both output and prices relative to what would otherwise have been the case, so long as there are sufficient resources. If resources are limited, however, and the capacity constraint bites restricting output, then the rise in demand will lead to an increase in imports, destocking, and faster rises in prices than would otherwise have been the case. In these circumstances the monetary policy that caused the rise in the money supply will also have caused a persisting increase in inflation. The rest of the time money growth follows, and is associated with, a rise in prices rather than causing it.

(b) Effect of demand

The price equation described in section 2.5 contains two terms reflecting the path of economic activity. The effect of policy on the path of demand will influence inflation through both of these.

The dynamic part of the equation contains a term in the rate of growth of manufacturing output. Because of this, if manufacturing output increases by more than the trend rate (subsumed into the intercept to the equation) then prices will rise by more than they would otherwise have done; if it increases by less they will rise less fast. It follows that if activity falls, remains at a low level and then rises back to its original level, this term in the price equation will put downward pressure on inflation when activity is falling, and while activity remains at a low level (a low level of output relative to capacity but with growth on trend) there will be no effect on inflation (once the lagged effects have fed through). When output grows faster than trend, taking the level back to the trend line, the rate of inflation will increase again, returning, according to this equation, to exactly the rate it would have taken in the absence of the recession (other things being equal).

The other term relating to activity is the term in capacity utilization in the long-run equilibrium part of the equation. The effect of this term is complex. First, it is defined as the deviation of capacity utilization from its optimal level (the data come from the survey carried out each month by the CBI). It is therefore different from zero only in the short run since in the long run (time for investment) capacity will adjust to the value implied by the level of activity. Second, it influences the price rise through the long-run equilibrium term in the equation: if the level of the profit margin is consistent with low capacity utilization, the whole long-run equilibrium term will be zero and so will have no effect on price-setting. However, if capacity utilization is low and the profit margin at the time price levels are revised does not take adequate account of that fact and is too high, then the long run equilibrium term will be positive and, because it has a negative coefficient, the price rises will be lower than they would otherwise have been.

(c) Role for influence of exchange rate

Later in our story, when the paths of wages and input prices are replaced by their determinants, the dependence of the dynamics of the spiral on the reactions of the exchange rate will become apparent. Here we merely note that the magnitude of this effect depends on the share of total unit costs that represents imported inputs and on the effect of foreign competitors' prices on the profit margin.

(d) Implications for inflation inertia

The theoretical derivation of our price equation suggests that, given no money illusion, the total long-term coefficient on explanatory inflation variables will be unity. Put another way, the equation implies full inflation indexation in the goods and services market. If this is the case for all the equations that make up the model of the spiral then it will have full inflation indexation: in equilibrium, when all real variables are at their long-run equilibrium levels, inflation this year will be the same as inflation last year. In these circumstances there would be no tendency for inflation to return towards zero or to some acceptable 'core' rate (3 per cent or 5 per cent, say) in the long term.

The data support this hypothesis of 'no money illusion' in the price equation.

(e) Potential for generating inflationary pressure

The effect of variations in demand and competitors' prices (relative to domestic prices) on price-setting seems to be slight (Figure 7.11 shows the contribution of the 'X' variables in the price-setting equation to the rate of inflation). It can therefore be argued that price-setting, motivated by the decision-taker's desire to maximize profits, in fact sets the price, given nominal wages, at around the level that gives the real wage a value consistent with the fundamentals (productivity, the terms of trade and the level of taxes).[11] Sometimes, when price rises are such as to reduce the real wage (perhaps because productivity growth has slowed, or the terms of trade have changed) this will lead to higher margins and tend to increase inflation. At other times, when the real wage consistent with the fundamentals is increasing, this may involve smaller profit margins and so tend to reduce inflation.[12]

APPENDIX 2A: THE RETAIL PRICES INDEX

The generally accepted measure of price inflation in the UK is the Retail Prices Index (RPI), rather than the Producer Price Index (Output) which is modelled by the equation developed here. As a result it is the RPI that is the main influence on the rate of increase of earnings in the UK. It follows that one needs an equation that relates these two indicators of inflation in order to model the UK inflation spiral.

The RPI is constructed as the weighted sum of the changes in the prices of a great number of goods and services from the value they took in a base period. The weights are revised each year on the basis of the information in the Household Expenditure Survey. The base period is January of each year and the index is spliced together in January.

The equation used for the RPI expresses it as the weighted sum[13] of price indices for food, PRF, housing, PRH, services provided by nationalized industries or local councils, PRN, and the rest, PRO:

$$RPI = 0.6170\,PRO + 0.2059\,PRF + 0.1186\,PRH + 0.0651\,PRN$$

In this equation PRO is given by:

$$PRO = (1 + VAT)\,PROXT$$

where PROXT ('other' prices excluding VAT) is proxied by the Producer Price Index. The food price index, PRF, is also proxied by the Producer Price Index. The housing price index, PRH, is given by:

$$PRH = 0.2222\,PRENT + 0.1905\,PRATE + 0.3782\,PRMIP + 0.2287\,PRHO$$

with the price indices for rent, PRENT, rates, PRATE, and the 'other' housing costs, PRHO (repair, maintenance, insurance) proxied by the Producer Price Index. The index for owner occupiers' housing costs is modelled by the equation:

$$PRMIP = r_m DEBT\,(1 - ITX)$$

where r_m is the mortgage interest rate, DEBT is mortgage debt outstanding (a long distributed lag on house prices, proxied by the Producer Price Index) and ITX is the standard rate of income tax. The real value of the Nationalized Industry Price Index (defined relative to the Producer Price Index) is treated as exogenous.

Besides picking up the effect of the changing weights, the residual on the equation for the rate of change of the RPI therefore picks up the difference between the rate of increase of the Producer Price Index and the sum of all the RPI components that are proxied by it. The difference between the path of the RPI and the PPIO is small, as shown in Figure 7.11.

APPENDIX 2B: MODELLING IMPORT PRICES

2B.1 Introduction

The rate of increase in prices in the rest of the world impinges on the domestic economy via the change in the prices of imported inputs and finished goods. In order to understand the inflation process it is therefore necessary to explain the mechanism by which the world currency prices of foreign goods and services, adjusted for the exchange rate, become sterling prices in the UK. This Appendix describes this link.

2B.2 Modelling import prices in sterling

The above analysis of domestic price-setting has implications for modelling the prices of imported goods, whether they be primary commodities or finished goods. It suggests that the prices of these goods for sale in the UK market will take account of overseas costs but will have a margin that is dependent on the prices charged for domestic output in the domestic market and on the level of activity in the UK. These prices will therefore be determined by an equation with the same general form as equation 2.10 or its dynamic (estimatable) counterpart, equation 2.14. For example, it might take the form:

$$\Delta p_i = \lambda_1(\Delta p_i^w - \Delta rx) + \lambda_2 \Delta p + \lambda_3 \Delta(y - \bar{y})$$
$$- \mu(L)[p_i - \delta_1(p_i^w - rx) - \delta_2 p - \delta_3(y - \bar{y})] \quad i = c, f \qquad (2B.1)$$

where rx is the exchange rate (weighted basket) and p_i^w represents the cost of the imported primary commodities or finished goods in world currencies. This should include labour costs, administered prices and any taxes as appropriate, as well as primary commodity prices; it should not reflect those aspects of the overseas market that may be incorporated in the mark-up for the price charged for sale in the foreign market.

For the purpose of analysing the inflation spiral in Chapters 5 and 6 the above equation for the change in domestic currency prices of imported goods can be written:

$$\Delta p_i = e_i(L)(\Delta p_i^w - \Delta rx) + f_i(L)\Delta p + X_{2i}. \quad i = c, f \qquad (2B.2)$$

where X_{2i} contains variables similar to those in X_1 but relating to sales in the domestic market rather than in the market of the country of origin. The no money illusion assumption (as defined in section 2.4.4) implies:

$$e_i(1) + f_i(1) = 1 \quad i = c, f \qquad (2B.3)$$

2B.3 Equations for import prices

This section lists the empirical equations for import prices in domestic currency that are used in the Inflation Spiral Equation. In fact these equations, which were estimated in the early 1980s and taken from a version of the Treasury model used in the mid-1980s, express the import prices as simple homogeneous log-linear combinations of domestic and world prices and the exchange rate. They do not include the dependence on domestic activity suggested by the theory outlined above but do include the dependence on competing domestic prices. As a result of the omission, the effect of domestic activity on the inflation spiral may be slightly understated.

Two import price variables are required for the equations for prices and wages in the model, one for competing finished goods and one for inputs into the domestic production process, as in equations 2.22 and 2.23. The latter combines the prices of primary commodities with the prices of finished or intermediate goods produced abroad and imported for use in domestic production.

These two import price variables are constructed from four import price indices. These relate to:

finished manufactures p_{fm}
semi-manufactures p_s
fuel p_{fu}
basic materials p_b

The first two weighted together using market shares to give an index for competing finished goods prices, p_f^* (equation 2.23). All four contribute, according to their input–output weights, to the series for the imported input price index (equation 2.22). In the model we relate these to a set of world price variables by the equations listed below.

The explanatory world price variables in these equations are:

trade-weighted manufactured export prices p_f^w
price of basic materials p_b^w
price of oil p_o^w
prices of non-ferrous metal and agricultural non-food p_n^w

The following are the equations used:

(i) Sterling price of imported finished manufactures

$$p_{fm} = 0.404p(-1) + 0.596(p_f^w - rx) \tag{2B.4}$$

(ii) Sterling price of imported semi-manufactures

$$\begin{aligned} p_s = {} & 0.093p + 0.907\{0.033p_b^w + 0.033p_o^w + 0.015p_o^w(-1) + 0.007p_o^w(-2) \\ & + 0.594p_n^w + 0.222p_n^w(-1) + 0.096p_n^w(-2) \\ & - [0.582rx + 0.221rx(-1) + 0.197rx(-2)]\} \end{aligned} \tag{2B.5}$$

(iii) Sterling price of imported fuel

$$p_{fu} = 0.424p_o^w + 0.424p_o^w(-1) + 0.116p_f^w + 0.036p_f^w(-1) - [0.540rx + 0.460rx(-1)] \tag{2B.6}$$

(iv) Sterling price of imported basic materials

$$\begin{aligned} p_b = {} & 0.173p_{bf}^w + 0.493p_{bf}^w(-1) + 0.132p_{bf}^w(-2) + 0.202p_{bf}^w(-3) \\ & + 0.329rx + 0.319rx(-1) + 0.240rx(-2) + 0.112rx(-3) \end{aligned} \tag{2B.7}$$

where

$$p_{bf}^w = \ln(0.88P_b^w + 0.12P_f^w) \tag{2B.8}$$

REFERENCES

Arrow, K. J. (1959) Towards a theory of price adjustment, in Abramovitz, M. (ed.) *The Allocation of Economic Resources*, Stanford University Press, Stanford, California.

Arrow, K. J. and Hahn, F. H. (1971) *General Competitive Analysis*, Holden-Day Inc., San Francisco.

Atkin, B. and Skinner, R. (1975) *How British Industry Prices*, Industrial Market Research Ltd.

Baumol, W. (1959) *Business Behaviour, Value and Growth*, Macmillan, New York.

Baumol, W. J. and Quandt, R. E. (1964) Rules of thumb and optimally imperfect decisions, *The American Economic Review*, **54**, 23–46.

Brechling, F. P. R. (1972) Some empirical evidence on the effectiveness of prices and incomes policies, in Parkin, J. M. and Sumner, M. T. (eds.) *Incomes Policy and Inflation*, Manchester University Press, Manchester.

Coutts, K., Godley, W. and Nordhaus, W. (1978) *Industrial Pricing in the United Kingdom*, Cambridge University Press, Cambridge.

Dorward, N. (1987) *The Pricing Decision: Economic Theory and Business Practice*, Harper and Row, London.

Dow, J. C. R. and Dicks-Mireaux, L. A. (1958) The excess demand for labour, *Oxford Economic Papers*, **10**.

Hague, D. C. (1971) *Pricing in Business*, George Allen and Unwin Ltd, London.

Hall, R. L. and Hitch, C. J. (1939) Price theory and business behaviour, *Oxford Economic Papers*, **2**, 12–45.

Leland, H. E. (1982) Theory of the firm facing uncertain demand, *The American Economic Review*, **52**, 278–91.

Lerner, A. P. (1944) *The Economics of Control*, Macmillan, New York.

McCallum, B. T. (1970) The effect of demand on prices in British manufacturing: another view, *Review of Economic Studies*, **37**, 147–56.

McFetridge, D. G. (1973) The determinants of pricing behaviour: a study of the Canadian cotton textile indutry, *Journal of Industrial Economics*, **22**, 141–52.

Machlup, F. (1946) Marginal analysis and empirical research, *American Economic Review*, **36**, 514–54.

Marris, R. (1964) *The Economic Theory of Managerial Capitalism*, Macmillan, London.

Marris, R. (1991) *Reconstructing Keynesian Economics with Imperfect Competition*, Edward Elgar, Aldershot.

Mills, E. S. (1959) Uncertainty and price theory, *Quarterly Journal of Economics*, **73**, 116–30.

Nield, R. R. (1963) *Pricing and Employment in the Trade Cycle*, Cambridge University Press, Cambridge.

Nordhaus, W. D. and Godley, W. (1972) Pricing in the trade cycle, *The Economic Journal*, **82**, 853–82.

Paish, F. W. (1962) *Studies in an Inflationary Economy*, MacMillan, London.

Penrose, E. T. (1959) *The Theory of the Growth of the Firm*, Basil Blackwell, Oxford.

Rao, V. R. (1984) Pricing research in marketing: the state of the art, *Journal of Business*, **57**, S39–S60.

Rowlatt, P. A. (1986) A model of wage bargaining, *Government Economic Service Working Paper No. 91*, HM Treasury, London.

Rowlatt, P. A. (1987) Analysis of the inflation process, *Government Economic Service Working Paper No. 99*, HM Treasury, London.

Rushdy, F. and Lund, P. J. (1967) The effect of demand on prices in British manufacturing industry, *The Review of Economic Studies*, **34**, 361–73.

Sandmo, A. (1971) On the theory of the competitive firm under price uncertainty, *The American Economic Review*, **61**, 65–73.

Scitovsky, T. (1943) A note on profit maximisation and its implications, *The Review of Economic Studies*, **11**, 57–60.

Shipley, D. D. (1981) Pricing objectives in British manufacturing industry, *The Journal of Industrial Economics*, **29**, 429–43.

Skinner, R. C. (1970) The determination of selling prices, *Journal of Industrial Economics*, **18**, 201–17.

Smith, G. W. (1982) The normal cost hypothesis: a reappraisal, in Artis, M. J., Green, C. J., Leslie, D. L. and Smith, B. W. (eds.) *Demand Management, Supply Constraints and Inflation*, Manchester University Press, Manchester.

Solow, R. M. (1969) *Price Expectations and the Behaviour of the Price Level*, Manchester University Press, Manchester.

Zabel, E. (1972) Monopoly and uncertainty, *Review of Economic Studies*, **39**, 205–19.

ENDNOTES

1. For example, Scitovsky (1943) investigates the implications of profit maximization for the entrepreneur's preference function, Penrose (1959) explores the relation between the manager's desire to make profits and the desire that the firm should grow, and Marris (1991) models the firm as maximizing a weighted combination of discounted future cash-flow and discounted future employment (size). Dorward (1987) contains an excellent summary of work on motivation and other issues relating to price decisions.

2. Rao (1984) has a discussion of tactical pricing behaviour.

3. For example, Mills (1959), Sandmo (1971), Zabel (1972) and Leland (1982).

4. Unsurprisingly, they also confirmed Neild's results, finding the demand variable was not significant in the regressions in which costs were 'normalized' using an exogenous trend productivity measure.

5. This depends on the capital stock, K, and is determined in a prior decision relating to longer term considerations in which the cost of capital plays a role (section 2.2.2).

6. Unless demand elasticities are precisely constant along demand schedules. This is unlikely. It implies strongly convex demand schedules. It raises the possibility that the production function may be such that no solution exists to the profit maximization problem. It becomes difficult to explain how the return to capital can be equalized across industries.

7. Lower case letters indicate the logarithms of variables represented by upper case letters; Δ is the difference operator $1 - L$ where L is the lag operator.

8. Section 2.4.2.

9. Here, the coefficients in equation 2.14 have been generalized into lag distributions, thus $a(L) = a_0 + a_1L + a_2L^2 + \cdots$ and so on.

10. One of the dynamic price explanatory variables, $\Delta ulc(-1)$, was subtracted from the dependent variable, Δp, and from each of the other dynamic price explanatory variables, Δp^i, as in the equation:

$$\Delta p - \Delta ulc(-1) = \sum \alpha_i(\Delta p^i - \Delta ulc(-1)) + \cdots$$

giving:

$$\Delta p = (1 - \sum \alpha_i)\Delta ulc(-1) + \sum \alpha_i \Delta p^i + \cdots$$

11. Section 3.2.3 has a discussion of this.
12. In the mid-1980s profit maximizing price rises reflected falls in commodity prices and permitted an increase in the real wage consistent with this change in the terms of trade.
13. These weights are based on the composition of the RPI in 1985. They sum to a number different to unity because the values of the component price indices were not normalized in that year.

3

The labour market

3.1 INTRODUCTION

The analysis of wage-setting is crucial to the modelling of the inflation process. Indeed, the labour market has been by far the most heavily worked area in the attempt to understand inflation and to specify policy prescriptions. In this chapter we explain the rationale for our wage equation.

Casual observation suggests that wages are generally determined in a process of collective negotiation – bargaining – between employers and employees, rather than simply responding to the interaction of demand and supply in the market. This view is supported by the New Earnings Survey (1989) which found that the wages of around 80 per cent of UK workers are determined by 'collective agreement'. It is clear that the main interests of employers and employees are opposing: employers, in their attempt to maximize profits (as discussed in Chapter 2) will wish to hold wages down as low as is consistent with employing enough staff of an adequate quality to perform the relevant tasks. Employees, possibly organized into a union or staff association, will try to maximize their take-home pay and therefore their nominal wage, subject to continuing in employment.

This being so, it seems strange that so much theoretical and empirical work should have been concentrated on the Phillips curve and the role of excess demand and supply in wage-setting. However, to the extent that the price in the labour market is set in a bargaining situation, the power[1] that each side holds will be important in determining the outcome. If, as seems likely, the allocation of power in the wage bargaining process is influenced by the level of excess supply or demand in the market, then this will have a significant role to play, along with other factors, in determining the outcome of the bargain.

Section 3.2 contains an assessment of the usual approach to modelling the path of wages: the Phillips curve. The possibility of hysteresis is explored and its relevance for policy prescriptions is noted. Various other theories that relate to special features of the labour market are discussed in section 3.3. In section 3.4 some empirical evidence relating to the approaches cited is summarized.

In section 3.5 we use the chosen approach, a bargaining model, to derive an equation that can be estimated. The results of the estimation are reported in section

3.6, where the equation used in our model is presented along with tables and charts to indicate its performance. Section 3.7 notes the implications this equation is likely to have for policy.

3.2 THE PHILLIPS CURVE

3.2.1 The Phillips curve and expectations

The historical starting point for most theoretical approaches to modelling the way in which wages are set has been the empirical observation of Phillips (1958). He observed that the rate of wage inflation in the UK seemed to vary inversely with the level of unemployment in such a way that equal falls in unemployment were associated with progressively larger increases in wage inflation (Figure 3.1).[2]

A theoretical justification for the relationship was produced afterwards,[3] citing the pressure of excess demand in individual labour markets operating on the nominal wage (unemployment was seen as a proxy for labour market disequilibrium).

This relationship suggested that there was a stable trade-off between inflation and unemployment. It has the implication that the government has a choice: it could gear fiscal and monetary policy towards having high unemployment with low price inflation or towards having a small number out of work but high inflation, or to some intermediate situation.

However, this historical relationship was not robust to the large swings in the business cycle that began in the 1960s. In each upswing the rate of inflation increased, but there was little fall in the level of unemployment. In the downswings unemployment increased with little effect on inflation.[4] The Phillips curve was

Fig. 3.1 Phillips curve.

unstable during this period, shifting progressively further upwards and outwards, as illustrated in Figure 8.1.

Both Phelps (1967) and Friedman (1968) suggested that this breakdown of the Phillips relationship related to the large increase in the rate of price inflation that followed the rapid rise in commodity prices. They argued that this had raised expectations regarding the rate of price inflation and that expected future price rises play a role in the relationship between unemployment and nominal wage rises: that the labour market sets the expected real wage, rather than the nominal wage, in the light of labour market disequilibrium. Accordingly, this amendment to Phillips' original inflation–unemployment trade-off included inflation expectations within the model. The relationship was respecified as what is now known as the Expectations Augmented Phillips Curve (EAPC),[5] as in Figure 3.2.

The Friedman–Phelps amendment fundamentally changes the implications of this relationship for policy. As well as reducing unemployment, a reflationary policy, by increasing inflation, would lead to increased inflation expectations. It follows that a reflationary policy which takes unemployment below the level U* in Figure 3.2, will cause a rise in inflation. This will lead to an increase in inflation expectations which will cause the old unemployment–inflation trade-off to shift upwards and outwards. The result is a situation in which there is a higher rate of inflation for any given unemployment level. Conversely, a policy that raises unemployment above U*, and so reduces inflation and inflation expectations, will lead to a downward and inward shift in the trade-off. Since U* is the level of unemployment that will obtain when expectations of inflation are fulfilled, it is known as the non-accelerating inflation rate of unemployment (NAIRU).

The EAPC therefore predicts that in the long run, when inflation expectations

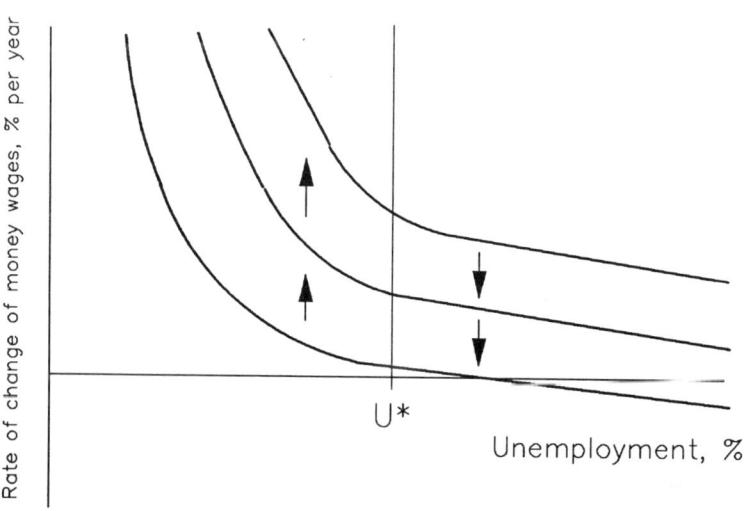

Fig. 3.2 Constant expectations Phillips curves.

are consistent with the outcome, there is only one level of unemployment that is possible (U*): there can be no trade-off between unemployment and inflation in the long run with this equation. Indeed, with this modification the long-run Phillips curve has become vertical. Any rate of inflation can be consistent with equilibrium in the labour market.

The implication of the EAPC for policy is that, in the absence of instantaneous market clearing, inflation can be controlled by careful manipulation of excess supply (or demand) in the labour market (as discussed in Chapter 8). In the extreme case, in which instantaneous market clearing is assumed to be combined with rational expectations,[6] the rate of unemployment would always be at its equilibrium level. Attempts to reduce unemployment below the NAIRU would be unsuccessful and would result only in a rapid revision of inflation expectations leading to a higher prevailing rate of inflation.

3.2.2 Determinants of the NAIRU

During the 1970s and 1980s, many OECD countries suffered increasing levels of unemployment combined with inflation rates that did not decline. If wage rises are determined by the EAPC, it is not surprising to find that economists attribute this to a rise in the NAIRU. Further, it comes as no surprise that empirical estimates suggest that the NAIRU rose. If the NAIRU is not constant, but varies with economic variables, then these need to be included in a model of wage setting since, clearly, they would have an influence on the inflation spiral. A number of alternative models have been proposed.

First, Minford has argued that the factors underlying the NAIRU are to be found on the supply side of the economy (Minford, 1988). He cites the likely influence of unemployment benefit rates, tax rates, demographic trends, employers' NI contributions and the unionization rate.

A second approach suggests that the simple EAPC equation itself may be misspecified. For example, it omits such factors as the effect on the equilibrium real wage of varying productivity growth and changes in the terms of trade.

A third explanation assumes that the NAIRU has increased but, rather than attributing this to supply side variables, assumes that it is because of what has come to be known as 'hysteresis'[7] operating in the labour market. The idea here is that the long-term unemployed ('outsiders' from the wage bargaining process) do not exert much downward pressure in the labour market since their chances of getting a job decline the longer they remain unemployed. A proper specification of the unemployment term in the EAPC equation would therefore exclude them.

Fourth, a broadly similar effect would be achieved if the level of the NAIRU depends on the past history (lagged values) of the level of unemployment. In the extreme case it should be the change in unemployment that is included in the wage equation, not the level. This possibility would change the policy implications of the EAPC (Chapter 8). If the NAIRU depends on lagged unemployment, then higher unemployment can no longer be confidently expected to defeat inflation. For if the NAIRU is, in fact, wholly determined by lagged unemployment such a policy will only defer inflation: when unemployment falls again, inflation will rise.

Finally, it may be that the NAIRU depends on the amount of productive capacity in the economy. If productive capacity is inadequate, inflationary bottlenecks will be encountered at a lower level of employment than if it were not.

3.2.3 Whole economy budget constraint

From time to time we refer to the situation in which the real wage or the profit margin is consistent with the 'fundamentals' or is higher than the 'warranted' level (section 2.6, for example). This relates to the total amount that is available in the economy for distribution between employees (the post-tax real wage) and employers (profit per unit of output). This amount is determined by labour productivity, the terms of trade and the quantity taken in taxes for public sector distribution. It is, so to speak, the whole economy budget constraint. If, when nominal wages are set **given** the level of prices, they are set at a level higher than is warranted by these fundamental factors, this will put upward pressure on inflation. This aspect of the inflation generating process is stressed by both Panic (1973) and Baxter (1973).

This so-called whole economy budget constraint is indicated by the following (simplified) set of equations. Given that unit profits, π, the real wage, rw, and the terms of trade, tt, can be defined in terms of the price, p, the wage, w, and the price of imports, p_{im}, by the following equations:

$$\pi = p - \alpha(w - pr) - (1 - \alpha)p_{im}$$

$$rw = w - p + rr$$

$$tt = p - p_{im}$$

(where pr is productivity and rr the retention ratio) it is easy to see that the following constraint holds:

$$\pi + \alpha rw = \alpha(pr + rr) + (1 - \alpha)tt \tag{3.1}$$

Equation 3.1 is, effectively, a budget constraint expressing the amount available in the economy to be shared between real wages and the profit margin.

When an entrepreneur chooses the price and output etc. to maximize expected profit, the relevant levels of productivity, the terms of trade and various tax rates are automatically taken into account, as well as the result of the most recent wage settlement. There is a sense, therefore, in which price-setting determines the real wage rather than inflation. Wage-setting may be more instrumental in determining the rate of inflation. However, both price-setting and wage-setting are of course relevant to the outcome on both the real wage and the rate of inflation. In this context it is interesting to note the cumulated contributions of price-setting in these markets to UK inflation rates according to our model in Figures 7.10 and 7.12.

3.2.4 Discussion of Phillips curve models

The EAPC is a model that explains the determination of the real wage. Clearly, if the labour market produces a nominal wage that implies a real wage level higher than warranted by the economic fundamentals, then this will put upward pressure on inflation. For when the firms concerned next set their prices, these will be raised by more than would otherwise have been the case. This will then reduce the real wage, perhaps to around the warranted level. To achieve the previously agreed, unrealistically high, real wage the nominal wage set in the next wage round will have to be higher than it would otherwise have been. This process will continue, and will put upward pressure on the inflation spiral.

However, the EAPC model described above is simply one of the possible models explaining the change in the expected real wage. Clearly there are other variables besides disequilibrium in the labour market that could have an effect on inflation through this route. Any factor that affects the real wage set in the labour market, causing it to deviate from the level implied by the fundamentals, will have the same effect. The following section contains some further reasons why the real wage agreed may be out of line with the fundamentals.

3.3 OTHER APPROACHES

3.3.1 Introduction

The labour market is subject to a number of institutional influences and constraints. Over the years these have been identified and studied by numerous economists. The results are summarized briefly in this section along with their relevance for the modelling of wage-setting.

First, 'search models' examine the determinants of the wage outcome for those seeking a job. These provide a microeconomic justification for the EAPC. Second, the implications of labour market 'implicit contracts' are examined. These relate to the wage outcome for those who remain in the same job. Third, there are the 'efficient wage hypotheses'. These suggest various reasons why firms may offer to pay workers more than can be justified by their productivity.

Finally, the development of approaches that emphasize the role of the union is described. These lead to the bargaining model, spelt out in sections 3.5 and 3.6, that underlies the wage equation incorporated into our model of the inflation spiral.

3.3.2 Search models

Search models[8] examine the implications for the labour market of the fact that workers have to spend time searching for jobs and employers spend time seeking suitable employees. These models provide an heuristic explanation for the EAPC, in that they explain why an excess of searchers over job vacancies leads to lower real wages being agreed and a scarcity of searchers to a higher real wage. In doing so they provide a source for modelling the NAIRU; they identify the factors which are likely to affect the length of the 'queue' when there are enough jobs to go round.

The simplest form of search model assumes that each prospective worker knows the distribution of potential wage offers, chooses a minimum acceptable wage (known as the reservation wage) and receives one job offer per search period. The reservation wage is assumed to be set at the level at which the expected gain from future search (an increase in expected lifetime earnings) equals the cost (the direct search cost less unemployment benefits and the opportunity cost of lost wages). The reservation wage declines as the search becomes prolonged.

Search theory is predicated on the absence of scales of pay that have been agreed with trade unions by collective bargaining. It suggests that in these circumstances wage offers are likely to be flexible, adjusting towards the level that would clear the market, but that searchers take time to acquire information about revisions to wage distributions and make the necessary adjustments to their reservation wages.

These models therefore enable the factors which determine the rate of unemployment when there is no shortage of vacancies to be identified and incorporated into the modelling of the NAIRU. For example, increases in the unemployment benefit paid to job searchers will reduce the net cost of search and so increase the time spent searching. If the wage distribution in the searcher's market changes but there is no change in the reservation wage, the average time spent searching will change. If job searchers raise their reservation wage for some reason this will increase the average search duration.

Although some economists[9] have had success with including variables representing some of these in equations to explain the change in the real wage, the work reported here gave little support to these findings (outlined in section 3.6.5).

3.3.3 Implicit contract theory

Whereas search models are concerned with the wages of those entering the labour force after a period of search, implicit contract theory concentrates on the wages of those who remain in employment with the same employer. Like the search models, these theories are predicated on the absence of collective bargaining.

One of the most striking differences between the real labour market and the standard view of a competitive market is the fact that workers tend to stay with the same firm for an extended period. This attachment between firm and worker has been particularly well documented for the Japanese economy (Hashimoto, 1979, for example) where most workers expect to remain with the same employer throughout their working life. A similar, if less extreme, situation obtains in the USA and other developed economies. Hall (1982) found the typical worker in the US was holding a job that had lasted, or would last, about eight years; and for a substantial proportion of older workers job duration was found to be more than twenty years. In the case of the UK, Main (1982) used data from the New Earnings

Survey (1968 and 1979) to show that the average completed length of a full-time job for UK males aged 21 and over was approximately 20 years. The strength and continuity of this association between firms and workers provided the initial stimulus for the development of the 'implicit contract' theories of real wage rigidity (as discussed by Azariadis 1975, Baily 1974, Gordon 1974).

Early versions of contract theory assumed that firms are relatively risk-neutral and are providing real income insurance for risk-averse workers (workers who prefer a fixed real wage to a variable one with a slightly higher mean). Workers and employers are assumed to have access to the same information: they each know the probability *ex ante* that a boom or a slump will occur, and *ex post* each can readily observe both the state of the economy and how the firm has been performing. The optimal labour contract is then one in which the worker accepts a lower average wage in exchange for being insured against the risk of a recession. The firm is able to extract higher profits from the lower expected value of its costs, given that it is prepared to bear the risk.

This version of implicit contract theory predicts that the real wage will generally be **below** that implied by the fundamentals (productivity, the terms of trade and tax rates (section 3.2.3)) and that the magnitude of fluctuations in employment will be dampened:[10] the fluctuations in demand will be reflected in productivity rather than employment. However, there is little empirical support for this theory. For example, if money wage settlements are below the level implied by the fundamentals so that the real wage tends, on average, to be below the level implied by the fundamentals, this would put downward pressure on inflation; prices would rise less than they would otherwise have done and nominal wages would rise by less again, next time they were reset. In this case there should be evidence of downward pressure on inflation from the labour market, and in our model this would take the form of a negative intercept in the wage equation. But this is not the observed pattern. Further, although it is true that productivity varies with demand, so does employment.

A variety of results can be obtained from implicit contract theory: the predictions vary with the precise specification of the assumptions. For example, the prediction that variations in demand are not reflected in unemployment is reversed if it is assumed that the firm 'insures' workers by offering redundancy payments that make workers indifferent between retention and layoff rather than by continuing to employ them through a recession. In this case, the level of employment would vary with the cycle (as in Grossman and Hart, 1981). This area of theory seems to have little to offer to our modelling.

3.3.4 Efficiency wage models

Efficiency wage models offer an explanation of why *ex ante* real wage levels remain high even when labour is in excess supply. The idea is that employers maintain a high real wage because by doing so they improve the productivity of their work-force. Originally, these models were formulated with reference to less developed countries where improvements in nutrition levels obtained through higher wages led to an increase in work effort.[11] In developed countries, any relevance of the efficiency wage hypothesis must stem from other effects relating to high wages.

Maintaining a high real wage could be a device used by employers to increase their employees' productivity if workers have some discretion over their performance and if employers are unable to observe work effort costlessly. The model proposed by Shapiro and Stiglitz[12] assumes that employees gain a disutility from having to carry out the work and hence would choose to 'shirk' if they could do so costlessly. In a conventional competitive labour market where all workers receive the market rate and there is no (involuntary) unemployment, a shirking worker who is caught and fired can immediately be rehired elsewhere with minimal costs. In order to induce workers not to shirk firms raise wages so that a penalty will be imposed on fired workers. However, if all firms increase wages simultaneously and to the same extent relative pay would, of course, remain unchanged.

Another reason why a firm may pay a higher wage than justified by labour productivity would be to reduce labour turnover. Substantial costs can arise from hiring and firing workers. Training costs will often be large and even where new employees are highly trained, there may be firm-specific skills which take time to acquire. When workers are fired, redundancy payments often have to be made. Increasing the wage reduces the number of voluntary quits and the rate of staff turnover by lowering the probability that a worker will be able to find a higher paid job elsewhere. This 'labour turnover' model shares many characteristics of the shirking model, for they both explain high real wages in terms of creating a penalty for workers who, either voluntarily or involuntarily, stop working for a firm, and both cease to be effective if all firms behave in the same way.

If workers are heterogeneous in ability and firms are unable to distinguish good from bad workers, the firm may have an incentive to pay a high wage if by doing so it can attract high quality workers. The 'adverse selection' model proposed by Weiss (1980) assumes that the firm cannot distinguish the calibre of workers and a low wage both discourages good workers from applying and induces currently employed good workers to quit. This firm finds it profitable to pay a high wage. It turns away applicants offering to work for less because if workers' reservation wages are correlated with their ability, an offer to work for less money signals a limited ability. A firm that cannot distinguish quality but knows that productivity is correlated with the alternative income would not cut wages in the face of declining demand as the best workers would quit. It would lay off (arbitrarily chosen) workers instead. The adverse selection model predicts an inflexible real wage and quantity adjustments to variations in demand.

These models provide reasons why the real wage may be above that justified by the fundamentals. Potentially they provide an input into the modelling of the real wage acceptable to the firm.

3.3.5 The role of the union

A rather more plausible approach, recently given more attention by macro-economic modellers, allows wages to be affected by unions' behaviour. Initial work in this area often assumed that unions have monopoly power and set their own wages with the firm then choosing the level of employment. Later approaches have bargaining taking place between firm and union over wages or over both wages and employment.

(a) Union monopoly approach

There is a sizeable body of literature[13] describing models in which, in order to arrive at a determinate solution to the bargaining problem, it is assumed that the union has the power to set wages unilaterally. This approach, which originated with Dunlop's work, assumes that the union is concerned about employment, as well as the wage, and this constrains the level of pay chosen by the union.

Following the lead of Farber (1978) and McDonald and Solow (1981), the union can be thought of as having the objective of maximizing the expected utility of the representative member. Not all of the union's members can expect to be employed at the going wage rate. The representative union member faces a probability of being employed and earning the going wage, and a probability of being laid off and receiving the best income available from outside opportunities (unemployment benefit, for example). The union chooses the wage that will place it on the highest indifference curve compatible with its view of the firm's labour demand function. The firm then chooses the quantities of the inputs, given their costs, to maximize its profit.

(b) Efficient bargaining models

It is shown by McDonald and Solow (1981) that an efficient bargain can be achieved by allowing negotiations between the union and firm to take place simultaneously over the wage/employment pair, rather than having the union unilaterally set wages and the firm respond with an employment decision.

They, along with others, have taken the view that the monopoly approach to union behaviour suffers from a major flaw: the outcome is inefficient because it does not lie on the bargaining contract curve[14] so there is a Pareto superior outcome. Efficient bargains are characterized by the fact that they are on the contract curve, the locus of tangency points between the set of union indifference curves and the firm's isoprofit curves. This is illustrated in Figure 3.3.

The outcome of bargaining in the monopoly union model results in a wage rate w^* and employment L^* at the point of tangency between the union's indifference curve and the firm's labour demand function. (The firm's labour demand curve is the locus of the points of tangency between the firm's isoprofit curves and the (horizontal) constant wage lines.) An efficient bargain, however, will lie on the contract curve (the locus of the points of tangency between the union indifference curves and the firm's isoprofit curves). It is clear that the union could achieve a

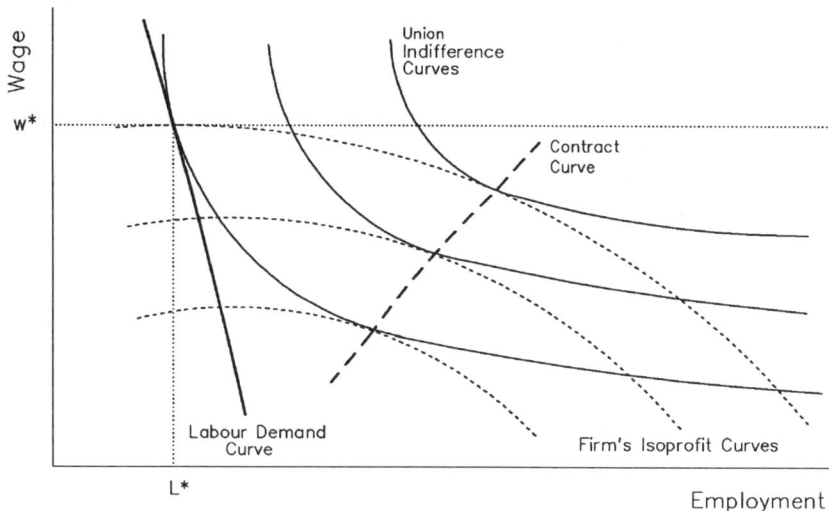

Fig. 3.3 Contract curve.

higher utility and/or the firm a higher profit than the outcome implied by the monopoly union model.

3.3.6 Conclusion

Out of the alternative approaches, listed above, we choose a collective bargaining model for the reasons noted in the introduction: after all, this is, in fact, the method by which most wage bargains are agreed and the outcome on wage bargains settled in this way is an important factor in determining the outcome in other cases.

Some of the other approaches we have summarized contribute insights which may be relevant within a bargaining model, but taken on their own they neglect the most obvious feature of the labour market, the negotiation that takes place. They are clearly unrealistic.

The model of wage setting used for the equation in our model is described in Rowlatt (1987). It starts from an approach similar to that of McDonald and Solow in that a bargain is picked out by maximizing a function comprising jointly of the union's and the firm's welfare functions. However, the bargain is assumed to take place only over the wage. The analysis is spelt out in section 3.5.

3.4 RESULTS OF EMPIRICAL WORK

3.4.1 Introduction

Most of the empirical work testing these theoretical approaches has adopted the Phillips curve framework and has examined the effect of different measures of labour market disequilibrium on changes in nominal wages and hence on changes in aggregate (expected) real wages.[15] Recently, empirical work has included an attempt to model the NAIRU, incorporating measures of union power and other supply side factors as explanatory variables. The elasticity of real wages with respect to variables such as these has been used to draw conclusions for policy prescriptions (e.g. Minford *et al.*, 1983, and Layard and Nickell, 1985).

There have as yet been few attempts to test the validity of the various micro models of real wages against the data. There has, however, been some empirical work examining models of trade union behaviour.

3.4.2 Empirical tests of Phillips curves

There has been an enormous amount of empirical work on the Phillips curve. In its simplest, expectations augmented, form it has been estimated over varying time periods and using data from a great many different economies. The results have been variable. In some countries, over some periods there is evidence of a significant Phillips curve effect (a significant negative coefficient on the level of unemployment). In other countries and using other periods this is not the case. Much seems to depend on the precise definition of the dependent variable, the price expectations variable, the unemployment indicator. Differing results are obtained depending on the inclusion or otherwise of productivity, of dummy variables to pick up periods of incomes policy, of lags on the unemployment variable and of variables to model the path of the NAIRU.

This work demonstrates the universality of the belief that the Phillips curve is fundamental to the understanding of the inflation process. Here, we summarize the results of one recent empirical study of the Phillips curve, that of Layard and Nickell (1985).

Layard and Nickell develop and estimate a Phillips curve type of model which is, in fact, based on a bargaining approach. In their model wage bargainers set the nominal wage as a mark-up on GDP prices with the mark-up dependent on two sets of variables, unemployment and what they term the 'push' variables (unemployment benefit, intensity of search, mismatch between vacancies and the unemployed, and trade union power as well as productivity, the terms of trade and tax rates).

Their study included the estimation of two additional equations, one for prices and one for employment. This enabled them to estimate the reduced form effect on unemployment of a number of exogenous variables.

The estimated equation for the level of the real wage, which used annual data over the period 1954 to 1983, found a highly significant coefficient on the level of the unemployment variable.

3.4.3 Tests of role for trade unions

Prevalent amongst theoretical models built to describe trade union behaviour are two assumptions: first, the conventional hypothesis for explaining decision taking with risk (Schoemaker, 1982), maximization of the union's expected utility; and second, that bargaining takes place over the wage-employment pair so the outcome will be Pareto efficient, lying on the contract curve. There is at present little empirical support for either of these assumptions.

Pencavel, in his 1985 survey of research into behavioural models of trade unionism (Pencavel, 1985), found no empirical test of the hypothesis that trade union behaviour reflects the maximization of the expected utility of a typical union member. Instead, empirical investigations of trade union behaviour have concentrated on the idea that the union's objective is to maximize the premium on the wage (the rent) that follows from unionization. The work of Ashenfelter and Brown (1983), Carruth and Oswald (1983) and MaCurdy and Pencavel (1986) can all be interpreted as including tests of this assumption. In each case the parameter restrictions implied by the hypothesis are rejected (though this may be because some auxiliary hypothesis is unjustified).

MaCurdy and Pencavel (1986) report the result of a test of the union monopoly hypothesis (in which the firm chooses employment and so is on its labour demand curve) against the efficient bargaining model (in which the outcome will be on the contract curve). Data relating to the International Typographical Union were pooled over a 28 year period and over 13 US towns. Parameter restrictions enabled the labour demand curve model to be rejected at conventional levels of significance for all specifications of the production function considered. Only weak support was given to the proposition that the union–firm agreements lay on the contract curve.

However, there is little evidence, either circumstantial or statistical, in support of the proposition that unions and firms negotiate over employment as well as pay. Collective agreements do not generally involve the level of employment. This suggests that efficient bargaining models are unlikely to give a satisfactory explanation of how wages are actually determined in bargaining situations.

3.5 DERIVATION OF MODEL EQUATION

3.5.1 Behavioural hypothesis

The theoretical model developed here, and reported in Rowlatt (1987), follows broadly the same approach as the study by Nickell (1983) which developed out of the analysis in McDonald and Solow (1981) and Oswald (1982).

In order to derive an equation explaining the path of wages it is assumed that, in unionized sectors, wage rises are settled in a bargaining process between employees (the union) and employers (the firm). Wage rises in the non-unionized sector are assumed to follow those of the unionized sectors. In the bargaining process, the firm aims for a wage outcome as low as possible, subject to its need to hire the labour it requires to operate at the optimal level. The union wants the wage to be as high as possible, subject to an acceptable outcome for employment.

The approach taken involves defining welfare functions for both parties to the bargain and specifying their 'reference' or fall-back levels of welfare. So long as the reference pair is within the feasible set the bargain can lead to an outcome Pareto superior to the fallback levels.

3.5.2 Modelling bargaining

(a) Employees

On the employees side it is assumed that the welfare function Ψ depends on the expected real wage rw^e (equal to $w - p^e$ where w is the nominal wage and p^e represents the expected level of retail prices) and the probability of redundancy ρ:

$$\Psi = \Psi(rw^e, \rho) \tag{3.2}$$

where ρ is taken to depend on disequilibrium in the labour market as indicated by the level and change in the rate of unemployment, U and ΔU.

It is assumed that Ψ has partial derivatives $\Psi_1 > 0$ and $\Psi_2 < 0$. In order to keep the analysis simple we assume that, over the regions relevant to the analysis, the first derivatives of Ψ and ρ can be treated as constant, so the equation can be treated as being locally linear:

$$\Psi = \Psi_1(w - p^e) + \Psi_2\rho$$

and

$$\frac{d\Psi}{dw} = \Psi_1 + \Psi_2\frac{\partial\rho}{\partial w} = \Psi' \tag{3.3}$$

with Ψ_1, Ψ_2 and Ψ' treated as locally constant.

(b) Employers

The approach taken to the firm's bargaining behaviour is analogous to that taken for the employees. Consistent with the behaviour specified in choosing output, price and inputs (section 2.4) it is assumed that the firm's long-term objective is to maximize its expected profit. In the short term, given the capital stock, this objective is achieved by maximizing operating cash-flow, Π. The firm's preference over alternative levels of profit is represented by the decision function $\Phi(\Pi)$ with derivatives $\Phi'(\Pi) > 0$ and $\Phi''(\Pi) < 0$. Given some proposed outcome on the wage, w, the firm assesses the cash-flow that is implied by going through the profit maximization process described in section 2.4 to discover the optimum output, price, employment and material and fuel inputs consistent with the proposed wage,[16] given the cost of material and fuel inputs, P_i, the perceived demand function, f (which depends on competitors' prices P_f^*), and the short-term production function, g. As a result the firm's decision regarding the wage is subject to the values taken by the variables exogenous to this decision:

$$\Phi(\Pi) = \Phi(W|P_i, P_f^*, \bar{P}, g, f) \tag{3.4}$$

where $\bar{P}$ is the general price level. It is assumed that, in the relevant region, the first derivative of Φ can be treated as constant.

The analysis in section 2.4 can be used to derive an expression for cash-flow in terms of the wage and the exogenous variables. The real level of cash-flow is given by:

$$\Pi = (P - C)Y \qquad (3.5)$$

where C is unit costs. Unit costs are given by equation 2.12:

$$C = \alpha_1 ULC + \alpha_2 P_{im} + \alpha_3 P_a + \alpha_4 TX \qquad (3.6)$$

in which ULC is unit labour costs (a function of the wage, W, labour taxes, LT, and productivity, PR), P_{im} is the sterling cost of imported inputs (a combination of the prices of primary commodities and finished goods), P_a is the cost of other inputs, such as those whose prices have been set by the UK authorities (during the estimation period these included fuel, telephone, post, etc.) and TX is taxes incurred by the firm (vehicle excise duty, industrial rates, etc.). This equation is subject to the constraint:

$$\alpha_1 + \alpha_2 + \alpha_3 + \alpha_4 = 1 \qquad (3.7)$$

as explained in section 2.4.3.

Using equation 2.10 for the price:

$$P = (1 - \beta)C + \beta P_f^* Y / \bar{Y} \qquad (3.8)$$

it is easy to show that:

$$\begin{aligned} \Pi &= [(1 - \beta)C + \beta P_f^* Y / \bar{Y} - C]Y \\ &= \beta[P_f^* Y / \bar{Y} - (\alpha_1 ULC + \alpha_2 P_{im} + \alpha_3 P_a + \alpha_4 TX)]Y \end{aligned} \qquad (3.9)$$

so

$$\Pi - \bar{\Pi} = -\alpha_1 \beta [ULC - (P_f^* Y / \bar{Y} - \alpha_2 P_{im} - \alpha_3 P_a - \alpha_4 TX)/\alpha_1]Y - \bar{\Pi}$$

where $\bar{\Pi}$ represents the level of operating cash-flow that corresponds to the reference level of Φ, $\bar{\Phi}$.

(c) The outcome of the bargain

The outcome of the bargain is picked out, using a method similar to that of Nash (1950). By maximizing a function of the two welfare functions we ensure that the chosen outcome is on the Pareto optimal frontier. Scaling factors included in the estimation allow the point on this frontier to be estimated from the data. The function is:

$$F = \mu(\Phi - \bar{\Phi})(\Psi - \bar{\Psi}) \qquad (3.10)$$

where $\bar{\Psi} = \Psi(\overline{rw} + k, 0)$. This is the reference level of Ψ. It corresponds to a real wage given by $\overline{rw} + k$ with $\overline{rw}$ the 'warranted' real wage (the real wage that is justified by the level of productivity, the terms of trade and the level of taxation) and k a premium that may be pressed for by unions. It is assumed that the reference level of the probability of redundancy is zero.

Choosing the wage w to maximize F leads to the marginal condition:

$$\frac{\partial \Psi}{\partial w}(\Phi - \bar{\Phi}) + \frac{\partial \Phi}{\partial \Pi}\frac{\partial \Pi}{\partial w}(\Psi - \bar{\Psi}) = 0 \qquad (3.11)$$

and, substituting using equation 3.3 (based on the local linearity assumptions), this becomes:

$$\Psi'\Phi'(\Pi - \bar{\Pi}) + \Phi'\frac{\partial \Pi}{\partial w}[\Psi_1(rw^e - \overline{rw} - k) + \Psi_2\rho] = 0 \qquad (3.12)$$

The weight given to the two sides in the bargaining outcome reflects their power in the bargaining situation (section 3.6.6 reports the result of the estimation regarding this aspect of the equation).

3.5.3 The equation to be estimated

For the most part wage levels are settled in terms of annual percentage changes, making reference to the annual rate of increase of a price index (among other things). This feature is captured by setting up the estimated equation in 'error correction' form; as a combination of two components. Equation 3.12 is differenced and the lagged value of the levels equation is included in the resulting equation to model the effect on the wage settlement of the deviation of the lagged level of relevant variables from their expected or acceptable values. The form of the estimated equation is:

$$\zeta_1\Delta(rw^e - \overline{rw} - k) - \zeta_2\Delta[(\Pi - \bar{\Pi})/(\alpha_1\beta Y)] + \zeta_3\Delta\rho$$
$$+ \mu_1(rw^e - \overline{rw} - k)_{-i} - \mu_2[(\Pi - \bar{\Pi})/Y]_{-j} + \mu_3\rho_{-s} = 0 \qquad (3.13)$$

Substituting for rw^e and $\Pi - \bar{\Pi}$ in the dynamic terms of this, approximating changes in levels by changes in logs (section 2.4.4) and redefining ζ_2 accordingly, gives:

$$\zeta_1\Delta(w - p^e - \overline{rw} - k) + \zeta_2'\Delta(w + lt - pr^e - [p_f^* - \alpha_2 p_{im} - \alpha_3 p_a - \alpha_4 tx]/\alpha_1)$$
$$+ \zeta_3\Delta\rho + \mu_1(rw^e - \overline{rw} - k)_{-i} - \mu_2[(\Pi - \bar{\Pi})/Y]_{-j} + \mu_3\rho_{-s} = 0 \qquad (3.14)$$

This, when solved for the change in nominal earnings, becomes:

$$\Delta w = \zeta(\Delta p^e + \Delta\overline{rw})$$
$$+ (1 - \zeta)\left[\frac{(\Delta p_f^* - \alpha_2\Delta p_{im} - \alpha_3\Delta p_a - \alpha_4\Delta tx)}{\alpha_1} + \Delta pr^e - \Delta lt\right]$$
$$- \zeta_3'\Delta\rho - \mu_1'(rw^e - \overline{rw})_{-i} + \mu_2'[(\Pi - \bar{\Pi})/Y]_{-j} + \mu_3'\rho_{-s} + \mu_1'k \qquad (3.15)$$

Here, the reference real wage level, $\overline{rw}$, is modelled as a function of expected or trend productivity, pr^e or tpr (when productivity increases the employer gets the benefit unless employees press for a share), the retention ratio, rr (employees will induce the firm to carry a share of any increase in direct taxes), and, in the long run, the terms of trade, tt (the firm will aim to share the cost of a worsening in the terms of trade with its employees):[17]

$$\Delta\overline{rw} = \Delta tpr + \Delta tt - \Delta rr$$

In deriving equation 3.15 it has been assumed that:

$$\Delta(\overline{\Pi}/Y) = 0 \quad \text{and} \quad \Delta k = 0$$

while $\zeta = \zeta_1/(\zeta_1 + \zeta_2')$, $\zeta_3' = \zeta_3/(\zeta_1 + \zeta_2')$ and $\mu_i' = \mu_i/(\zeta_1 + \zeta_2')$ with $i = 1, 2, 3$.

The result of estimating equation 3.15, for incorporation into our model of the inflation spiral, is described in section 3.6. The estimated version also incorporates dummy variables to pick up the effects of incomes policies, the effect of the Clegg settlements in the public sector on private sector bargaining behaviour, and to correct for strike effects.

A number of prior constraints have been imposed on the coefficients. In particular, the derivation of this equation, from the parties' concern for the real wage and profits, entails homogeneity constraints similar to those described in section 2.4.4 and consistent with an absence of money illusion. These comprise both static homogeneity, which ensures that the outcome on the real wage is independent of the price level in the long term, and dynamic homogeneity, which ensures that, other things being equal, wages grow at the rate at which prices rise plus the trend rate of productivity growth (included in the model of the fall-back real wage).

3.5.4 Implications for the inflation spiral

(a) Separation of endogenous from exogenous terms

In order to construct the reduced form model of the inflation spiral and to analyse its dynamics the terms in this equation are divided between those that are endogenous to the domestic inflation spiral and those that are not. The equation is therefore written in the form:

$$\Delta w = \Delta prt + g(L)\Delta p + h(L)\Delta p_f - j(L)\Delta p_c + X_3 \qquad (3.16)$$

As in the price equation (section 2.4.5), the price of imported inputs, p_{im}, has been divided into the finished goods part (incorporated into the term in Δp_f along with the competitors' price term Δp_f^*), and the primary commodities part (in Δp_c). The term X_3 encompasses all the factors that are not part of the spiral. The price variable relevant to employees' wage-bargaining is different from the factory-gate prices which we have chosen as inflation indicator (represented by Δp in equation 3.16) and the effect of this difference is included in the term X_3. Changes in administered prices, Δp_a, and in taxes per unit of output, Δtx, have been included in the term X_3 in real terms, and the implied lagged price change terms are incorporated in the term $g(L)\Delta p$.

Variables that impinge on the inflation spiral as a result of wages being determined in the bargaining process described by equation 3.16 include changes in the world currency levels of world prices and the variables that have been incorporated into the term X_3:

- the rate of increase of the cost of primary commodities in world currencies $- \Delta p_c^w$
- the rate of increase of finished goods prices in world currencies $- \Delta p_f^w$
- disequilibrium in the labour market (unemployment) $- U$
- the change in unemployment $- \Delta U$
- the deviation of unit profits from the reference level $- (\Pi - \bar{\Pi})/Y$
- the deviation of the lagged real wage from its warranted level (involving retention ratio, terms of trade and trend productivity) $- (rw - \overline{rw})$
- changes in trend (or expected) productivity growth $- \Delta tpr$
- changes in relevant taxes $- \Delta lt$ and Δrr
- the effect of special factors causing retail price rises, (Δrpi), to differ from those of the producer output price (such as real changes in local authority rents and rates, mortgage interest payments, seasonal food prices) $- (\Delta rpi - \Delta p)$
- the labour market premium (the extra the union may press for above the rise in the 'warranted' real wage) $- k$
- the effect of special factors in the labour market, such as incomes policies, etc. $- d$.

(b) Features likely to be important to the spiral

The following features of this equation are relevant to the operation of the inflation spiral.

(i) When the level of unemployment or profits differs from the equilibrium level, this situation tends to persist for a while. As a result it has a cumulative effect on inflation.

(ii) Settlements may tend to be larger (or smaller) than is justified by productivity growth, changes in the terms of trade or tax changes. This happens if the labour market incorporates a 'premium' (represented by k in the equation). If this were the case it would be important in terms of its effect on inflation because this would persist and its effect on inflation would cumulate.

(iii) Changes in the real value of administered prices or of the tax rate are likely to cause only a once-off shock to the inflation spiral.

(iv) In general the dummy variables will have a once-off effect on the inflation spiral; however, the effects of a sustained successful incomes policy will cumulate during the period over which it is operating and feed into the spiral producing an inflation rate lower than it would otherwise have been.

Finally, the effect of equation 3.16 on the degree of inertia in the inflation spiral depends on the value of:

$$g(1) + h(1) - j(1). \tag{3.17}$$

If this is equal to unity, as would be implied by the dynamic homogeneity condition arising from the 'no money illusion' assumption, then this equation will pass last period's inflation through into the current period.

3.6 AN EQUATION FOR EARNINGS

3.6.1 The chosen equation

This section describes the empirical work that was done to arrive at an equation suitable for inclusion in the model.[18] As with the price equation, we are concerned with the validity of various constraints on the coefficients, rather than their precise estimated values. Although the best estimates of particular coefficients presented here are likely to change, given the data that has become available since, the homogeneity properties and the significance (or otherwise) of the contribution from individual variables to the path of wages are likely to remain valid.

The preferred equation was estimated over the period from 1967Q4 to 1985Q1. It contains six terms (apart from the intercept and the dummies):

$$\Delta \ln ERMF = 0.79(\tfrac{1}{4}\Delta_4 \ln WACC_{-1}) + 0.21(\tfrac{1}{4}\Delta_4 \ln WAFF_{-1}) - 0.16 DISRW_{-3}$$
$$(9.1) \qquad\qquad (-) \qquad\qquad (4.4)$$
$$+ 0.017 PROFY_{-3} - 0.014 \ln UNUKS_{-2} - 0.057\Delta \ln UNUKS$$
$$(2.2) \qquad\qquad (2.0) \qquad\qquad (3.2)$$
$$+ \text{dummies} \tag{3.18}$$

The dependent variable,[19] $\Delta \ln ERMF$, the quarter on previous quarter proportionate increase in average earnings in manufacturing, is modelled here as a compromise between the wage rise the employees would find acceptable, $\Delta_4 \ln WACC$, and that which employers can afford, $\Delta_4 WAFF$. The estimated coefficients are constrained to sum to unity. The magnitude of the coefficient on the union's 'acceptable' wage provides an indication of the 'power' of the union. The outcome is modified by three factors: $DISRW$, the deviation of the pre-tax real wage, $ERMF/RPI$, from its reference level, $RWWAR$; $PROFY$, the deviation of real profits from its reference level; and $UNUKS$, a measure of UK short term unemployment that occurs in the equation both in level and in difference form.

This section starts by describing the checks that were done on the functional form of the equation and the dummies that were included. It then goes on to describe the construction of each of the terms in the equation, examining the constraints imposed and, where relevant, comparing the sizes of the freely estimated coefficients with the values implied by the theory.

Table 3.1 Functional form

Dependent variable $\Delta \ln ERMF$		RPI only		RPI and a few other variables		Preferred specification		
Explanatory variables[1]		I	II	III	IV	V	VI	VII
$\Delta \ln ERMF$	1	0.15 (1.1)		0.04 (0.3)		−0.15 (1.3)		
	2	0.11 (1.1)		0.10 (1.0)		0.00 (0.0)		
	3	−0.25 (2.9)		−0.19 (2.3)		−0.02 (0.2)		
	4	−0.07 (0.7)		−0.05 (0.6)		−0.01 (0.2)		
$\Delta \ln RPI$	0	−0.03 (0.3)		−0.04 (0.5)		0.07 (0.7)		
	1	0.16 (1.7)	0.14[2] (4.7)	0.19 (2.1)	0.22 (6.1)	0.28 (2.8)	0.23 (5.1)	0.20 (9.1)
	2	0.11 (1.2)	0.14	0.23 (2.4)	0.22	0.50 (4.0)	0.23	0.20
	3	0.09 (1.1)	0.14	0.16 (1.9)	0.22	0.14 (1.6)	0.23	0.20
	4	0.23 (2.9)	0.14	0.29 (3.8)	0.22	0.28 (3.4)	0.23	0.20
$\frac{1}{4}\Delta_4 \ln WAFF_{-1}$						0.35 (2.6)	0.28 (2.3)	0.21
$\frac{1}{4}\Delta_4 \ln TPMF_{-1}$						3.43 (2.7)	2.08 (2.5)	1.00
$\frac{1}{4}\Delta_4 \ln RETRAT_{-1}$						−0.26 (0.6)	−0.23 (0.6)	−0.47
$\ln ERMF_{-3}$		0.09 (2.7)	0.05 (1.9)	0.05 (1.6)	0.01 (0.5)	−0.31 (2.7)	−0.18 (3.4)	−0.16 (4.4)
$\ln RPI_{-3}$		−0.10 (2.8)	−0.06 (2.0)	−0.05 (1.4)	−0.01 (0.2)	0.33 (2.8)	0.19 (3.4)	0.16
$\ln RWWAR_{-3}$						0.26 (2.8)	0.17 (3.0)	0.16
$PROFY_{-3}$				−0.006 (0.7)	−0.008 (0.9)	0.040 (2.2)	0.027 (1.6)	0.017 (2.2)
$\ln UNUKS_{-2}/100$				−2.19 (2.1)	−2.28 (2.3)	−1.80 (1.7)	−1.83 (1.7)	−1.40 (2.0)
$\Delta \ln UNUKS/100$				−7.75 (3.0)	−9.59 (4.1)	−7.04 (2.8)	−6.39 (2.7)	−5.70 (3.2)
Dummies		✓	✓	✓	✓	✓	✓	✓
SEE		0.73	0.77	0.67	0.68	0.59	0.61	0.60
$\bar{R}^2$		0.75	0.73	0.80	0.79	0.84	0.83	0.89
DW		1.6	1.5	1.8	1.9	1.7	2.1	2.0
DF		48	56	45	53	41	49	54
Period				1967Q4 to 1984Q1				

[1] Data definitions are in Appendix 3A.
[2] The lines indicate constraints imposed.
[3] χ^2 indicates the significance of the parameter constraints. Equation of comparison and degrees of freedom in parentheses.

3.6.2 Functional form and dummy variables

(a) Functional form

Most wage settlements take place annually and operate for one year. Throughout the empirical work it was assumed that the quarter on previous quarter percentage change in the average earnings data picks up the effect of the annual wage settlements operative within the quarter on the level of average earnings. This means that the one-quarter change in earnings will be related to the four-quarter percentage change in the explanatory price variables. Few empirical analyses take this fact on board, and it is important in ensuring that efficient estimates are obtained for the coefficients in this equation.

The effect of testing this hypothesis is shown in Table 3.1. In this table the explanatory price variables are one-quarter changes, so four consecutive coefficients of equal magnitude indicate that the four-quarter percentage change is acceptable to the data.

Three sets of equations are shown in Table 3.1, in each case the first is estimated without constraints on the functional form and the second (and third) with the constraints. The first pair tests the relationship between earnings and prices, as they are seen by employees, with no additional explanatory variables. The second pair examines an equation similar to the Phillips curve by including terms in short-term unemployment; it also incorporates the level of profits. The third set examines the 'preferred' equation. In addition to the variables in the second pair of equations, these contain variables representing the firm's view of the wage that is affordable (*WAFF*). They also contain two non-price aspects of the employees' view of the wage that is acceptable: trend productivity growth in manufacturing (*TPMF*), which indicates how much there may be to share out; and the retention ratio (*RETRAT*), which indicates how much the employees keep after income tax has been taken into account. The equation also contains a variable indicating the level of the real wage that is warranted by such fundamentals as the level of labour productivity, the terms of trade and the rate of taxation (*RWWAR*, section 3.6.4).

Comparing columns I and II, columns III and IV and columns V, VI and VII, suggests that the zero constraint on the lags of $\Delta \ln ERMF$ becomes increasingly acceptable as the model is developed and that the constraint of four consecutive equal coefficients on the lags of $\Delta \ln RPI$ is acceptable to the data.

(b) Dummy variables

Dummy variables were included in the regressions to pick up the effects of incomes policies, strikes and the effects of public sector pay policy on private sector settlements. Table 3.2 indicates the importance of these dummies to the fit of the equation, to the estimate of the relative influence of the firm and of the employees on the outcome of the bargaining process, and on the important functional form with which unemployment affects wage settlements (see also Chapter 8).

The labour market

Table 3.2 Preferred equation with and without dummies

Dependent variable $\Delta \ln ERMF$		
Explanatory variables[1]	I with dummies	II without dummies
$\frac{1}{4}\Delta_4 \ln WACC_{-1}$	0.79|[2] (9.1)	0.90| (6.1)
$\frac{1}{4}\Delta_4 \ln WAFF_{-1}$	0.21|	0.10|
$DISRW_{-3}$	−0.16 (4.4)	−0.14 (1.9)
$PROFY_{-3}$	0.017 (2.2)	0.037 (2.5)
$\ln UNUKS_{-2}/100$	−1.40 (2.0)	−0.22 (0.2)
$\Delta\ln UNUKS/100$	−5.70 (3.2)	−5.36 (1.6)
Dummies	√	×
SEE	0.60	1.30
$\bar{R}^2$	0.89	0.49
DW	2.0	1.5
DF	54	60
χ^2		108.6[3] (6 df)
Period	1967Q4 to 1984Q1	

[1]Variables are defined in Appendix 3A.
[2]Indicates constraints imposed.
[3]Tests exclusion restrictions (χ^2 (6,5%) = 13).

The estimated coefficients on the dummies included are shown in Table 3.3. The periods they refer to are indicated in Figure 3.4.

The effect of **incomes policies** was modelled by means of a 'norm', indicating the level of nominal wages implied by the policy, appropriate to each quarter in which an incomes policy was operating.[20] In running the regressions it was assumed that the norm partially takes over the role of price inflation. A dummy (IPDUM) was constructed which took the value unity when an incomes policy was operating and was zero at all other times. The variable:

$$IPDN = IPDUM\,(NORM - \%\,PRICE) \tag{3.19}$$

was then included on the regressions as well as % PRICE. The estimated coefficient on this incomes policy variable turned out at around 0.7 to 0.9, indicating that the incomes policies were generally about 70–90 per cent successful in holding wage rises to the norm.

A **catch-up** dummy (CACHUP) was also included in the regressions. This dummy takes the value unity in each of the four quarters of the wage round immediately following the end of each period of policy. It is zero elsewhere. The estimated coefficients, shown in Table 3.3, indicate that a catch-up of over two percentage points on earnings (4 times 0.59) generally takes place at the end of a period of incomes policy. Figure 7.9 indicates that, while this has been just sufficient to cancel out the effect on inflation of a one year incomes policy, a three year policy has a net downward effect on inflation that persists for a number of years.

The three main **strikes** that affected the data during the estimation period took place in 1974Q1 (three-day week), 1979Q3 (engineering) and 1980Q1 (steel). The Department of Employment provided estimates of the effects of the last two and the earnings data used in the estimation were adjusted to take account of this (Appendix 3A). The three-day week was dealt with by including a three period Almon distribution on a dummy variable that took the value unity in 1974Q1 (zero elsewhere) and constraining the long-term coefficient to zero.

Two further features of the data seemed to warrant attention. A 'Clegg dummy' was included that took unit values in the four quarters of the 1979–80 pay round to pick up the effect of the **Clegg awards** in the public sector on private sector pay settlements. This is not very significant, and it is possible that it has picked up some of the effect of the catch up after the end of the 'social contract'. An **outlying** residual in 1981Q3 was observable in most of the regressions and led to the inclusion of a dummy for that quarter (Rowlatt, 1986).

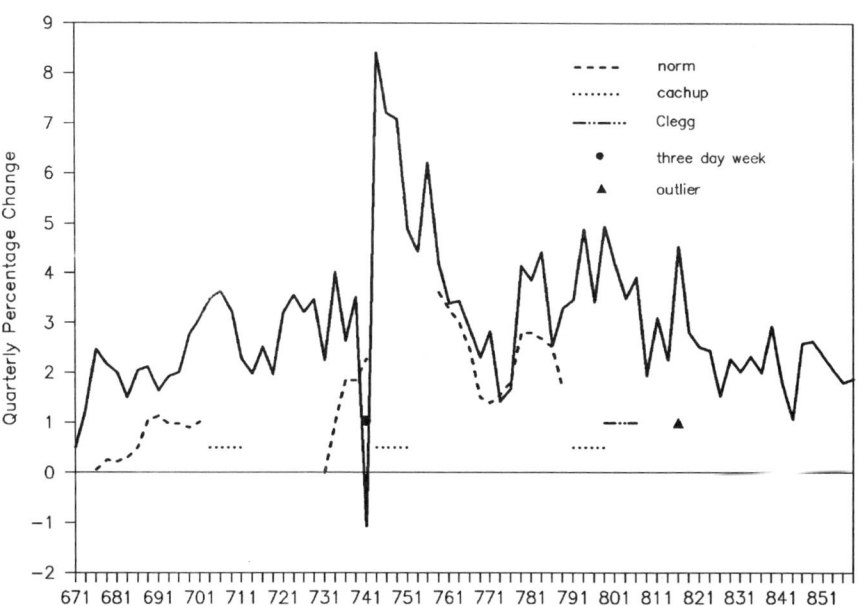

Fig. 3.4 Quarterly change in average earnings.

Table 3.3 Inclusion of dummies

Dependent variable $\Delta \ln ERMF$

Explanatory variables[1]	I	II	III	IV	Preferred equation V
741 DUM	−4.37|[2]	−5.01|	−4.86|	−4.45|	−4.90|
	(6.4)	(8.8)	(7.9)	(6.9)	(8.7)
741 DUM$_{-1}$	1.77|	2.99|	2.89|	2.90|	2.96|
	(2.0)	(6.0)	(5.5)	(4.9)	(5.9)
741 DUM$_{-2}$	2.60|	2.01|	1.98|	1.55|	1.94|
	(3.0)|	(3.7)|	(3.4)|	(2.5)|	(3.6)|
IPDN	0.73	0.74	0.78	0.79	0.77
	(4.0)	(5.1)	(5.0)	(7.3)	(8.0)
CACHUP	0.65	0.54	0.54	0.87	0.59
	(2.0)	(2.1)	(1.9)	(3.1)	(2.4)
CLEGDM	0.54	0.65	0.35	0.56	0.43
	(1.1)	(1.6)	(0.7)	(1.2)	(1.1)
DUM813	2.00	1.94	1.99	1.51	1.89
	(2.8)	(3.0)	(2.8)	(2.1)	(3.0)
Other variables	√	√	√	√	√
SEE	0.59	0.60	0.62	0.71	0.60
$\bar{R}^2$	0.84	0.84	0.88	0.85	0.89
DW	1.7	2.0	2.2	1.5	2.0
DF	41	52	48	56	54
Period	1967Q4–84Q1	1967Q4–84Q1	1967Q4–84Q1	1967Q4–84Q1	1967Q4–84Q1
Equation[3]	Table 3.1 col V	Table 3.4 col III	Table 3.5 col VII	Table 3.7 col VIII	Table 3.8 col IV

[1]Variables are defined in Appendix 3A.
[2]Indicates constraint imposed—coefficients sum to zero.
[3]Estimates of the effects of the dummies on a representative collection of equations reported in other tables in this Chapter are displayed in this table. The one in column IV omits variables included in the preferred specification—shown in column V. The equations in columns I, II and III are estimated without some of the constraints imposed in the preferred specification.

3.6.3 The union's view and the firm's view

The specification of the earnings equation as the outcome of a bargain between union (or employees) and the firm (or employer) means that the estimation entails modelling the fall-back position of each party. This section describes the modelling of the rise in the nominal wage that the union considers acceptable (given the increase in productivity and changes in the income tax rate) and the wage rise that the firm considers is affordable (given market considerations and the rises in the other costs it faces).

Table 3.4: Tests of constraints in dynamic terms

Dependent variable $\Delta \ln ERMF$

Explanatory variables[1]	Preferred equation I	II	III	IV	V	VI
$\frac{1}{4}\Delta_4 \ln RPI_{-1}$	0.79|[2]	0.83|	0.85|	0.90|	0.70|	0.67
	(9.1)	(7.5)	(7.7)	(6.3)	(4.2)	(3.1)
$\frac{1}{4}\Delta_4 \ln RETRAT_{-1}$	−0.47	−0.50	−0.51	−0.54	−0.42	−0.52
						(1.1)
$\frac{1}{4}\Delta_4 \ln TPMF_{-1}$	1.00	$\left\{\begin{array}{l}0.83\|\\0.24\|\end{array}\right.$	1.96	1.61	1.81	1.79
			(2.9)	(1.8)	(2.1)	(2.1)
$\frac{1}{4}PPEX$	0.14	0.16	0.18|	0.12	0.09|	0.10
		(2.5)	(2.9)	(1.2)	(1.0)	(0.9)
$\frac{1}{4}\Delta_4 \ln UMFM_{-1}$	0.07	0.08	0.09|	0.04	0.04|	0.03
				(0.3)		(0.2)
$\frac{1}{4}\Delta_4 \ln UKCP_{-2}$	0.07	0.08	0.09	0.20|	0.32	0.33
				(2.4)	(3.2)	(3.1)
$\frac{1}{4}\Delta_4 \ln RXD_{-1}$	−0.07	−0.08	−0.09	−0.20|	−0.15	−0.15
				(1.8)		(1.7)
$\frac{1}{4}\Delta_4 \ln PM_{-1}$	−0.08	−0.09	−0.11	−0.14	−0.11	−0.12
				(2.4)	(2.0)	(1.8)
$\frac{1}{4}\Delta_4 \ln LABTX_{-1}$	−0.21|	−0.24|	−0.27|	−0.80	0.03	0.09
				(0.7)	(0.0)	(0.1)
$DISRW_{-3}$	−0.16	−0.16	−0.20	−0.22	−0.19	−0.20
	(4.4)	(4.5)	(4.5)	(4.5)	(3.8)	(3.3)
$PROFY_{-3}$	0.017	0.019	0.029	0.029	0.015	0.017
	(2.2)	(2.3)	(2.6)	(2.2)	(1.1)	(0.9)
$\ln UNUKS_{-2}/100$	−1.40	−1.41	−1.04	−1.51	−1.47	−1.39
	(2.0)	(2.0)	(1.4)	(1.7)	(1.7)	(1.4)
$\Delta \ln UNUKS/100$	−5.70	−6.23	−5.22	−5.78	−5.64	−5.48
	(3.2)	(3.1)	(2.5)	(2.2)	(2.2)	(1.9)
Dummies	√	√	√	√	√	√
SEE	0.60	0.60	0.60	0.61	0.58	0.59
$\bar{R}^2$	0.89	0.83	0.84	0.83	0.85	0.84
DW	2.0	2.0	2.0	2.1	2.3	2.3
DF	54	53	52	48	48	46
χ^2	0.5[3]	2.3	3.6	5.4	0.2	
	(II,1)	(III,1)	(IV,4)	(VI,2)	(VI,2)	
	2.8		8.8			
	(III,2)		(V,6)			
Period	1967Q4 to 1984Q1					

[1]Defined in Appendix 3A.
[2]Indicates constraints imposed.
[3]Tests of constraints imposed. The equation of comparison and the degrees of freedom are in parentheses.

Fig. 3.5 Wage rise acceptable to employees.

(a) The union's view

It was assumed that the employees' view of the acceptable real wage depends on an appropriate measure of price inflation, a view of the likely trend rate of productivity growth and the level of direct taxation (incorporated in the form of the retention ratio). The trend productivity variable is a smoothed version of actual productivity in UK manufacturing. The retention ratio was included in four-quarter moving average form to pick up the seasonality of changes in its value. The resulting expression for the union's acceptable wage rise was the following:

$$\Delta_4 \ln WACC = \Delta_4 \ln RPI + \Delta_4 \ln TPMF - 0.6\Delta_4 \ln RETRAT \qquad (3.20)$$

Table 3.4 shows the wage equation with and without the constraints implied by this form. Figure 3.5 shows the path of $\Delta_4 \ln WACC$ alongside that of our dependent variable.

(b) The firm's view

The model of the firm's view of the affordable wage rise includes a price variable designed to represent the firm's view of the likely change in the prices charged by their competitors (CP), a weighted average of import price deflators (PM), a trend productivity variable ($TPMF$), and an indicator of the effect of labour taxes ($LABTX$). The first is constructed from three price series: a price expectations series constructed from CBI survey data (*PPEX*) picks up expectations relating to domestic sales in domestic markets; the import price deflator for finished manufactures (*UMFM*) picks up expectations relating to overseas sales in the domestic market; for the overseas market a UK-weighted dollar index of world manufacturing export prices is used (*UKCP*) along with the sterling–dollar exchange rate (*RXD*).

The other components of the affordable wage are the following. A weighted average of import costs (*PM*, constructed using input–output weights on price deflators for different categories of imports) was used to indicate rises in import costs. This is expected to have a negative effect on wage settlements because, if it rises, it will decrease the firm's ability to afford wage increases. It was assumed that the same trend productivity variable as above was relevant. The labour tax variable was included in four-quarter moving average form.

The final expression for the wage rise which firms view as being affordable was the following:

$$\Delta_4 \ln WAFF = 1.4\Delta_4 \ln CP - 0.4\Delta_4 \ln PM + \Delta_4 \ln TPMF + \Delta_4 \ln LABTX \quad (3.21)$$

where

$$\Delta_4 \ln CP = 0.75\Delta_4 \ln CPD + 0.25\Delta_4 \ln CPX$$
$$\Delta_4 \ln CPD = 0.333\Delta_4 \ln UMFM + 0.667\,PPEX$$
$$\Delta_4 \ln CPX = \Delta_4 \ln UKCP - \Delta_4 \ln RXD$$

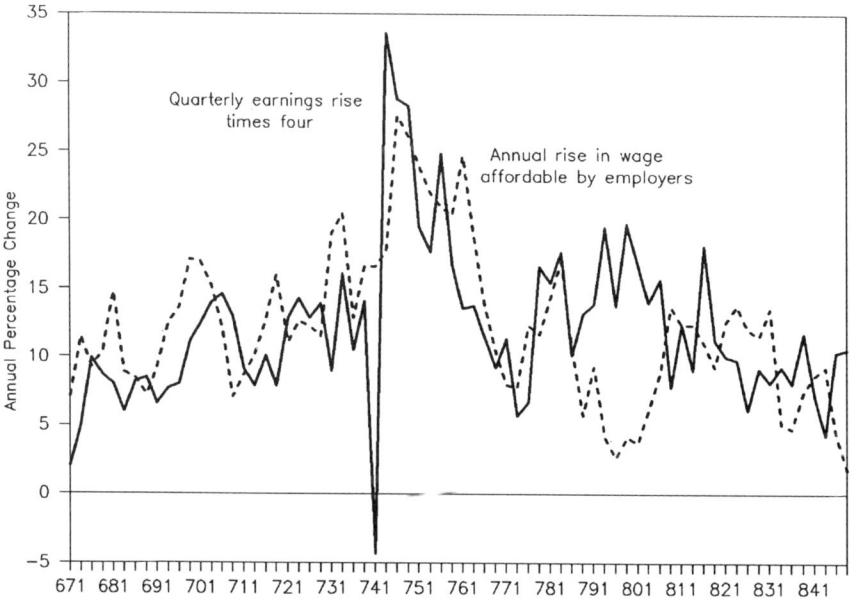

Fig. 3.6 Wage rise affordable by employers.

The weights imposed in these equations relate to the shares of imports in the domestic market and the share of domestic output exported. They were not rejected by the data. Table 3.4 shows the effect on the equation explaining the. path of $\Delta \ln ERMF$ of estimating with and without the constraints. Figure 3.6 shows the path of $\Delta_4 \ln WAFF$ alongside that of the rise in average earnings.

The hypothesis that wages are settled in a bargaining process in which the firm has a significant influence implies that the coefficient on material input costs in the wage equation is negative. The equation reported in this section, which finds a significant value for this coefficient, therefore lends support to this hypothesis. An alternative hypothesis suggests that a rise in import prices affects the wage settlement because of the likely effect of import prices on the real wage. But this predicts that increases in import prices would lead to higher wage settlements and so implies that there should be a **positive** coefficient on this variable.

(c) Expectations

Two alternative variables were included initially to pick up the price inflation component of the wage rise the union considers to be acceptable, the latest actual RPI figures and a consumer price expectations series constructed from Gallup survey data, *CPEX*. The price expectations series, which was available over a relatively short period, made virtually no contribution to the fit of the equation and was omitted from the final specification. Casual empiricism suggests that an important role is played in wage bargaining by the latest available data for RPI increases; the data supported this. However, it cannot be concluded with any confidence that price expectations play no role in unions' bargaining behaviour since a 'better' series for price expectations could always indicate the contrary.

Three price series are included as candidates for modelling the competitors' price element of the nominal wage rise affordable by the firm. Two of these, the import price deflator for finished manufactured goods, *UMFM*, (for foreign goods competing in the domestic market) and the UK-weighted dollar index of world manufactured export prices, *UKCP*, converted into sterling using the sterling-dollar spot rate are backward looking series derived from actual data. The third is a price expectations series constructed from CBI data, *PPEX*. There was some slight support for including the price expectations series, as shown in Table 3.4.

The assumption that price expectations play a part in determining wage settlements is relevant to many of the policy options used to reduce inflation. This was true of the 'monetarism' of the early 1980s. It is true again in 1991 to the extent that it is assumed that joining the ERM will result in wage settlements lower than would otherwise have been the case because of an **expected** fall in price inflation. If price expectations in fact play no role in wage settlements, then any policy initiative which depends solely on this will be doomed to fail. The data suggest that the employees' side of the wage bargain may be backward-looking and dependent on the published data; the employers' side, on the other hand, may reflect expected increases in competitors' prices and so may be influenced by UK membership of the ERM (Barrell, 1990 and Smith, 1990).

3.6.4 The levels terms

The theory suggested three terms for inclusion in the equation that are specified in 'levels' rather than in difference form: an 'error correction term' representing the deviation of the real wage from its long-run equilibrium level (the warranted real wage), the deviation of the profit rate from the level it would take in a long-run equilibrium and the deviation of the unemployment rate from the NAIRU.

(a) Warranted real wage

Economic theory suggests that the warranted real wage, the real wage that is consistent with the economic fundamentals (section 3.2.3) depends on the long-term trend level of labour productivity, and varies with the level of taxes and the terms of trade. Further, if 'real wage aspirations', often cited as a sociological explanation of inflation (Baxter, 1973, and Panic, 1973), have any credibility then it is in this term of the estimated equation that it will appear. If wage rises tend to be higher than can be justified by the fundamentals, as these works suggest, then there will be a positive intercept on the term in the equation that describes the level of the real wage consistent with long run equilibrium in the labour market.

The specification of $DISRW$, the deviation of the real wage from its reference level, involves modelling the long-run warranted or acceptable real wage ($RWWAR$). Our specification of this is similar to our specification of the dynamic term in the real wage found acceptable to the employees, but in addition it includes a dependence on the terms of trade (TT). The specification of $DISRW$ is therefore:

$$DISRW = \ln RW - \ln RWWAR$$
$$= (\ln ERMF - \ln RPI) - (\ln TPMF + \beta \ln TT - \eta \ln RETRAT) \quad (3.22)$$

where the relevant definition of the terms of trade involves the ratio of the producer output price ($PPIO$) to the unit cost of imported imputs (PM):

$$\ln TT = \ln PPIO - \ln PM$$

and the retention ratio is defined as:

$$\ln RETRAT = \ln NWSB - \ln WSB$$

where $NWSB$ and WSB are the UK total wage and salary bill net and gross of direct taxes respectively.

Table 3.5 shows tests of the various constraints implicit in the real wage level term of our equation. Given these tests, the coefficients on the terms of trade and on the retention ratio were imposed at 0.15 and 0.6 respectively. Given that the warranted real wage is constrained to have a coefficient equal and opposite to that of the actual real wage and this is estimated at 0.16, the implied coefficient on the terms of trade variable is 0.02 and on the retention ratio is 0.10 as shown in Column I of the table. The table also indicates that the estimates of the coefficient on the retention ratio always took the correct sign, though they were not generally significantly different from zero. The terms of trade effect, though small, was also consistently of the right sign.

Table 3.5 Tests of constraints in real wage levels terms

Dependent variable $\Delta \ln ERMF$

Explanatory variables[1]	Preferred equation I	II	III	IV	V	VI	VII
$\ln ERMF_{-3}$	−0.16[2] (4.4)	−0.14 (3.0)	−0.18 (4.5)	−0.16 (3.2)	−0.15 (3.9)	−0.17 (2.7)	−0.17 (2.3)
$\ln RPI_{-3}$	0.16	0.14	0.18	0.16	0.15 (4.1)	0.16 (3.0)	0.14 (2.0)
$\ln TPMF_{-3}$	0.16	0.14	0.18	0.18 (2.9)	0.16 (3.5)	0.20 (2.1)	0.23 (2.3)
$\ln PPIO_{-3}$	0.02	0.03 (1.2)	0.04 (2.2)	0.02 (0.9)	0.02	0.02 (0.8)	0.09 (1.4)
$\ln PM_{-3}$	−0.02	−0.02 (1.0)	−0.04	−0.02	−0.02	−0.02	−0.03 (1.2)
$\ln NWFP_{-3}$	−0.10	−0.11 (1.3)	−0.04 (0.5)	−0.06 (0.6)	−0.10	−0.05 (0.5)	−0.05 (0.5)
$\ln WFP_{-3}$	0.10	0.11	0.05 (0.7)	0.06	0.10	0.05	0.02 (0.2)
$\frac{1}{4}\Delta_4 \ln WACC_{-1}$	0.79 (9.1)	0.79 (8.2)	0.79 (8.0)	0.77 (7.4)	0.79 (8.9)	0.76 (7.0)	0.77 (6.9)
$\frac{1}{4}\Delta_4 \ln WAFF_{-1}$	0.21	0.21	0.21	0.23	0.21	0.24	0.23
$PROFY_{-3}$	0.017 (2.2)	0.015 (1.8)	0.016 (1.9)	0.016 (1.9)	0.015 (1.9)	0.016 (1.9)	0.008 (0.7)
$\ln UNUKS_{-2}/100$	−1.40 (2.0)	−2.09 (1.8)	−1.96 (1.8)	−1.80 (1.8)	−1.96 (2.1)	−1.69 (1.4)	−2.26 (1.7)
$\Delta \ln UNUKS/100$	−5.70 (3.2)	−6.84 (3.1)	−6.69 (3.0)	−6.26 (2.9)	−6.44 (3.2)	−6.11 (2.5)	−6.68 (2.7)
Dummies	√	√	√	√	√	√	√
SEE	0.60	0.61	0.61	0.61	0.60	0.61	0.62
$\bar{R}^2$	0.89	0.89	0.89	0.89	0.89	0.88	0.88
DW	2.0	2.1	2.1	2.1	2.1	2.1	2.2
DF	54	51	51	51	52	50	48
χ^2	3.9[3] (VII,6)	2.4 (VII,3)	2.6 (VII,3)	2.0 (VII,3)	2.2 (VII,4)	2.0 (VII,2)	
Period	1967Q4 to 1984Q1						

[1]Variables are defined in Appendix 3A.
[2]Indicates constraints imposed.
[3]Tests of constraints imposed. Equation of comparison and degrees of freedom are in parentheses.

(b) Role of unemployment

Questions arise as to the appropriate measure of the unemployment rate to use in the earnings equation. These concern both the functional form in which the unemployment rate appears in the equation (in levels or in difference form,

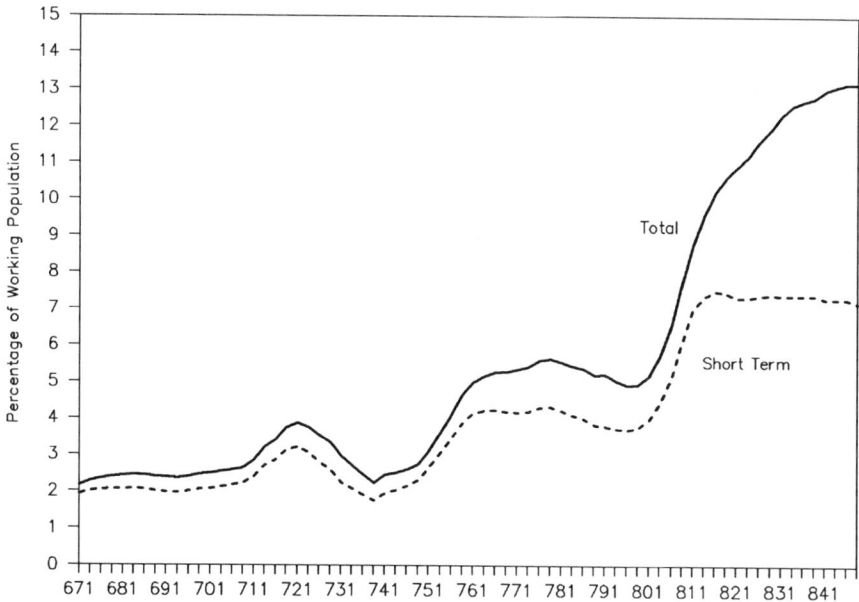

Fig. 3.7 Unemployment.

Chapter 8) and the measure of unemployment that is appropriate (total un-employed or short-term unemployed; percentage of the work-force or logarithmic form, see Figure 3.7).

Table 3.6 demonstrates the effect of including three lags of two alternative measures of unemployment, total and short term (less than 52 weeks), in levels and in logarithmic form.[21] In all four cases the coefficients on the lags alternate in sign, suggesting that there is a role for the change in unemployment (a hysteresis effect with the NAIRU depending on past unemployment) as well as, possibly, a longer term levels effect (with the conventional implications of the NAIRU). The long-term effect is very unstable when the levels of the unemployment variables are used; it is much more stable with the logarithms of unemployment, but still not convincingly significant at the 90 per cent level. This result is very important. If the level of unemployment is not significant in this equation then the conventional macroeconomic policies that are used for reducing inflation are unlikely to be effective (Chapter 8).

(c) Role of profits

The theory underlying our wage equation suggests that profits per unit of output may have an effect on the wage outcome. The variable included for the flow of profits is taken from the ICC's company accounts with the North Sea netted out

Table 3.6 Effects of unemployment

Dependent variable $\Delta \ln ERMF$

Explanatory variables[1]	Total unemployment				Short-term unemployment			
	Level		Logarithm		Level		Logarithm	
	I	II	III	IV	V	VI	VII	VIII
$Unemp^2/100$	−2.36 (2.3)	−2.27 (3.2)	−8.66 (2.5)	−9.03 (2.7)	−2.48 (2.1)	−1.51 (1.9)	−7.14 (2.2)	−6.63 (2.1)
$Unemp_{-1}/100$	3.53 (2.1)	3.34 (2.5)	12.52 (2.2)	12.38 (1.9)	3.36 (1.7)	1.67 (1.1)	9.27 (1.7)	7.89 (1.3)
$Unemp_{-2}/100$	−1.55 (1.6)	−0.96 (1.3)	−5.07 (1.8)	−3.97 (1.1)	−1.47 (1.3)	−0.23 (0.3)	−3.53 (1.3)	−2.54 (0.8)
Total	−0.38 (1.5)	0.11 (1.1)	−1.21 (1.5)	−0.61 (0.9)	−0.59 (1.6)	−0.07 (0.3)	−1.41 (1.5)	−1.27 (1.5)
$\frac{1}{4}\Delta_4 \ln WACC_{-1}$	0.83[3] (7.1)	0.86 (8.3)	0.85 (7.8)	0.76 (8.1)	0.83 (6.6)	0.81 (7.4)	0.86 (7.5)	0.76 (7.7)
$\frac{1}{4}\Delta_4 \ln WAFF_{-1}$	0.17	0.13	0.15	0.24	0.17	0.19	0.14	0.24
$DISRW_{-3}$	−0.18 (3.2)	−0.09 (3.1)	−0.17 (3.8)	−0.13 (3.3)	−0.18 (3.4)	−0.12 (3.7)	−0.17 (3.9)	−0.15 (3.9)
$PROFY_{-3}$	0.027 (1.5)	0.034 (3.5)	0.025 (1.5)	0.020 (2.1)	0.024 (1.3)	0.028 (2.7)	0.023 (1.3)	0.018 (2.1)
Dummies	✓	✓	✓	✓	✓	✓	✓	✓
SEE	0.62	0.59	0.62	0.62	0.63	0.64	0.63	0.63
$\bar{R}^2$	0.89	0.91	0.89	0.90	0.88	0.89	0.88	0.89
DW	1.9	2.1	2.0	2.0	1.9	2.1	2.0	2.1
DF	41	43	41	43	41	43	41	43
Period[4]	663–801	702–841	663–801	702–841	663–801	702–841	663–801	702–841
χ^2	195.3[5] (16,26)	14.6 (13,22)	34.5 (16,26)	11.0 (13,22)	98.3 (16,26)	12.1 (13,22)	25.6 (16,26)	9.6 (13,22)

[1] Variables are defined in Appendix 3A.
[2] The measure of unemployment included is indicated at the top of the column.
[3] Indicates constraints imposed.
[4] 663–801 means 1966Q3 to 1980Q1 inclusive, and so on.
[5] Forecasting test. Degrees of freedom and 5% significance level in parentheses. Sample period 1966Q3 to 1984Q1.

Table 3.7 Inclusion of levels terms

Dependent variable $\Delta \ln ERMF$

Explanatory variables[1]	Preferred equation I	II	III	IV	V	VI	VII	VIII
$\frac{1}{4}\Delta_4 \ln WACC_{-1}$	0.79|[2] (9.1)	0.82| (9.3)	0.77| (8.7)	0.82| (8.2)	0.88| (8.0)	0.89| (8.6)	0.86| (8.7)	0.88| (8.1)
$\frac{1}{4}\Delta_4 \ln WAFF_{-1}$	0.21|	0.18|	0.23|	0.18|	0.12|	0.11|	0.14|	0.12|
$DISRW_{-3}$	−0.16 (4.4)	−0.18 (5.0)	−0.11 (5.9)		0.01 (0.6)			
$PROFY_{-3}$	0.017 (2.2)		0.030 (5.9)	0.026 (3.0)			0.012 (4.6)	
$\ln UNUKS_{-2}/100$	−1.40 (2.0)	−2.60 (5.8)		+0.92 (1.7)		−0.55 (2.5)		
$\Delta \ln UNUKS/100$	−5.70 (3.2)	−7.68 (4.7)	−4.67 (2.6)	−6.39 (3.1)	−9.41 (4.7)	−9.68 (5.1)	−8.28 (4.6)	−9.16 (4.7)
Dummies	√	√	√	√	√	√	√	√
SEE	0.60	0.62	0.62	0.70	0.78	0.74	0.71	0.78
$\bar{R}^2$	0.89	0.88	0.88	0.85	0.81	0.83	0.85	0.82
DW	2.0	2.0	1.8	1.5	1.3	1.4	1.5	1.3
DF	54	55	55	55	56	56	56	57
χ^2		5.8[3] (I,1)	4.8 (I,1)	20.7 (I,1)	37.2 (I,2)	30.5 (I,2)	24.1 (I,2)	43.9 (I,3)
Period	1967Q4to 1984Q1							

[1] Variables are defined in Appendix 3A.
[2] Indicates constraints imposed.
[3] Tests of constraints imposed. Equation of comparison and degrees of freedom in parentheses.

(because its profit stream reflects special factors), deflated by private sector output and by the TFE deflator. The series is volatile and has been included as a four-quarter moving average.

(d) Role of 'levels terms'

Table 3.7 shows the roles played by all three levels terms in various alternative specifications of the equation. The three variables move in a relatively smooth manner. As a result, their influence on the deviation of actual earnings rises from those deemed 'acceptable' or 'affordable' (modelled by the dynamic terms) varies fairly slowly over time. They are not expected to explain the jaggedness of the path of average earnings changes. Because of this aspect of their time profile, the information content in these series is not high, so the data are unlikely to allow a precise indication of the magnitude of their effect to be estimated.

The table shows the effect of omitting these variables from the equation, of including them one or two at a time and of including all three. The results shown in the table were interpreted as justifying the inclusion of all three terms (Figures 3.8 and 3.9).

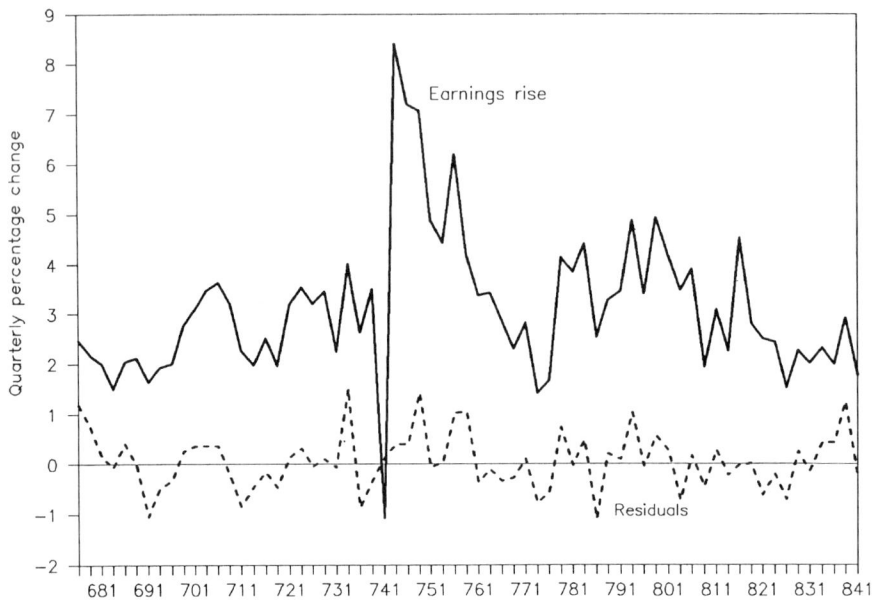

Fig. 3.8 Residuals on earnings equation.

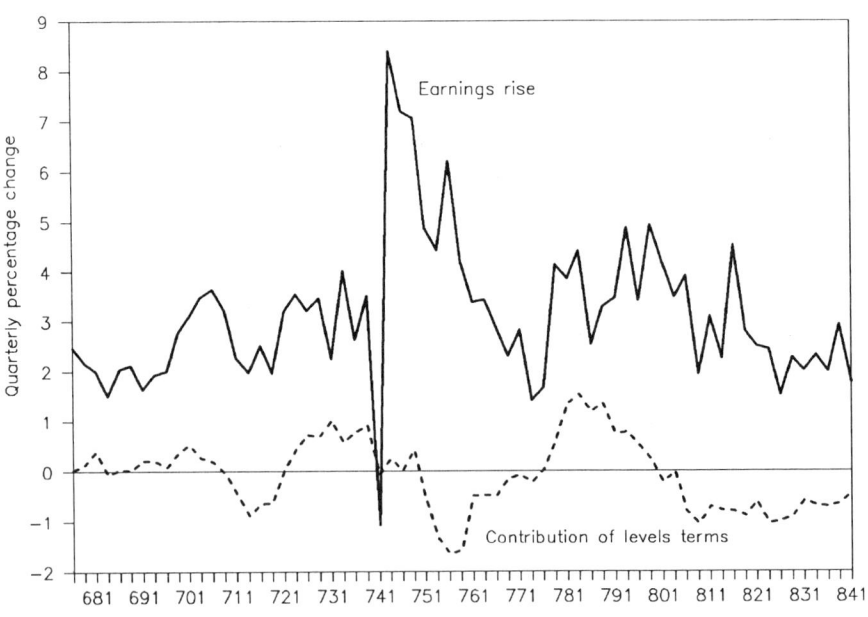

Fig. 3.9 Contribution of levels terms.

3.6.5 Modelling the NAIRU

Experiments were performed with variables designed to model the NAIRU: the unionization rate (membership as a proportion of labour force employed), the real level of benefits and measures of structural change. In each case the equation was first estimated with five lags of the relevant variable and then reduced to the most parsimonious specification. The only one of these variables that appeared to be helpful was the measure of structural change – defined as the absolute value of the change in the ratio of employment in manufacturing to total employment. This variable, one quarter lagged, just passed the exclusion test at the 5 per cent level. It was not included in the preferred specification because of reservations relating to the probability that the result was spurious (data-mining) and about the role that such a variable might be playing.

3.6.6 Stability

Table 3.8 shows the result of estimating the equation over widely varying periods. It indicates that the estimated equation is relatively stable. However, it does suggest that there may have been some change of structure during the period 1980–82. For example, the results suggest that the union side of the bargaining process has become less powerful since 1980 (because the estimated coefficient on $\frac{1}{4}\Delta_4 \ln WACC_{-1}$ is smaller when estimated using more recent data). There is also some evidence to suggest that the effect of excess demand may have been more powerful before 1980. Experimentation with inclusion and omission of periods suggests that the change in structure is not attributable to a temporary episode but has continued. Changes in the institutional structure of the market or in the extent to which real wage aspirations affect the outcome of settlements will result in variations in the intercept or in other coefficients in the equation.

3.7 IMPLICATIONS FOR POLICY

As in the final section of Chapter 2, we note here the implications of this equation for a number of policy issues. These include the role of money growth as a determinant of the inflation rate, the use of demand management as a policy for controlling inflation, the role this equation allows for the exchange rate to affect inflation, the degree of inflation inertia arising from this market, the likely effect of membership of the ERM and the potential for inflationary pressure to arise in the labour market.

(a) The role of money

There is no direct role for money in this equation, just as there was none in the price equation. A possible role for money growth would arise if the rate of increase in the money supply were to influence price expectations and if wage bargainers

Table 3.8 Stability

Dependent variable $\Delta \ln ERMF$

Period	I 1971Q3– 1984Q1	II 1970Q2– 1984Q1	III 1969Q1– 1984Q1	IV 1967Q4– 1984Q1	V 1966Q3– 1984Q1	VI 1966Q3– 1981Q4	VII 1966Q3– 1980Q1	VIII 1966Q3– 1978Q4
Explanatory variables[1]								
$\frac{1}{4}\Delta_4 \ln WACC_{-1}$	0.70[2]	0.77	0.79	0.79	0.79	0.90	0.87	0.91
	(7.2)	(8.3)	(8.7)	(9.1)	(9.1)	(9.0)	(7.8)	(7.5)
$\frac{1}{4}\Delta_4 \ln WAFF_{-1}$	0.30	0.23	0.21	0.21	0.21	0.10	0.13	0.09
$DISRW_{-3}$	−0.14	−0.15	−0.16	−0.16	−0.16	−0.14	−0.17	−0.17
	(3.8)	(3.9)	(4.1)	(4.4)	(4.6)	(3.8)	(3.9)	(3.7)
$PROFY_{-3}$	0.016	0.019	0.020	0.017	0.015	0.007	0.019	0.015
	(1.9)	(2.2)	(2.4)	(2.2)	(2.0)	(0.5)	(1.2)	(0.8)
$\ln UNUKS_{-2}/100$	−1.39	−1.22	−1.11	−1.40	−1.65	−1.60	−1.56	−1.79
	(1.7)	(1.5)	(1.5)	(2.0)	(2.5)	(2.1)	(1.7)	(1.8)
$\Delta \ln UNUK/100$	−4.65	−5.60	−5.32	−5.70	−6.03	−7.90	−5.71	−6.43
	(2.3)	(2.9)	(2.8)	(3.2)	(3.4)	(3.6)	(2.1)	(2.2)
Dummies	√	√	√	√	√	√	√	√
SEE	0.61	0.62	0.62	0.60	0.60	0.65	0.62	0.63
$\bar{R}^2$	0.91	0.90	0.89	0.89	0.88	0.88	0.88	0.88
DW	2.4	2.1	2.0	2.0	1.9	2.2	2.0	1.9
DF	39	44	49	54	57	49	42	38
Hendry χ^2	21[3]	11	8	4		12	24	21
	(18,29)	(13,22)	(8,16)	(3,8)		(9,17)	(16,26)	(20,31)

[1]Variables are defined in Appendix 3A.
[2]Indicates constraints imposed.
[3]Forecasting test. Degrees of freedom and 5 per cent significance level in parentheses. Sample period 1966Q3 to 1984Q1 in total.

used expected price inflation rather than lagged actual price inflation when setting their 'reference' wage settlement rates. However, the empirical evidence lends little support to this hypothesis. Indeed, the explanatory power of the RPI in the wage equation, with all the kinks in its path reflecting special factors, is impressive. Further, the 'casual empiricism' of reports on wage bargaining is strongly suggestive of hard data regarding the latest available published figures on RPI inflation being used by the employees' side in the wage bargaining process.

There remains a role for monetary policy (as opposed to money growth), in the form of a rise in interest rates for example, to affect wage settlements indirectly. It may influence the level of unemployment, or the path of some other variable included in the equation. In this case money growth and the rate at which wage settlements take place would both be affected by the same stimulus rather than either one causing the other.

(b) Effect of demand

The term in the level of unemployment which occurs in the wage equation is the basis of the commonly held view that a recession will lead to a sustained fall in the rate of inflation. If unemployment were to occur in difference form in this equation then, as with the similar term in the price equation, the model would predict that the rate of inflation would return to its previous level (other things being equal) when activity returned to its long-run equilibrium level after the recession was over.

It is not clear from the statistical analysis what functional form unemployment takes in this equation (Tables 3.6 and 3.7). There is some evidence to support the hypothesis that the level of unemployment plays a role in determining wage rises, but the data are not such as to allow the important issue of the functional form to be resolved definitively. This may be because the data generating process is not stable and the form of the effect varies from one cycle to another.

(c) Role for influence of exchange rate

There is a small role for the exchange rate to influence inflation as a result of the equation chosen for wage-setting. This will enhance the effect the exchange rate has on inflation as a result of the price equation, which was noted at the end of Chapter 2. It arises because the equation is derived from a bargaining model. When import prices change as a result of a change in the exchange rate, this will affect firms' profits. It will therefore affect their bargaining behaviour.

(d) Implications for inflation inertia

Again, as in the price equation, the theory suggests that the coefficients on the terms in explanatory price inflation variables in the wage equation sum to unity: that there is full inflation indexation in the labour market. This is a consequence of the 'no money illusion' assumption and implies a full pass through of inflation from one period to the next in the context of the wage equation. The data are consistent with this assumption.

(e) Membership of ERM

If the UK currency is to maintain its value against the currencies of other countries then, given that the UK has a more inflationary labour market than elsewhere, there will need to be a substantial change in the UK wage settlement process. For if the domestic pressures impinging on the spiral in the UK are different from those in the rest of Europe, then the UK is likely to price itself out of the market. At present we have the option of realigning our currency, as described in the next chapter, to maintain its real value. If that option is removed it will be necessary for our labour market to adjust to the pressures or lack of pressures in the rest of Europe, rather than those in the UK, if high unemployment is to be avoided. We need, therefore, to see a structural change in the wage settlement process, with the role of the RPI in the wage equation played by a European inflation measure, if the move towards one currency is to progress as planned.

(f) Potential for causing inflation

It is clear that the labour market has a considerable potential for causing high inflation. In particular, unrealistic wage aspirations, influencing the outcome on wage settlements, will put upward pressure on the inflation spiral. There are a number of other possible causes of such upward pressure, excess demand in the labour market being the most obvious.

APPENDIX 3A: DEFINITIONS OF VARIABLES

ERMF   The dependent variable is the quarter on previous quarter proportionate change in the Department of Employment series for actual manufacturing earnings (seasonally adjusted):

$$\Delta \ln ERMF = \ln ERMF - \ln ERMF(-1)$$

On a simplistic view of the wage round this measures the effect on average earnings in manufacturing of the annual increase for those whose settlements become effective in the relevant quarter.

DE data for 1963Q1 to 1979Q4 (January 1970 = 100) have been rescaled and combined with data from 1980Q1 to 1985Q1 (January 1980 = 100). The figure for 1979Q3 has been increased by 2.05 per cent and that for 1980Q1 by 1.86 per cent, on advice from DE, to allow for industrial disputes. The effect of the 3-day week (1974Q1) has been dealt with by including a dummy with two lags and constraining its long-term effect to zero.

WACC   This variable is included in four quarter change form and is defined by the equation:

$$\Delta_4 \ln WACC = \Delta_4 \ln RPI - 0.6\Delta_4 \ln RETRAT + \Delta_4 \ln TPMF$$

where: RPI   is the Retail Prices Index;
         RETRAT is the four-quarter moving average of the retention ratio, NWSB/WSB;
         NWSB   is the net wage and salary bill;
         WSB   is the gross wage and salary bill;
         TPMF   is trend productivity in manufacturing.

WAFF   This variable is included in four-quarter percentage change form and is defined by the equation:

$$\Delta_4 WAFF = \Delta_4 \ln CP - 0.4(\Delta_4 \ln PM - \Delta_4 \ln CP) - \Delta_4 \ln LABTAX + \Delta_4 \ln TPMF$$

where:
$$\Delta_4 \ln CP = 0.75 \Delta_4 \ln CPD + 0.25\Delta_4 \ln CPX$$
$$\Delta_4 \ln CPD = 0.667 PPEX + 0.333\Delta_4 \ln UMFM$$
$$\Delta_4 \ln CPX = \Delta_4 \ln UKCP - \Delta_4 \ln RXD$$

and: PPEX   is a price expectations series derived from CBI data;
       UMFM   is the price deflator for imported finished manufactures;
       UKCP   is the UK trade weighted dollar price index of world manufactured exports;
       RXD   is the sterling–dollar spot rate;
       PM   is the price deflator for imported inputs;
       LABTAX is the four-quarter moving average of the labour tax ratio:

$$LTXRAT = (WSB + NIS + EMCON + OCON)/WSB$$

with   WSB the wage and salary bill;
         NIS the National Insurance Surcharge;
         EMCON employers' contributions to NH, etc.;
         OCON employers' other contributions.
TPMF   is trend productivity in manufacturing.

PROFY   is the logarithm of the four-quarter moving average of profits per unit of private sector output, defined as:

$$PROFY = \ln \{ [PRFY + PRFY(-1) + PRFY(-2) + PRFY(-3)]/4 \}$$

where:

$$PRFY = PROF/YPR$$
$$PROF = (SAVIC + NODVIC + UKIP - SAC - NSOP + DNSOI + UKTP)/PTFE$$
$$YPR = Y - YOG - 74.025 YPU$$

and: SAVIC   is savings of industrial and commercial companies;

NODVIC   is ICC's dividends and long-term interest payments;
UKIP   is private companies' interest payments to banks on North Sea operations;
SAC   is companies' stock appreciation;
NSOP   is private companies' profits on NS activities gross of depreciation and taxes;
DNSOI   is North Sea oil debits on interest, profits and dividends;
UKTP   is private companies' tax payments on NS operations;
PTFE   is the price deflator for total final expenditure;
Y   is real gross domestic product at factor cost;
YOG   is real value added in NS oil and gas extraction;
YPU   is the output of public services.

$DISRW$ is the logarithm of the deviation of the real wage from its 'warranted' level:

$$DISRW = \ln RW - \ln RWWAR$$

where:

$$\ln RW = \ln ERMF - \ln RPI$$

$$\ln RWWAR = \ln TPMF + 0.15 \ln TT - 0.6 \ln RETRAT$$

and: ERMF   is average earnings in manufacturing;
       RPI   is the Retail Prices Index;
       TPMF   is trend productivity in manufacturing;
       TT   is the terms of trade, PPIO/PM;
       PPIO   the producer price index (output);
       PM   the price deflator for imported inputs;
       RETRAT is the four-quarter moving average of the retention ratio.

UNUKS   is the percentage of the labour force that has been unemployed for less than 52 weeks.

REFERENCES

Akerlof, G. A. and Miyazaki, H. (1980) The implicit contract theory of unemployment meets the wage bill argument, *Review of Economic Studies*, **47**, 321–38.

Ashenfelter, O. and Brown, J. N. (1983) Testing the efficiency of employment contracts, Hoover Institution Conference on Labor Economics.

Azariadis, C. (1975) Implicit contracts and underemployment equilibria, *Journal of Political Economy*, **83**, 1183–202.

Baily, M. N. (1974) Wages and employment under uncertain demand, *Review of Economic Studies*, **41**, 37–50.

Barrell, R. (1990) Has the EMS changed wage and price behaviour in Europe? *National Institute Economic Review*, **34**, 64–72.

Baxter, J. L. (1973) Inflation in the context of relative social deprivation and social justice, *Scottish Journal of Political Economy*, **20**, 263–82.

Bliss, C. and Stern, N. (1978) Productivity, wages and nutrition, *Journal of Development Economics*, **5**, 363–98.

Carruth, A. and Oswald, A. (1983) Miners' wages in post-war Britain: an application of a model of trade union behavior. Unpublished paper.

Dean, A. J. H. (1978) Incomes policies and differentials, *National Institute Economic Review*, **85**, 40–8.

Dunlop, J. T. (1944) *Wage Determination Under Trade Unions*, Macmillan, New York.

Farber, H. S. (1978) Individual preferences and union wage determination: the case of the united mine workers, *Journal of Political Economy*, **86**, 923–42.

Friedman, M. (1968) The role of monetary policy, *The American Economic Review*, **58**, 1–17.

Gordon, D. F. (1974) A neoclassical theory of Keynesian unemployment, *Economic Enquiry*, **12**, 431–59.

Grossman, S. J. and Hart, O. D. (1981) Implicit contracts, moral hazard and unemployment, *American Economic Association Papers and Proceedings*, **71**, 301–7.

Hall, R. E. (1982) The importance of lifetime jobs in the US economy, *The American Economic Review*, **72**, 716–24.

Hashimoto, M. (1979) Bonus payments, on-the-job training and lifetime employment in Japan, *Journal of Political Economy*, **87**, 1086–104.

Layard, R. and Nickell, S. (1985) The causes of British unemployment, *National Institute Economic Review*, 62–85.

Layard, R., Nickell, S. and Jackman, R. (1991) *Unemployment*, Oxford University Press, Oxford.

Leibenstein, H. (1957) *Economic Backwardness and Economic Growth*, Wiley, New York.

Leontief, W. (1946) The pure theory of the guaranteed annual wage contract, *Journal of Political Economy*, **54**, 76–9.

Lipsey, R. G. (1960) The relation between unemployment and the rate of change of money wage rates in the United Kingdom, 1862–1957: a further analysis, *Economica*, **27**, 1–31.

MaCurdy, T. E. and Pencavel J. H. (1986) Testing between competing models of wage and employment determination in unionized markets, *Journal of Political Economy*, **94**, S3–S39.

McDonald, I. M. and Solow, R. M. (1981) Wage bargaining and employment, *The American Economic Review*, **71**, 896–908.

Main, B. G. M. (1982) The length of a job in Great Britain, *Economica*, **49**, 325–33.

Minford, P. (1988) A new classical model of the labour market, in Beenstock, M. (ed.) *Modelling the Labour Market*, Chapman and Hall, London.

Minford, A. P. L., Davies, D. H., Peel, M. J. and Sprague, A. (1983) *Unemployment – Cause and Cure*, Martin Robertson, Oxford.

Mortensen, D. T. (1984) Job search and labour market analysis, in Ashenfelter, O. and Layard, R. (eds.) *Handbook of Labour Economics, Volume II*, Elsevier Science Publishers, Amsterdam.

Nash, J. F. (1950) The bargaining problem, *Econometrica*, **18**, 155–62.

New Earnings Survey (1989) Central Statistical Office, London.

Nickell, S. J. (1983) A bargaining model of the Phillips Curve, Centre for Labour Economics, London School of Economics, Discussion Paper No. 130.

Oswald, A. J. (1982), Trade unions, wages and unemployment: what can simple models tell us? *Oxford Economic Papers*, **34**, 526–45.

Panic, M. (1973) The origin of increasing inflationary tendencies in contemporary society, in Hirsch, F. and Goldthorpe, J. H. (eds.) *The Political Economy of Inflation*, Martin Robertson, London.

Pencavel, J. (1985) Wages and employment under trade unionism: microeconomic models and macroeconomic applications, *Scandinavian Journal of Economics*, **87**, 197–225.

Phelps, E. S. (1967) Phillips curves, expectations of inflation and optimal unemployment over time, *Economica*, **34**, 254–81.

Phillips, A. W. (1958) The relation between unemployment and the rate of change of money wage rates in the United Kingdom, 1861–1957, *Economica*, **25**, 283–99.

Rees, A. (1962) *The Economics of Trade Unions*, University of Chicago Press, Chicago.

Rowlatt, P. A. (1986) A model of wage bargaining, *Government Economic Service Working Paper No. 91*, HM Treasury, London.

Rowlatt, P. A. (1987) A model of wage bargaining, *Oxford Bulletin of Economics and Statistics*, **49**, 347–72.

Schoemaker, P. J. H. (1982) The expected utility model: its variants, purposes, evidence and limitations, *Journal of Economic Literature*, **20**, 529–63.

Shapiro, C. and Stiglitz, J. (1984) Equilibrium unemployment as a worker discipline device, *American Economic Review*, **74**(3), 433–44.

Smith, J. G. (1990) Pay strategy for the 1990s, *Institute for Public Policy Research Economic Study No. 8*, London.

Weiss, A. (1980) Job queues and layoffs in labor markets with flexible wages, *Journal of Political Economy*, **88**, 526–38.

ENDNOTES

1. Section 3.5.2 contains a definition of this power in the context of our model.
2. The relation took the form:

$$\Delta w_t = \alpha + \beta U_t^{-\gamma}$$

   where Δw_t is the change in money wage rates and U_t is the percentage of the labour force registered as unemployed.
3. Lipsey, 1960.
4. The unemployment rate rose progressively from around 1.5 per cent in the 1950s to the 5 per cent level of the late 1970s (Figure 3.7).
5. The Expectations Augmented Phillips Curve relates wage inflation, Δw_t, to expected price inflation, Δp_t^e, and the deviation of the rate of unemployment, U_t, from the market clearing rate, $\bar{U}_t$:

$$\Delta w_t = \Delta p_t^e - \alpha(U_t - \bar{U}_t) + u_t.$$

   where u_t is a randomly distributed residual. If price changes, Δp_t, were determined by the changes in wages: $\Delta p_t = \Delta w_t + v_t$ (with v_t a random residual) and price expectations were extrapolative: $\Delta p_t^e = \Delta p_{t-1} + w_t$ (w_t is another random residual), this equation would become:

$$\Delta p_t = \Delta p_{t-1} - \alpha(U_t - \bar{U}_t) + \varepsilon_t$$

   where ε_t incorporates the random error terms u_t, v_t and w_t. This equation has the *change* in inflation dependent on the *level* of the deviation of the unemployment rate from the market clearing rate.
6. This has been espoused by some economists, e.g. Minford *et al.* (1983).
7. Layard *et al.* (1991).
8. A useful survey may be found in Mortensen (1984).
9. E.g., Minford *et al.* (1983) and Layard and Nickell (1985).
10. Akerlof and Miyazaki (1980), for example.
11. Leibenstein (1957), or Bliss and Stern (1978).
12. Shapiro and Stiglitz (1984) is the classic article.
13. Dunlop (1944); Rees (1962); Farber (1978) or Oswald (1982) *inter alia*.
14. The concept is due to Leontief (1946).
15. Usually taking no account of the functional form implicit in the relationship, given the construction of the data used (section 3.6.2).

16. Assuming that productivity is independent of the wage paid (section 3.3).
17. Section 3.2.3.
18. Rowlatt (1986) gives a more detailed report.
19. Variable mnemonics are defined in Appendix 3A.
20. For the values taken by NORM refer to Figure 3.4 and Rowlatt (1987) or Dean (1978).
21. The implication of using the logarithmic form is that the effect on the real wage of a change in the level of unemployment becomes smaller the higher the initial level of unemployment. With the logarithmic form a fall in unemployment from 20 to 10 per cent will have the same effect on the real wage as a fall from 5 to 2.5 per cent. With the levels form the effect of a fall from 20 to 10 per cent will be four times as big as that of a fall from 5 to 2.5 per cent.

4

The foreign exchange market

4.1 INTRODUCTION

Unlike most other empirical analyses of inflation (for example, Gordon 1985), we treat the exchange rate as an integral part of the inflation spiral. We do this because the effect on domestic inflation of shocks to the economic system depends on the dynamic reaction of the exchange rate to differential rates of price inflation at home and abroad (Chapters 5 and 6). Given the way in which the market in currencies works, a policy requirement that the nominal exchange rate remains unchanged may have profound implications for policy instruments and could indeed prove untenable.

The approach taken to modelling the exchange rate is broadly the same as that taken to modelling prices and wages. In section 4.2 we examine the likely motivation of those that buy and sell in foreign currency markets and note relevant features of the institutional structure of the market. This is followed by a discussion of the main alternative theoretical approaches to explaining the path of the exchange rate. Section 4.3 summarizes the published results of some empirical tests of the various hypotheses.

Section 4.4 draws on the theory developed in section 4.2, given the empirical support noted in section 4.3, to derive an equation for the exchange rate path that can be estimated and notes the properties that are most relevant to the inflation spiral. The estimation results are reported in section 4.5. The equation for the exchange rate used in our model of the inflation spiral is then presented, its performance is illustrated in a chart and its main implications noted. Section 4.6 summarizes its significance for various aspects of policy.

4.2 THEORETICAL APPROACHES[1]

4.2.1. Introduction

The exchange rate is the price (or rate) at which one currency is exchanged for another. It may be defined either way up, in relation to one other currency (the bilateral exchange rate) or in relation to a basket of currencies (the European

Currency Unit, ECU, for example), and in real or in nominal terms. Here, the nominal exchange rate is defined as the foreign price of domestic currency, dollars per pound sterling, for example.

The price competitiveness of one economy's goods compared to those of another is indicated by the real rate at which the currencies are exchanged. If P is the price of domestic goods (UK, say), P^w the foreign currency price of foreign goods (US) and RX the spot exchange rate ($/£), the real exchange rate is given by:

$$RRX = RX\,(P/P^w) \tag{4.1}$$

It follows that, if the nominal exchange rate remains constant, a larger increase in domestic than foreign prices results in a rise in the real exchange rate (and a loss of international competitiveness) similar to that resulting from an appreciation in the nominal exchange rate.

As in any market, the relation between the supply and the demand for a currency is crucial to the determination of its price. Thus, in order to model the path of the exchange rate, we find ourselves examining the reasons why people would wish to obtain one currency rather than another. There are three main classes of motive. First, foreign currency is needed in order to buy goods or services from foreigners. The demand for foreign currency for this purpose makes up the visible trade account and the services component of the invisibles in the balance of payments statistics. Second, foreign currency is required to buy assets abroad. These may be either physical assets or financial ones for long- or short-term investment (including those held for speculation purposes). These make up the capital account statistics. Third, the returns on assets owned by foreigners, profits, interest payments and dividends, may be converted into the currency of origin. These are included in the statistics for invisible trade. Corresponding to each of these we can model the demand for currency. In each case there may be disparities in timing between the transaction triggering the demand and the actual foreign currency conversion.

The spot value of the exchange rate is determined in the market. The continual transactions that take place, in which purchasers of a currency seek sellers and *vice versa*, ensure that the price moves to the level that results in a zero *ex post* net demand in the spot market. In the absence of public sector intervention it will therefore be determined in such a way as to match the flows that respond virtually instantaneously (speculation in short-term financial assets) to the underlying, less responsive demands for currency (longer term investments, income flows from international investments and trade).

The price of foreign exchange may be set within any of several possible regimes. At one extreme an exchange rate may be freely floating, in which case its price reflects the relation between whatever supply and demand arises for the currency in the market place, with no deliberate intervention by the authorities. At the other extreme, central banks guarantee to buy and sell an unlimited quantity of a currency at a given price, so that its price may be held fixed relative to some other currency or bundle of currencies.

In practice there has been considerable variation in exchange rate regimes in recent decades. At the Bretton Woods conference towards the end of the Second World War a fixed rate system was introduced in which exchange rates were held fixed in relation to the dollar, although there was scope for limited fluctuations around this level. The final breakdown of the Bretton Woods system in 1973 led to the general adoption of a floating system, although in reality this meant a 'dirty float' for many countries (central banks intervening to smooth and stabilize rates). Since then the European Exchange Rate Mechanism (ERM) has been set up. This allows a degree of latitude while maintaining a broad parity between the rates of those that join.

In any exchange rate regime the current account surplus or deficit will be exactly blanced by an equivalent capital account deficit or surplus *ex post*, after taking account of any intervention by the authorities. It follows that the total demand for (supply of) a currency depends on the factors that determine the current account and the capital account whatever the regime. A structural approach to understanding the factors influencing the path of the exchange rate will involve the *ex ante* disequilibrium, and therefore the demand and supply for foreign currency by private sector operators at home and abroad, regardless of the regime that operates.

In a fixed rate system the *ex ante* disequilibrium in the exchange market affects the behaviour of the authorities (given the permitted range for the exchange rate); public sector intervention of one sort or another prevents the path of the exchange rate from being affected by the disequilibrium because it offsets the effect on the exchange rate which the disequilibrium would otherwise have had. The authorities need to be able to respond to any such disequilibrium with short-term intervention in the market as well as adjusting longer term monetary and fiscal policy. It follows that although membership of the ERM or any other fixed rate agreement may have a short term beneficial effect on the economy (by enabling lower interest rates, by changing the balance of power in wage bargaining or by affecting expectations of future wage or price rises, for example), it will also have important implications for fiscal and monetary policy, will considerably restrict the authorities' freedom of action and may prove untenable in the longer term.

4.2.2 Trade account factors

Theories of exchange rate determination can be divided into those that emphasize factors relating to the trade account and those in which the rate is assumed to move in response to capital account factors. The approach taken in the equation used in our model combines both theories.

We begin with theories which emphasize the international goods market or trade account. The purchasing power parity (PPP) theory of exchange rate determination identifies a reference point which is useful in the analysis of the inflation spiral, although of little relevance to the short-term path of the exchange rate. It rests on the hypothesis that the path of the exchange rate is such as to ensure that the 'Law of One Price' holds. The Law of One Price states that in the absence of transport and other transactions costs, prices will be the same in all countries that trade freely amongst themselves. Put another way, it asserts that £100 should buy as much in the UK as £100-worth of dollars buys in the US, because if this were not the case the goods will be purchased wherever they can be bought cheapest.

The implication of the PPP approach in its simplest form is that the exchange rate adjusts to maintain the Law of One Price. Thus, in a world of differential rates of inflation, bilateral exchange rates would continuously move to keep real exchange rates constant. For example, if the UK were to experience an annual inflation rate 5 per cent above that of its major trading partners over some period, PPP in this form implies that the sterling spot rate would depreciate by 5 per cent a year during this time. In this case any difference in the sterling price of goods bought in the UK and abroad would be removed by the exchange rate movement and competitiveness would remain constant.

The hypothesis that the path of the exchange rate is consistent with PPP is an example of the general principle that behaviour is determined by real variables rather than nominal ones. However, there is a number of theoretical reasons why this hypothesis cannot be expected to explain the short-term path of the nominal exchange rate, quite apart from the fact that the data fail to lend it support (Figure 4.1).[2]

First, the Law of One Price can only apply to the prices of traded goods; it can be of little direct significance to goods for which transport costs make export impractical, or to services which must be consumed in the country in which they

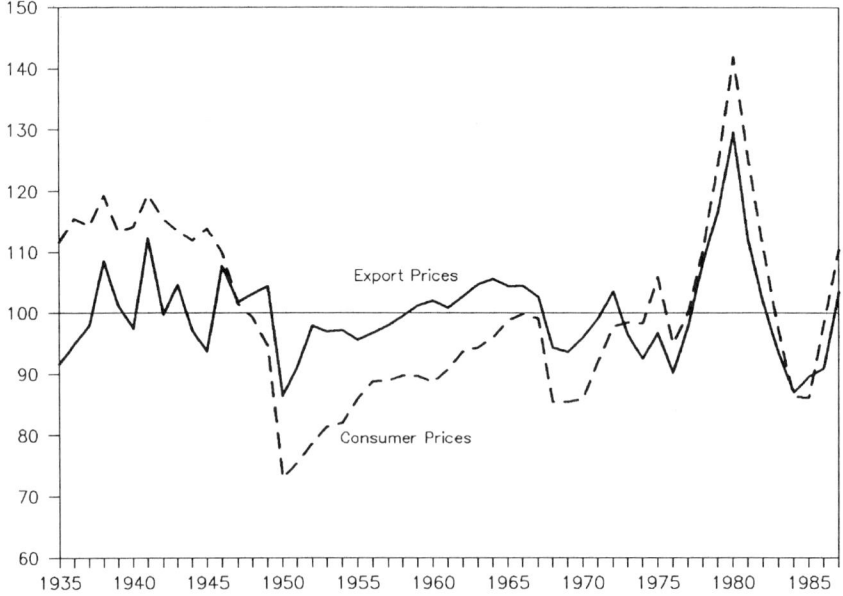

Fig. 4.1 Ratios of UK to US prices in sterling.

are produced. Thus, if labour markets maintain the broad relativities between wages in different sectors, productivity grows faster in manufacturing than in service sectors and only the output of manufacturing sectors is traded, then different rates of productivity growth between countries will result in a violation of the simplest form of the PPP assumption. The use of PPP as the basis of a (long-run) model of exchange rate determination must therefore make a distinction between traded and nontraded goods (Figure 4.1), or take account of differential productivity growth.

Second, even if traded goods' prices approximated broadly to the level implied by the Law of One Price, it would not necessarily follow that PPP determined the path of the exchange rate. Instead, variations in competitiveness resulting from an exchange rate movement may have an effect on price-setting and profit margins. For example, the substantial costs faced by firms entering markets may mean that, given an adverse exchange rate movement, companies will prefer to reduce their prices, squeezing profit margins, instead of withdrawing from a market until a reverse movement in the exchange rate once again allows competitive trading. A seeming consistency with PPP could arise because prices adjust rather than because exchange rates adjust. This effect enters our model through the term in competitors' prices in the price-setting equation (Chapter 2).

Third, PPP implicitly assumes that internationally traded goods are perfect substitutes. This implies that the level of the underlying equilibrium real exchange rate is uniquely determined by relative prices, and that this equilibrium rate achieves current account balance. Moreover, it suggests that any deviation of the rate from its equilibrium level would result in very large current account imbalances. However, it is evident that variations in other factors (the level of activity, for example) change the level of competitiveness which will maintain the trade account in balance. Therefore the equilibrium exchange rate is not uniquely determined by relative prices, and quite small changes in the rate do not precipitate very large imbalances. Price elasticities of demand are not infinite, the demand schedules have a downward slope. Further, variations in the quality of the goods produced, swings in fashion or the discovery of new reserves of natural resources[3] will all have an influence on trade flows and therefore on the implied market clearing level of the exchange rate.

Fourth, the market clearing level of the current account (and therefore of competitiveness) will depend on the net balance of long-term inward and outward investment. There may be a continuing build-up of net foreign balances over a period, which needs to be financed by a continuing net deficit on the current account. This would allow the level of competitiveness at which the currency market clears to decline for a while.

Finally, a return must be paid on any existing foreign balances, and a return will be earned on foreign assets owned by residents. This will change the flows on the invisible account. Other things being equal, this will affect the volume of net exports required to achieve external balance on current account and therefore the level of competitiveness at which *ex ante* equilibrium is achieved.

In conclusion, there are good reasons for supposing that PPP may be of limited help in explaining how the price of foreign exchange moves in the short run. Empirical evidence supports this view, as can be seen from the duration and size of fluctuations of the real sterling–dollar rate during the period from 1935 to 1985. The volatility that the real values of these and other currencies have exhibited in recent years certainly suggests that factors other than differential rates of inflation are important in determining the short-run paths of nominal exchange rates. However, considerations along the lines of PPP, that is, relating to international competitiveness, adjusted to take account of finds of new resources and so on, are likely to have some relevance to the determination of the long-run real rate of exchange. In the long run the real exchange rate will be compatible with *ex ante* balance in the exchange markets and in international asset portfolios.

We now turn our attention to theories of exchange rate determination which emphasize the capital account of the balance of payments.

4.2.3 Capital account factors

Since the breakdown of the Bretton Woods agreement in the early 1970s and the consequent change from a fixed to a floating exchange rate regime, the exchange controls that restricted short-term speculative flows across the exchanges have been dismantled and there is now little regulation of the flow of capital.[4] This, along with the ever more sophisticated information technology (which allows for rapid international asset trading at negligible transactions costs), has meant that the capital market has become increasingly global in nature. There are now huge quantities of speculative funds moving freely between the world's financial markets looking for profit. The path of the exchange rate is determined, in the short run, by these short-term speculative flows financing the currency requirements of other traders.

(a) Uncovered interest parity

The central assumption of the asset market approach to exchange rate determination is the capital account counterpart of PPP, Uncovered Interest Parity (UIP): the path of the exchange rate is such that the expected rates of return on assets are equalized across countries. That is, the spot rate RX and the expected value of speculators' views regarding the future exchange rate $E(RX^e_{+1})$ are simultaneously determined in asset market equilibrium, given the relevant interest rates (r and r^w), to leave investors indifferent between the currencies in which they hold their assets:[5]

$$rx = E(rx^e_{+1}) + (r - r^w) \qquad (4.2)$$

where the lower case letters for the exchange rate variables indicate that logarithms have been taken.

The justification for the UIP equation involves the assumption that capital has perfect international mobility, that is, that there are no exchange controls, no transaction costs, and that investors are risk neutral. This implies that all assets in all currencies are considered by investors to be perfect substitutes. Hence, the Law of One Price will hold for asset returns (rather than for the prices of tradable goods). If the expected movement in the nominal exchange rate reflects the differing expected inflation rates in two countries, so the real exchange rate is expected to remain constant, UIP implies that real interest rates will be the same in the two countries.

If a different rate of return is offered on assets in two countries, and the exchange rate were expected to remain constant, then investors would see that they could increase the expected return by buying assets denominated in one of the currencies and would transfer their wealth into that currency. Potentially this could generate a vast flow of funds from one currency into another. However, this flow would quickly lead to an exchange rate adjustment that would eliminate the differential. In practice exchange rate operators continuously adjust the rates in the light of the changing situation and this prevents massive flows of funds from taking place. They leave the speculator broadly indifferent to the currency denomination of assets by quoting prices that approximately equalize expected returns.[6] Thus, it is not actual movements of capital across the exchanges which cause the exchange rate to shift; instead it is the possibility of the capital flows that would occur if the price of foreign exchange did not move that causes the exchange rate movement. The exchange rate moves to choke off these capital flows before they occur.

What can the UIP relation tell us about movements in the rate of exchange? If domestic interest rates are high compared to the rate in the rest of the world then, for this equation to hold, it must be the case that the domestic exchange rate is expected to depreciate and provide a capital loss which will offset the gain on the interest differential. Suppose that investors in sterling denominated assets receive a return of 20 per cent per annum on their investments, while there is a 10 per cent rate of interest on corresponding dollar denominated assets. With an initial exchange rate of $2 per pound sterling, investors could earn a return of either £20 or $20 for each £100 (or $200) invested. For the total expected returns to be equalized so the UIP relation holds, investors must, on average, expect the sterling exchange rate to depreciate to $1.83 per pound[7] during the period since this would give a capital gain on dollar denominated assets (or loss on those that are sterling denominated) which would exactly offset the interest differential.

If, in addition, investors have rational expectations[8] then the only difference between the *ex post* change in the exchange rate and the interest differential will be due to random, unsystematic errors in forecasting the new rate.

The prediction that a high domestic interest rate relative to rates abroad is associated with an expected depreciation in the value of a currency is not, perhaps, what many would intuitively expect. It would seem natural to expect a relatively high domestic interest rate to imply flows of funds into a currency in search of higher returns and a consequent appreciation of that currency. This apparent paradox is resolved by making a distinction between anticipated and unanticipated changes in the interest differential (Dornbusch 1976). The UIP relation is based on the assumption that the expected change in the exchange rate will be such as to leave investors indifferent between the currencies in which they hold their assets. Investors will have a view about the long-run equilibrium level of the exchange rate, and their expectations regarding the likely future path of relative interest rates will influence their expectations about how and when it may be reached. The existing interest rate differential therefore determines the level at which the exchange rate must be today in order that the expected depreciation during the period just beginning exactly offsets it. High existing interest rates (relative to those abroad) are therefore associated with the expectation that the value of the currency will decrease (so that total returns are equalized), low interest rates are associated with the expectation of a rise in the currency.

The currency depreciation described above is consistent with an existing high rate of interest. If there is an unanticipated rise in the rate of interest the exchange rate must immediately appreciate since the higher interest rate will now require a larger expected depreciation towards the long-run equilibrium level in order to provide a greater capital loss to offset the increased interest differential. Thus, it is an unanticipated rise in interest rates which results in the immediate appreciation which many intuitively expect, and it is in this sense that UIP predicts that a rise in interest rates implies an appreciating currency: the rise in interest rates causes a currency appreciation so that a larger depreciation is expected in the future, given the long-run equilibrium level of the currency. This expected depreciation will be commensurate with the new difference in rates.

It is clear that the UIP hypothesis relates to the expected change in the exchange rate; it has nothing to say about the level of the spot rate unless a view is taken of its expected level at some point in the future. In order to make UIP operational as a model of the spot exchange rate path we therefore need another element in our model: we need to take a view as to the determinants of the expected future level of the exchange rate. The UIP equation, which takes asset market equilibrium as its base, therefore needs to be combined with a theory of how expectations of the future path of the exchange rate are determined. It is here that the Purchasing Power Parity assumption and the modifications it requires become relevant.

In this theory there are no actual flows across the exchanges and the equilibrium exchange rate is entirely determined by the requirement that expected returns are equalized. In particular it implies that current account disequilibrium has no direct effect on the spot rate. The unreality of this implication is troublesome.

The premise of perfect international capital mobility, on which the prediction of uncovered interest parity is based, relies on the assumption that international investors are risk neutral. Below we relax this assumption and this removes the troublesome feature referred to above.

(b) Risk adjusted uncovered interest parity

If investors are risk-averse and assets carry varying amounts and types of risk, the assets will not be perfectly substitutable. The quantities of individual assets that speculators wish to hold will depend on their risk characteristics as well as their expected returns.

This implies that in equilibrium the expected real return on different assets will depend on their relative supplies: if the supply of an asset perceived as carrying risk (foreign balances held by UK residents, for example) is to be increased, the expected return on it must be increased in order to induce people to hold more of it. For risk averse speculators will need a larger expected return to induce them to hold a risky asset when they could have chosen one with less risk. The UIP relationship (equation 4.2) must be rewritten to take account of the risk aversion factor; instead of uncovered interest parity we will have 'risk adjusted uncovered interest parity'. This is the basis of the equation incorporated into our model.

When investors are risk-averse they will acquire a portfolio of assets which trades expected value against riskiness. The risk premia mean that there will be differences in the expected returns on different assets even when asset markets are in equilibrium. A way of embodying risk-aversion into asset market theory is to assume that investors diversify their portfolios so as to optimize with respect to both the mean and variance of expected end-of-period wealth (section 4.4).

If there is an *ex ante* disequilibrium in the foreign exchange market, the exchange rate and therefore the expected return must (other things being equal) move to induce the flow that clears the market. The relaxation of the assumption of risk neutrality is equivalent to assuming that the demand curve for risky assets is downward sloping. The amount of the *ex ante* disequilibrium (the current account balance and the 'underlying' flows on capital account) now has an explicit role in the determination of the level of the exchange rate. Other things being equal, an increase in the current account deficit will give rise to an *ex ante* disequilibrium in the foreign exchange market and, at existing interest rates, an expected rise in the exchange rate will be needed to induce the equilibrating inflow on capital account. For the same long-run exchange rate level, this implies a lower level today: the spot rate must fall.

(c) Covered interest parity and the forward rate

In addition to the spot market for foreign exchange there is a forward market in foreign currency and it is worth noting, in the context of the determination of the spot rate, the relation between the spot and forward rates. The forward market allows traders to deal today in foreign exchange that will be supplied at some fixed date in the future at a price which is specified today.

A central prediction of the forward exchange market theory is that of Covered Interest Parity (CIP). This states that the difference between the forward exchange rate and the spot exchange rate should be exactly equal to the interest differential which prevails during the period. This relation is used in the empirical tests of the UIP hypothesis. If FX represents the forward exchange rate, RX the spot rate, and r and r^w the domestic and foreign rates of interest respectively, the covered interest parity condition states:

$$fx = rx + (r^w - r) \tag{4.3}$$

Evidence that CIP holds is an indication that the foreign exchange market is efficient.[9] If CIP did not hold there would be an opportunity for profit to be made from riskless arbitrage strategies. A speculator would be able to borrow funds in one currency at a rate r, convert them into the foreign currency and lend at the rate r^w, while simultaneously contracting to convert the proceeds back into domestic currency on the forward exchange market and make a risk free profit.

The empirical evidence (considered in section 4.3.3) strongly supports the theoretical prediction that CIP holds. Indeed, as Begg (1983) points out, this is not surprising since CIP is used by dealers as the basis for price setting in the forward market.

4.3. RESULTS OF EMPIRICAL WORK

4.3.1 Introduction

A great many empirical investigations have been performed in an attempt either to validate or to refute the various theories of exchange rate determination. The results are discouraging. Due partly to the limitations and weaknesses of the data they generally fail to give a definitive indication as to whether a theory is acceptable to the data or whether it should be rejected.

In this section the empirical evidence which has been amassed to evaluate the theories outlined in section 4.2 is assessed.

4.3.2 Purchasing power parity

If the Purchasing Power Parity (PPP) hypothesis were valid, then it might be thought that following a temporary nominal shock within an economy, international commodity arbitrage would cause the nominal exchange rate to adjust so as to take the real exchange rate back to its equilibrium level. However, this prediction holds little credibility. Casual observation of exchange rate movements over the past two decades reveals that all the major currencies have displayed a short-term volatility which cannot be explained by variations in relative rates of inflation. Indeed, there is no need to revert to the use of formal econometric testing procedures to establish this point.

Typical results of empirical investigation of this prediction are those obtained by Adler and Lehmann (1983). If the long run PPP hypothesis is a valid description of the data generating process then, according to Adler and Lehmann, deviations of the real exchange rate from the level implied by PPP should be positively serially correlated. This would follow if the initial deviations from parity are due to some cumulating process, and if the PPP hypothesis implies that there is a systematic tendency for the real rate to return to its original level when there is a deviation from parity. The evidence shows, however, that deviations from purchasing power parity resemble a martingale (a stochastic process in which successive increments cannot be predicted on the basis of past behaviour).

There is little formal statistical evidence to support the proposition that purchasing power parity is relevant to the long-term level of the exchange rate. However, as Adler and Lehmann point out, the mean of the deviations of real exchange rates from an (estimated) parity level tend to average to zero over sufficiently long periods. Casual empiricism thus supports the hypothesis that when international competitiveness moves too far out of line there is a process of adjustment that brings it back.

We can conclude from this that PPP is not a reliable guide to short-term currency price movements. Empirical evidence is unable to refute the proposition that PPP is relevant to exchange rate determination in the long term; however, it is hard to imagine that international competitiveness could play no part whatever in determining the level of the exchange rate.

4.3.3 Uncovered interest parity

The approach to assessing whether or not uncovered interest parity (UIP) is consistent with the data has generally been to test whether the forward rate is an unbiased predictor of future spot exchange rates. The logic of this test is demonstrated by the following simple algebra.

If $E_t(rx^e_{t+1})$ is the expected value of the (logarithm of the) spot rate rx expected at time t to pertain at time $t + 1$, and r_t and r^w_t are the domestic and foreign rates of interest respectively, then UIP is described by equation 4.2 and:

$$rx_t = E_t(rx^e_{t+1}) + (r_t - r^w_t) + \varepsilon_t. \qquad (4.4)$$

where ε_t is the zero mean, uncorrelated residual. If investors have rational expectations, then:

$$rx_{t+1} = E_t(rx^e_{t+1}) + u_{t+1} \qquad (4.5)$$

where u_t is not correlated with other economic variables, has constant variance, an expected value of zero and is not serially correlated.

Assuming that the covered interest parity condition holds[10] (equation 4.3) so that:

$$fx_t = rx_t + (r^w_t - r_t) + \eta_t \qquad (4.6)$$

with η_t a zero mean, uncorrelated residual, it follows that:

$$rx_{t+1} = fx_t + u^*_{t+1} \qquad (4.7)$$

where u^*_{t+1} is a combination of the residuals on equations 4.4, 4.5 and 4.6. Equation 4.7 states that the forward rate is an unbiased predictor of future spot rates.

Many empirical tests of the proposition embodied in equation 4.7 have been performed.[11] Generally, it is rejected. Most of the tests indicate that the forward rate is not an unbiased indicator of future spot rates: serial correlation in the residuals cannot be rejected at the 5 per cent level. It is important to note, however, that the proposition in equation 4.7 rests on three separate assumptions: UIP and its implications (in particular, the lack of risk aversion of the speculators whose transactions clear the market); a simple form of rational expectations; and the forward parity condition. The last is well supported by the data; the first two are more questionable.

One explanation of why the test in equation 4.7 might fail even if the perfect capital mobility assumption were correct relates to a problem with the rational expectations assumption. It is referred to as the 'Peso Problem'.[12] Consider a currency for which there exists a clear possibility of a large devaluation. The magnitude of the exchange rate change expected is large, but the probability of it occurring today is small: the product of these, the expected value, is small but not zero. For UIP to hold there must be a small, but non-zero, interest differential to offset the expectation of a change in the level of the currency. In most periods there will *ex post* have been no change in the actual exchange rate. This means that the residual in equation 4.5 will be serially correlated: the simple form of rational expectations encapsulated in this equation cannot cope with this situation.

The point is that it is 'rational' for expectations in the market to take account of low probability, low frequency events such as this, even though in most periods they do not in fact transpire. When an empirical test is performed of the UIP hypothesis, many of the periods from which data are sampled may contain no change in the exchange rate. It may then be wrongly concluded from the data either that expectations are biased or that deviations from UIP have occurred. But the problem may not be that the interest parity condition does not hold, or that expectations are not in some sense 'rational'; instead, the specification of the test does not adequately take account of events which have a low probability of occurring.

Various alternatives to rational expectations have been proposed in an attempt to explain deviations from UIP. Lewis (1988) suggests that market participants may not immediately understand the policies that are being pursued. She uses the hypothesis that learning will affect exchange rate behaviour to explain why during the early 1980s foreign exchange speculators seem to have systematically underestimated the strength of the dollar.

A competing explanation comes from Goodhart (1988) who, in an extension to an earlier model proposed by Frankel and Froot (1986), points out that all market participants will not have the same expectations. He characterizes participants into three groups according to how they formulate their expectations: chartists, who rely on extrapolation techniques; fundamentalists, who perceive the exchange rate as having a long-run equilibrium level to which it will tend to converge; and those who believe the rate follows a random walk.

Finally, a strong assumption used in the formulation of the UIP hypothesis is that capital has perfect international mobility so that assets denominated in different currencies are perfect substitutes for one another. Once this assumption is relaxed, as in the next section, to allow a degree of inelasticity in the demand for financial assets, UIP is no longer expected to hold.

4.3.4 Risk adjusted uncovered interest parity

Once the assumption of risk-neutrality is relaxed, it is no longer expected that all assets will yield equal returns. This is sufficient to account for the observed deviations from uncovered interest parity.

Empirical testing of the existence of risk premia[13] has generally been based on the proposition that investors diversify their portfolios so as to optimize with respect to a combination of the mean and the variance of expected end-period wealth. The tests have generally not lent support to the hypothesis (Frankel and Engel, 1984, interpreted their results as rejecting it). However, they were predicated on a number of strong assumptions: that expected utility is maximized over one period only; that relative risk aversion remains constant over time; that investors are homogeneous; that expectations are rational; that the relevant asset supplies are appropriately defined and accurately measured and that capital markets are perfect. A violation of any one of these assumptions would be sufficient to explain the lack of significant coefficient estimates on the relevant variables. Further, the equation reported in section 4.5 gives some support to the existence of a risk premium with its coefficient on *ex ante* demand significant at around 5 per cent on a one-sided test.

If the rate of return on individual risky assets is *ex ante* a function of their relative supply, the exchange rate level will depend on the degree of *ex ante* disequilibrium and the degree of exchange rate risk becomes a relevant issue. It determines the extent to which the exchange rate will move in response to a balance of payments disequilibrium. The empirical results obtained by Frankel (1986) suggested that exchange risk premia may be very small in magnitude. He estimated that if the supply of foreign assets were increased by 1 per cent of world wealth this would raise the risk premium which must be paid on dollar assets by only 0.02 per cent.

A further possible cause of differential rates of asset returns is political risk. Aliber (1973) suggested that deviations from interest rate parity can reflect political risk when assets are denominated in the same currency but issued in different political jurisdictions. Dooley and Isard (1980) examined the role of political risk by using a model of portfolio behaviour to explain the differential between the interest rate on Euromark deposits in Zurich and the rate on mark-denominated loans in Frankfurt for the period 1970 to 1974. The evidence suggested that whereas the main part of the observed interest differential was the result of an effective tax imposed by the capital controls which existed, there also seemed to be a risk premium. An interest differential of up to 2 per cent was required in order to induce non-residents to bear the political risk (that is, the risk that capital controls would be imposed).

4.3.5 Covered interest parity

Although empirical testing of the covered interest parity proposition (equation 4.3) has yielded widely varying conclusions in the past, the results of some recent tests seem conclusively to support it.

Early research[14] reported deviations from covered interest parity for a number of currencies and assets. However, these works have been criticized by Taylor (1986) as being invalid tests of the CIP theorem. A true deviation from parity represents a riskless opportunity for investors to make pure arbitrage profits. Taylor therefore argues that any data used to test covered interest parity must be data on which a trader would have dealt, that is, they must be contemporaneously sampled actual market data. Using contemporaneous, high frequency trading data recorded in the London foreign exchange market, and using the exact formula employed by market participants to calculate interest payments, Taylor's test comes closer than any other yet performed to a valid evaluation of the CIP hypothesis.

His results are pretty conclusive. Not altogether surprisingly, he finds that the foreign exchange and capital markets are perfectly efficient in the sense that there appear to be no opportunities for profit to be made from covered interest arbitrage, given the data considered. We conclude, therefore, that the covered interest parity hypothesis holds.

4.4 DERIVATION OF MODEL EQUATION

4.4.1 Behavioural hypothesis

In deriving an equation for the exchange rate for inclusion in our model of the inflation spiral, we take account of the theoretical discussion in section 4.2 and the existing empirical work reported in section 4.3. We assume that the price in the foreign exchange market moves to induce speculators to meet the net *ex ante* demand for foreign currency and so to clear the market. The path of the price therefore depends on the determinants of these investors' decisions concerning their portfolios, as well as depending on the profile of the *ex ante* disequilibrium in the market. If the authorities wish to influence the price, they will need to influence these decisions or offset their effect on the price.

It is assumed that investors aim to maximize a decision function involving both the expected return and, because they are risk-averse, the variance of the return. The result is an equation for the exchange rate consistent with 'risk adjusted uncovered interest parity' (section 4.2.3) in which the risk premium depends on the cumulated net *ex ante* disequilibria in the foreign exchange market, or, put another way, on the net balances of financial assets held in sterling by domestic and foreign investors for speculative purposes. This approach synthesizes the asset and PPP theories described in section 4.2.

4.4.2 Derivation of basic equation

On the above hypothesis the share of total financial wealth invested in foreign securities for speculative reasons will be chosen to maximize a decision function that depends on the variance of end-period wealth as well as its expected value.

Speculators are therefore assumed to maximize:

$$\Omega = \Omega[E(FW), \text{var}(FW)] \tag{4.8}$$

where $E(FW)$ is expected end-period financial wealth and $\text{var}(FW)$ is its variance. Expected end-period wealth is given by:

$$E(FW) = (1 - \mu)FW_{-1}[1 + r] + \mu FW_{-1}[1 + rx - E(rx^e_{+1}) + r^w] \tag{4.9}$$

where μ is the share invested in foreign currency assets, r and r^w are the domestic and foreign interest rates, while rx and $E(rx^e_{+1})$ are the logarithm of the spot exchange rate and the expected value of the logarithm of the future exchange rate.

With the uncertainty in end-period wealth arising only from uncertainty concerning the future exchange rate, the equation:

$$\text{var}(FW) = \mu^2 FW^2_{-1} \text{var}(rx^e_{+1}) \tag{4.10}$$

describes the variance of expected end-period wealth.

The marginal condition to this decision is

$$\frac{d\Omega}{d\mu} = \Omega_1 \frac{\partial E(FW)}{\partial \mu} + \Omega_2 \frac{\partial \text{var}(FW)}{\partial \mu} = 0 \tag{4.11}$$

Substituting the differentials with respect to μ of equations 4.9 and 4.10 into equation 4.11 gives:

$$2\mu FW^2_{-1}\Omega_2 \text{var}(rx^e_{+1}) = FW_{-1}\Omega_1[r - r^w - rx + E(rx^e_{+1})]$$

or, rearranging:

$$\mu = \frac{\Omega_1}{2FW_{-1}\Omega_2 \text{var}(rx^e_{+1})}[r - r^w - rx + E(rx^e_{+1})] \tag{4.12}$$

as a description of the share of foreign currency assets in the portfolio.

The stock of foreign assets held in the portfolio of domestic investors (expressed in the domestic currency) is therefore given by:

$$A = \mu FW_{-1}$$
$$= \xi[r - r^w - rx + E(rx^e_{+1})]FW_{-1} \tag{4.13}$$

where

$$\xi = \frac{\Omega_1}{2FW_{-1}\Omega_2 \text{var}(rx^e_{+1})} \tag{4.14}$$

and the coefficient ξ indicates the degree of capital mobility.

If speculators were not risk averse, so $\Omega_2 = 0$, or if there were no uncertainty about the future exchange rate, so $\text{var}(rx^e_{+1}) = 0$, then capital mobility would be infinite: an infinitesimal change in the spot rate would cause a substantial flow across the exchanges (other things being equal). In this case equation 4.13 can be written:

$$rx = E(rx^e_{+1}) + (r - r^w) \qquad (4.15)$$

so the uncovered parity condition holds, see equation 4.2.

It is assumed that the spot rate, rx in equation 4.13, moves to ensure that the change in speculators' demand for foreign currency assets is equal to the *ex ante* disequilibrium in the market – known as the basic balance *BB*. Apart from the official intervention, *OI*, the basic balance consists of the current account balance, *CB* (the trade balance, exports less imports, plus the balance on invisibles which includes the earnings on foreign currency assets held by residents less the earnings on sterling assets held by non-residents) and any underlying imbalance on capital account, *UCAP* (that is, the net balance on capital account of flows that are not sensitive to the value of the spot rate).

The market clearing condition is therefore:

$$BB = \Delta A + \Delta A^w \qquad (4.16)$$

where

$$BB = CB + UCAP - OI \qquad (4.17)$$

and A^w is the stock of domestic assets in foreign investors' portfolios (expressed in domestic currency). This is given by an expression similar to 4.13 but relating to FW^w, the financial wealth of the foreign investors (we assume the degree of capital mobility, ξ, is the same for domestic and for foreign investors). Substituting for A and A^w in equation 4.16, solving for the spot rate (omitting, because it is second order small a term in the level of the covered differential and the growth of wealth) gives:

$$\Delta rx = \Delta E(rx^e_{+1}) + \Delta(r - r^w) + B/\xi \qquad (4.18)$$

where we have written B for $[BB/(FW_{-1} + FW^w_{-1})]$.

Equation 4.18 is the equation we shall use in our model to describe the path of the exchange rate. It can be viewed either as an inverted asset demand function in flow form or as the first difference of a risk-adjusted uncovered interest parity condition.

4.4.3 Modelling exchange rate expectations

The question that remains concerns the determinants of exchange rate expectations, rx^e. Models of expectation formation range from the assumption of full rational expectations through various levels of partial rational expectations to models in which it is assumed that the rate is simply expected to adjust smoothly towards its long-run equilibrium rate, that is, the rate at which there will be an *ex ante* clearing of the foreign exchange market.

Here we assume, with Baumol and Quandt (1964), that exchange market operators do not have an 'irrational passion for rationality'. The marginal benefit (in terms of producing accurate exchange rate forecasts), if any, from constructing a full rational expectations model of the economy and predicting its path into the future, is most unlikely to exceed the cost of such a process. It seems more likely that speculators take account, in an *ad hoc* way, of the latest information on relevant variables such as the current balance and likely influences on the interest rate. We therefore specify an equation for exchange rate expectations based on a model of the likely paths of the equilibrium level of the exchange rate and of the factors likely to influence the adjustment to it.

The long-run equilibrium real exchange rate is written σ^q, so the nominal long-run equilibrium rate is given by:

$$rx^q = p_f^w - p + \sigma^q \tag{4.19}$$

where p_f^w and p are own-currency prices of traded finished goods and σ^q depends on the real oil price and the extent of UK oil reserves, the only factors likely to have a substantial effect on the long-run equilibrium exchange rate over this period. It is assumed that the nominal exchange rate is expected to adjust towards its long-run equilibrium level, with the path of adjustment affected by the interest rate differential, the likely path of the basic balance, B^e, the (expected) path of relative price inflation and the current value of North Sea oil reserves (subsumed within $\Delta\sigma^q$). Its change at time t is therefore given by:

$$\begin{aligned}
\Delta E(rx^e_{+1}) &= \alpha\Delta rx^q + \beta\Delta(r - r^w) + \gamma B^e/\xi - \mu(rx - rx^q) + u \\
&= \alpha(\Delta p_f^w - \Delta p) + \beta\Delta(r - r^w) + \gamma B^e/\xi + \alpha\Delta\sigma^q \\
&\quad - \mu[rx - (p_f^w - p + \sigma^q)]_{-1} + u
\end{aligned} \tag{4.20}$$

where u is the residual. In practice this residual picks up the influence of other, unquantified factors on exchange rate expectations and is likely to be of considerable importance in explaining the path of the exchange rate *ex post*.

The equation for the exchange rate is obtained by substituting equation 4.20 into 4.18:

$$\begin{aligned}
\Delta rx &= \alpha(\Delta p_f^w - \Delta p) + (1 + \beta)\Delta(r - r^w) + (B + \gamma B^e)/\xi + \alpha\Delta\sigma^q \\
&\quad - \mu[rx - (p_f^w - p + \sigma^q)]_{-1} + u
\end{aligned} \tag{4.21}$$

It is this equation that was estimated and, after some adjustments to coefficients (p. 113), is included in our model.

4.4.4 Implications for inflation spiral

(a) Separation of terms into endogenous and exogenous

For the purposes of the analysis in Chapter 5, the terms of equation 4.21 are separated into those that are part of the domestic inflation spiral and those that impinge upon it. The latter are incorporated into the variable labelled X_4 in the following formulation of the equation:

$$\Delta rx = m(L)(\Delta p_f^w - \Delta p) + X_4 \qquad (4.22)$$

Here the coefficient α in equation 4.21 is replaced by the more general lag function $m(L)$ (see p.46, note 9). This formulation of the equation is used in Chapter 5 where the inflation spiral equation is derived.

In equation 4.22, X_4 incorporates all the variables that do not move in line with price inflation:

$$X_4 = (1 + \beta)\Delta(r - r^w) + (B + \gamma B^e)/\xi + \alpha\Delta\sigma^q$$
$$- \mu[rx - (p_f^w - p + \sigma^q)]_{-1} + u \qquad (4.23)$$

Thus X_4 includes disequilibrium terms such as the net *ex ante* excess demand, and the deviation of the exchange rate from its expected long-run equilibrium level as well as terms in relative interest rates and the other factors thought to influence the path of exchange rate expectations.

If the path of the nominal exchange rate is determined by equation 4.22 and if the equation is derived from the hypothesis outlined in section 4.4.1, then the form of $m(L)$, which describes the dynamic adjustment of the exchange rate to relative price inflation and is of great importance to our story, depends on the manner in which exchange rate expectations are formed. Further, it is not clear whether a full dynamic adjustment can be assumed to take place, for this will depend on whether or not exchange market speculators find it helpful, in predicting the future path, to make this assumption. Thus it cannot be maintained on *a priori* grounds that $m(1) = 1$ (as was the case in the analogous situation for the wages and prices equations, sections 2.4.4 and 3.5.3). Instead we may reasonably assume:

$$0 \leq m(1) \leq 1 \qquad (4.24)$$

that is, that the cumulated effect of differential rates of price inflation is neither perverse (less than zero) nor overshooting (greater than unity).

The main factors impinging on the inflation spiral, as a result of this view of how the foreign exchange market operates, are:

- the path of the interest rate differential in the structural equation, $(r - r^w)$;
- the *ex ante* disequilibrium in the market as a proportion of total speculative balances, B;
- the factors, other than relative price inflation, which affect the expected value of the future exchange rate, $E(rx_{+1}^e)$, namely:
  —any further effect of the interest differential, $(r - r^w)$;
  —the change in the long run equilibrium real exchange rate, $\Delta\sigma^q$;
  —the deviation of the spot rate from the long-run equilibrium rate perceived by market, $[rx - (p_f^w - p - \sigma^q)]$;
  —the determinants of the long-run equilibrium rate, σ^q;
  —other factors, u.

(b) Features likely to be important to spiral

By far the most important role of the exchange rate in the inflation spiral arises from the possibility that the exchange rate reaction to differential inflation rates will be muted, that is, $m(1)$ is less than unity. Related to this is the extent of a role for the *ex ante* disequilibrium on the underlying flows, *BB*, in bringing the exchange rate back to an equilibrium level if $m(1)$ is less than unity. These issues are discussed in Chapters 5 and 6.

4.5 AN EQUATION FOR THE EXCHANGE RATE

4.5.1 Issues relating to estimation

Estimation of equation 4.21 raises three types of issue. The first concerns the econometric validity of the estimation procedure, the second relates to changes of structure in world currency markets, and the third to the precise definition of the data series used.

(a) Econometric issues

We start with the econometric issues. These concern the possibility of simultaneity bias and the identification of the dependent variable.

There are two reasons why this equation may be subject to simultaneity bias. First, the dependent variable is the quarter on previous quarter change in the nominal exchange rate. If a fall in the exchange rate near the beginning of a three month period were to affect the current balance, one of the explanatory variables, then the estimate of the coefficient on this variable would be biased. In fact, empirical analysis of the lag in the adjustment of exports and imports to a change in relative prices at home and abroad suggests that this is unlikely to cause a significant bias. There seems to be only a slight effect of relative prices on trade flows within the first few months.

The second possible source of simultaneity bias concerns the interest rate and may be more serious. If the exchange rate appears to be under pressure, the domestic interest rate is likely to be raised by the authorities. A correlation between a fall in the exchange rate and a rise in domestic interest rates would reduce the estimated coefficient on relative interest rates. In fact, the estimated value of this coefficient is considerably higher than implied by a simple uncovered interest parity condition (suggesting that an unanticipated rise in interest rates raises the expected future exchange rate as well as the spot rate). No attempt has been made to use instrumental variables to abstract from the possible simultaneity.

The other question that arises in connection with the estimation concerns the validity of estimating an asset demand function in inverted form. Which is the dependent variable of the structural equation, the asset demand or the price at which the market clears? Here we take the view that the asset supply and the variables other than the exchange rate that influence asset demands can be treated as being weakly exogenous in this market clearing equation. If this is the case, then it is correct to treat the equation as determining the path of the exchange rate rather than the asset demand.

(b) Changes in market structure

Changes in the structure of the market in foreign exchange include such factors as the exchange rate regime and the existence or otherwise of exchange controls. Similar concerns relate to anything that has a substantial impact on the quantity of financial wealth seeking a home, such as the oil price rise in the early 1970s, since these are difficult to incorporate in the equation automatically.

The equation was estimated over the period since the abandonment of the Bretton Woods system, when the sterling exchange rate had been floating, though subject to official intervention from time to time. The effect of the exchange controls, abolished in October 1979, was to constrain the quantity of funds of various types available for both 'underlying' and speculative investment on the exchanges. The main relevance of this to our exercise is its effect on the definition of the data series used for the underlying demand on capital account and the magnitude and path of the stock of funds available for speculative purposes. A particular feature of the period used for estimation has been the build-up of funds in OPEC countries, the counterpart of the oil surpluses. These were included separately in the estimated equation in order to pick up their effect on the exchange rate path.

(c) Definition of data

This brings us to the last of the issues relating to the estimation of this equation. The result of estimation is bound to depend on the definition of the data series used: on how the 'underlying' capital flows are defined and separated from those that are treated as being 'market clearing', and on the series used to represent the total quantities of funds available. In this work, the various capital flows identified in the balance of payments statistics were allocated between the two categories 'underlying' and 'speculative'. This allocation was inevitably done on an *ad hoc* basis. For this reason, if for no other, the estimates of this equation must be treated with care.

4.5.2 An estimated equation

A typical result of using OLS on an equation of the form of equation 4.21 is the following (roman numerals are explained below):

$$\Delta rx = \Delta rx^e + 0.0025\Delta(r - r^w) + 0.00001BB + 2.1\Delta OPEC/\pounds M3 \qquad (4.25)$$
$$\text{(i)} \qquad\qquad\qquad (1.6) \qquad (5.5)$$

where

$$BB = CB + UCAP - OI \tag{4.26}$$

$$\Delta rx^e = -0.06 + 0.62\Delta m^w - 0.32\Delta m + 0.0067\Delta(r - r^w) + 0.00051\Delta(S.P_o^w/P_f^w)$$
$$\text{(ii)} \quad (1.0) \qquad (1.9) \qquad (1.8) \qquad\qquad (0.7)$$

$$+ 0.00001BB - 0.51(rx_{-4} - rx^q_{-4}) + \text{residual} \tag{4.27}$$
$$\text{(v)} \qquad (3.6)$$

and

$$rx^q = 1.0m^w - 1.0m + 9.97 - 0.015T + 0.05(r - r^w) + 0.001(S.P_o^w/P_f^w)$$
$$\text{(iii)} \qquad \text{(iii)} \quad (3.5) \quad (2.9) \quad (1.4) \qquad\qquad \text{(iv)} \tag{4.28}$$

Period: 1971Q1 to 1980Q2 $\qquad R^2 = 0.91 \qquad DW = 1.7$

In these equations BB represents the total net *ex ante* demand for currency, constructed from the current balance, CB, the underlying demand on capital account, $UCAP$, and official intervention, OI. The definition of the net underlying demand on capital account, $UCAP$, is subject to a considerable degree of judgement and is unlikely to have taken proper account of the underlying inflows associated with the build-up of the oil balances following the oil price hike of 1974. As a result the equation includes the separate variable, $OPEC$, the exchange reserves held in sterling by the central monetary authorities in oil-exporting countries. This is deflated by the stock of money (£M3) to normalize for the likely 'real' effect. The variables M and M^w represent the domestic and world money supplies (lower case in the equation because in logarithms) and are playing the role of proxy for price expectations. S is the estimated recoverable reserves of North Sea oil with P_o^w the world price of oil in the same bundle of currencies as P_f^w. T is a (quarterly) time trend included in the long-run equilibrium model to pick up the effect of differences in trend productivity growth and other factors at home and abroad. This term implies that there has been a trend decline in the equilibrium sterling exchange rate of 1.5 per cent a year.

This equation has been written in the form shown above to distinguish between the structural part of the equation and the model of exchange rate expectations. The coefficient marked (i) is constrained to the value implied by uncovered interest parity (interest rates are in percentage form, the dependent variable is the quarterly change). Part of the estimated intercept marked (ii) is included in the equation for the expected change in the rate as a dynamic counterpart to the time trend in the long-run equilibrium model; the remainder is included in the equation for the long-run equilibrium rate and simply takes account of the units in which the variables are expressed. The residual has (arbitrarily) been allocated to the exchange rate expectations equation. The expected long-run equilibrium real exchange rate is modelled to depend on the variation in the resources in the economy (the value of the stock of North Sea oil) and interest rates at home and abroad. This will influence the path the exchange rate follows in relation to the long run equilibrium rate that would pertain if the interest rates were equal.

4.5.3 The chosen equation

A number of changes were made to the above equation in order to get it into a form likely to produce acceptable simulation properties, while at the same time taking account of the information contained in the data. As a result, the equation used to model the path of the exchange rate in our model of the inflation spiral is the following:

$$\Delta rx = \Delta rx^e + 0.0025\Delta(r - r^w) + 0.1BB/\pounds M3$$
$$\text{(i)} \qquad\qquad\qquad \text{(ii)} \qquad\qquad\qquad (4.29)$$

where:

$$BB = CB + UCAP - OI$$

$$\Delta rx^e = 0.5(\Delta p_f^w - \Delta p) + 0.0067\Delta(r - r^w) + 0.0014\Delta(S.P_o^w/P_f^w)$$
$$\text{(iii)} \qquad\qquad\qquad\qquad\qquad \text{(iv)}$$
$$- 0.277(rx_{-1} - rx^q) + \text{residual} \qquad\qquad\qquad (4.30)$$

and:

$$rx^q = (p_f^w - p) + 8.34 - 0.005\,T + 0.013(r - r^w) + 0.0014(S.P_o^w/P_f^w) \quad (4.31)$$

In equation 4.29 the coefficient marked (i) is constrained to conform to the risk-adjusted covered parity interpretation of this equation. The freely estimated

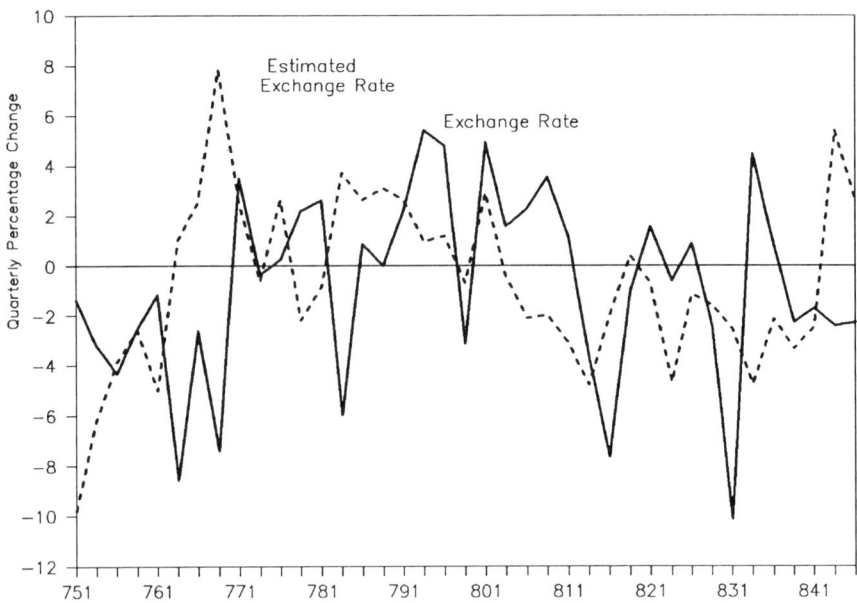

Fig. 4.2 Track of exchange rate equation.

coefficient on the change in the interest differential is far larger than this and the remainder has been attributed to the expectations model (equation 4.30). The underlying balance variable has been deflated by £M3 as a proxy for the financial wealth variable and the coefficient marked (ii) has been rescaled accordingly and set at a lower level (the higher value was found to give unacceptably volatile properties to the model).

Regression analysis ascribes a large standard error to the coefficient on the expected relative price inflation term, marked (iii). As a result, it is not possible to determine the value of this coefficient empirically and there is little basis for the choice of 0.5.[15] Further, the value taken by this coefficient is important in determining the properties of the inflation spiral (Chapters 5, 6 and 7). Our model uses actual traded goods prices in the model for the expected future value of the exchange rate, as indicated in equations 4.30 and 4.31. Any difference between actual and expected relative price inflation has therefore, by implication, been allocated to the residual.

The coefficient marked (iv) has been imposed at a higher value than was estimated. The value of the coefficient on the term describing the long run equilibrium in equation 4.30 and the coefficients in the model of the expected long-run real exchange rate were estimated using OLS subject to these constraints.

4.5.4 Properties of the equation

The dynamic properties of this equation for the exchange rate have implications for the way the government can hold parity at a given, predetermined level. They are the following:

- Official intervention amounting to a purchase of £1 billion (1980 prices) raises the exchange rate initially by about 0.4 per cent; in the absence of further intervention it would then subside slowly towards the level it would otherwise have taken.
- A rise of 3 percentage points in domestic interest rates (unanticipated) leads to an immediate rise in the exchange rate of 4 per cent and, if it persisted, this would be followed by an upward drift to a level 15 per cent higher than would otherwise have been the case.
- An increase of 10 per cent in the world price of oil (in dollars) causes a rise of 2 per cent in the sterling exchange rate immediately with a subsequent increase reaching a level 5 per cent higher than it would have been after four years (abstracting from any effect there might be on world prices or world activity).
- A once-off rise in the domestic price level of 1 per cent puts downward pressure on the exchange rate, which declines to reach a level 1 per cent below that which it would otherwise have taken after a period of about four years.

The track of the chosen equation is not impressive, it is shown in Figure 4.2. However, this is only to be expected: noone can consistently explain the path of the exchange rate successfully, if they could they would be rich. The dynamic

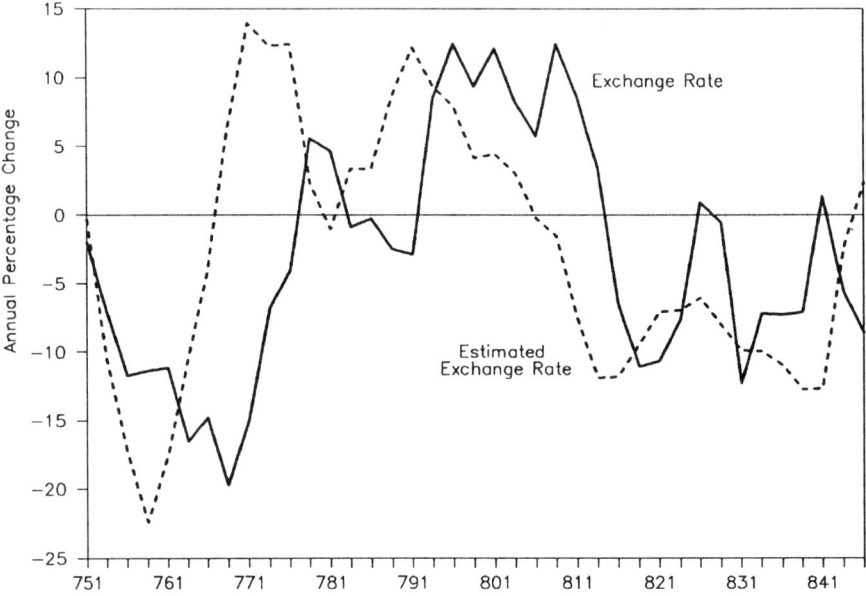

Fig. 4.3 Track of annual change in exchange rate.

track of this equation (that is, using the estimated value of the lagged exchange rate) over the later part of the estimation period, and including one year beyond, is shown in Figure 4.3.

The remainder of our story is not dependent on the precise specification of the exchange rate equation. What matters is whether or not the exchange rate equation has a coefficient of unity on the term in relative price movements and whether the variables incorporated in X_4 can cumulate indefinitely. In the following we spell out the consequences of the alternatives.

4.6 IMPLICATIONS FOR POLICY

(a) The role of money

As with the wage equation, there is a theoretical possibility that money growth affects price inflation through the role of expectations in the exchange rate equation. The route is quite tortuous. If the growth of the money supply affects price expectations and expected relative price inflation affects expectations regarding the future path of the exchange rate, then since exchange rate expectations are an essential ingredient of our exchange rate equation, it follows that money growth could affect the path of the exchange rate. In this case it would have an effect on the rate of inflation. However, given that our model of inflation, derived from structural equations describing price-setting in each relevant market, contains no direct role for money growth it is difficult to justify the proposition that price expectations are influenced by the rate of growth of the money supply. Further, there seems to be no support from the data for this proposition. We conclude that there is unlikely to be a significant effect of relative money growth on the rate of inflation as a result of this.

Monetary policy, however, through determining the path of relative interest rates, has a crucial role to play in determining the path of the exchange rate. It is through discrepancies between interest rates at home and abroad that speculative flows can be induced. These will prevent the exchange rate from responding to the effect of changes in competitiveness on trade flows, and may thereby prevent the full effect of domestic inflationary pressure from expressing itself in the observed rate of inflation, at least for a while. In the longer term the pressure may prove too great to handle in this way.

(b) Effect of demand

A fiscal or monetary policy that affects the level of demand in the economy will have an impact on the path of the exchange rate through its effect on the balance of trade account. Indeed, this is an important ingredient of a policy package designed to hold inflation down in the face of inflationary pressures. However, it is only a temporary palliative; when demand is allowed to expand to its full employment level, the exchange rate will revert to the level it would otherwise have taken (other things being equal), allowing the pent up inflation to run through the system.

(c) Implications for inflation inertia

Unlike in the goods and services market or the labour market, there is no reason to assume that there is a total pass through of inflation from one period to the next in the foreign exchange market. This is because the degree of pass through depends on the expectations of exchange market speculators regarding the effect of relative inflation rates on the future path of the exchange rate: given the path of the exchange rate in the past, it seems unlikely that a full adjustment for relative price inflation will be expected in the short term. However, any lack of pass through will, unless reversed by later events, result in a loss of competitiveness, and this will put downward pressure on the exchange rate in the future, other things being equal.

(d) Potential for causing inflation

Just as a rising exchange rate puts downward pressure on the spiral, as well as leading to an increasing competitive disadvantage in the short term, other things being equal, so a falling exchange rate creates inflationary pressure while leading to a short term competitive advantage. It follows that anything that takes the exchange rate below its long-run equilibrium level will inject inflationary pressure into the system.

REFERENCES

Adler, M. and Lehmann, B. (1983) Deviations from purchasing power parity in the long run, *The Journal of Finance*, **38**, 1471–87.

Aliber, R. Z. (1973) The interest rate parity theorem: a reinterpretation, *Journal of Political Economy*, **81**, 1451–9.

Baumol, W. J. and Quandt, R. E. (1964) Rules of thumb and optimally imperfect decisions, *The American Economic Review*, **54**, 23–46.

Begg, D. K. H. (1983) The economics of floating exchange rates: the lessons of the 70s and the research programme for the 80s, Fourth Report, Treasury and Civil Service Committee.

Dooley, M. P. and Isard, P. (1980) Capital controls, political risk, and deviations from interest-rate parity, *Journal of Political Economy*, **88**, 370–84.

Dornbusch, R. (1976) Expectations and exchange rate dynamics, *Journal of Political Economy*, **84**, 1161–76.

Forsyth, P. J. and Kay, J. A. (1980) The economic implications of North Sea oil revenues, *Fiscal Studies*, **1**, 1–28.

Frankel, J. A. (1986) The implications of mean-variance optimization for four questions in international macroeconomics, *Journal of International Money and Finance*, **5**, S53–57.

Frankel, J. A. and Froot, K. A. (1986) Using survey data to test some standard propositions regarding exchange rate expectations, *Research Papers in Economics*, 86–11, Institute of Business and Economic Research, University of California, Berkeley.

Frankel, J. and Engel, C. M. (1984) Do asset-demand functions optimize over the mean and variance of real returns? A six-currency test, *Journal of International Economics*, **17**, 309–23.

Frenkel, J. A. (1981) The collapse of purchasing power parities during the 1970s, *European Economic Review*, **16**, 145–65.

Goodhart, C. (1988) The foreign exchange market: a random walk with a dragging anchor, *Economica*, **55**, 437–60.

Gordon, R. J. (1985) Understanding inflation in the 1980s, *Brookings Papers on Economic Activity*, **1**, 263–99.

Hodrick, R. (1981) International asset pricing with time-varying risk premia, *Journal of International Economics*, **11**, 573–77.

Hodrick, R. J. (1987) *The Empirical Evidence on the Efficiency of Forward and Futures Foreign Exchange Markets*, Harwood Academic Publishers, New York.

Lewis, K. K. (1988) Can learning affect exchange rate behaviour? The case of the dollar in the early 1980s, *Journal of Monetary Economics*, **23**, 79–100.

Officer, L. H. and Willett, T. D. (1979) The covered-arbitrage schedule: a critical survey of recent developments, *Journal of Money, Credit and Banking*, **2**, 247–57.

Taylor, M. (1986) Covered interest parity: a high-frequency, high-quality data study, *Economica*, **54**, 429–38.

ENDNOTES

1. An excellent summary of the economics of the exchange rate is to be found in Begg (1983).
2. Frenkel (1981).
3. The discovery of North Sea oil in the UK is a case in point (Forsyth and Kay, 1980).
4. Under the fixed exchange rate regime, exchange controls were an important device for protecting the foreign exchange reserves of central banks against being depleted

by speculative capital flows. Without this protection, central banks might have been unable to maintain the agreed exchange parities.

5. The expected end-period value of £1 invested by a speculator at home for one period is $1 + r$, invested in foreign assets it is

$$RX(1 + r^w)/RX^e_{+1}$$

Equating these, taking logarithms, using the relation $\log(1 + r) \simeq r$ for $r < 1$ and taking the expected value gives equation 4.2.

6. Of course, speculators in fact hold differing expectations about the future.

7. At a rate of exchange of $1.83 to the pound the end of period total wealth held in dollars, $220, would be exactly equivalent to £120, the expected total end of period wealth denominated in steling $(220/120 = 1.83)$.

8. That is, they use all available information and knowledge so as not to make systematic forecasting errors.

9. A market is said to be efficient if prices in the market fully reflect all available information so market participants will not be able to make an abnormal profit on the basis of available information.

10. Empirical tests of the prediction of CIP are reported in section 4.3.5 and support this.

11. A review of the empirical literature can be found in Hodrick (1987).

12. The problem was first recognized in relation to the Mexican peso and the US dollar.

13. Hodrick (1981); Frankel and Engel (1984); Frankel (1986).

14. Officer and Willett (1979) provide a critical survey.

15. This value was chosen in a discussion within HM Treasury.

5

The Inflation Spiral Equation

5.1 INTRODUCTION

In this chapter we combine the equations that have been derived to explain price-setting in each market into a reduced form equation for the inflation spiral (the Inflation Spiral Equation, or ISE) and extract the main implications of the resulting model. These implications relate to three aspects of the inflation process: the dynamics of the spiral, the most likely causes of inflation, and the policy initiatives most likely to prevent or cure it. In particular, we identify the consequences for the dynamics of the spiral of the inflation indexation assumptions, that is, the dynamic homogeneity constraints that have been imposed as a result of the no money illusion hypothesis (as discussed in sections 2.4.4, 3.5.3 and 4.4.4).

Writing all the component equations of the model in percentage change (change of logarithm) form enables the reduced form equation, derived in section 5.2, to expose clearly the dynamic properties of the inflation spiral. Section 5.3 takes the equations derived in section 5.2 and uses them to list the most important dynamic features of the inflation spiral; in Chapter 6 the implications of the dynamic properties of the ISE for the inflation process are developed more fully.

Section 5.4 then identifies the variables which, according to this model, seem likely to be most important empirically in determining the path of the inflation process. An empirical analysis of the UK inflation process over the period 1969 to 1985, using the ISE, is described in Chapter 7. This analysis estimates the magnitude of the contributions from each of the variables included in the model. It is updated using easily available data in Appendix 7A.

Finally, section 5.5 picks out the variables and the coefficients in the model that have implications for the policy initiatives that might be used to prevent and to cure inflation. The policy implications are developed in more detail in Chapter 8.

5.2 DERIVATION OF THE INFLATION SPIRAL EQUATION

5.2.1 Introduction

The model consists of structural equations for changes in domestic prices, Δp, the prices of imported finished goods and primary commodities in domestic currencies,

Δp_f and Δp_c, wages, Δw, and the exchange rate, Δrx (equations 2.17, 2B.2, 3.16, 4.22):

$$\Delta p = a(L)(\Delta w - \Delta pr) + b(L)\Delta p_f + c(L)\Delta p_c + d(L)\Delta p + X_1 \qquad (5.1)$$

$$\Delta p_i = e_i(L)(\Delta p_i^w - \Delta rx) + f_i(L)\Delta p + X_{2i} \quad i = f, c \qquad (5.2)$$

$$\Delta w = \Delta prt + g(L)\Delta p + h(L)\Delta p_f - j(L)\Delta p_c + X_3 \qquad (5.3)$$

$$\Delta rx = m(L)(\Delta p_f^w - \Delta p) + X_4 \qquad (5.4)$$

In these equations p_i^w ($i = f, c$) are the prices of imported finished goods or primary commodities in world currencies and Δpr and Δprt are the actual and trend rates of productivity growth (assumed to be the appropriate productivity measures in the goods and services market and the labour market respectively). The terms X_1, X_{2i} ($i = f, c$), X_3, X_4 incorporate all the (real) variables which impinge on the inflation process in each market, causing inflation to increase or decrease, but which do not play a direct, primary role in promulgating price rises around the inflation spiral.[1] As we have seen, the price and wage levels terms appearing in the equations always occur as 'real' variables. They are incorporated into these 'X' variables. In this section we combine these equations to derive the reduced form equation for the inflation spiral (the ISE).

5.2.2 Price rises in domestic currency

First consider the domestic price setting process. Substituting equation 5.3 into equation 5.1 gives an equation that relates domestic price inflation, Δp, to the rise in import prices in domestic currency, Δp_f and Δp_c, the factors that impinge on inflation from domestic markets, X_1, X_3 and any differential between the two measures of productivity, $\Delta prt - \Delta pr$:

$$\Delta p = \psi_1(L)\Delta p + \psi_2(L)\Delta p_f + \psi_3(L)\Delta p_c + F_1(L, X_1, X_3, \Delta prt - \Delta pr) \qquad (5.5)$$

where F_1 is a function of lag distributions of X_1, X_3, and $\Delta prt - \Delta pr$. A consequence of the dynamic homogeneity constraints in the domestic markets for goods and services and for labour, is that domestic markets are subject to full inflation indexation in equilibrium. This is because the condition:

$$\psi_1(1) + \psi_2(1) + \psi_3(1) = 1 \qquad (5.6)$$

holds concerning the parameters in this equation. This condition does not require dynamic homogeneity in the foreign exchange market.

The importance of condition 5.6, applied to equation 5.5, in determining the dynamic properties of the spiral is explained below, in section 5.3. Here we address its economic rationale, which derives from the 'no money illusion' assumption. In the market for goods and services this assumption implies that if all input costs and competitors' prices rise at the same rate then the mark-up will be independent of the rate of inflation. This means that if the variables incorporated in X_1 exert no inflationary pressure the price must rise at the same rate as unit costs. It follows that the coefficients on the independent explanatory price inflation variables must sum to unity (equation 2.16).

In the labour market, the no money illusion hypothesis implies that, if all prices relevant to wage setting increase at the same rate and all the factors incorporated in X_3 are zero, then the real wage increase will reflect only the expected growth in labour productivity. That is, wages will rise at the same rate as the explanatory prices after adjusting for expected productivity growth. This means that the coefficients on the variables that model price inflation in the wage rise equation must sum to unity (equation 3.17).

These homogeneity properties, which follow from the assumption of no money illusion, directly yield the homogeneity constraint 5.6. They are examined in more depth in Chapter 6.

5.2.3 The role of the exchange rate

Substituting the exchange rate equation (equation 5.4) into the structural equation for changes in the price of imported finished goods and primary commodities (equation 5.2) enables the effect of pressures in the foreign exchange market to be incorporated into the equations for the domestic currency prices of imported goods. Given the dynamic homogeneity condition for import price setting (implied by the no money illusion assumption):

$$e_i(1) + f_i(1) = 1 \quad i = f, c \tag{5.7}$$

this gives:

$$\Delta p_c = \phi_c(L)\Delta p_c^w + (1 - \phi_c(L))\Delta p + \xi_c(L)(\Delta p_c^w - \Delta p_f^w) + F_{2c}(L, X_{2c}, X_4)$$
$$\Delta p_f = \phi_f(L)\Delta p_f^w + (1 - \phi_f(L))\Delta p + F_{2f}(L, X_{2f}, X_4) \tag{5.8}$$

with:

$$\phi_i(L) = e_i(L)(1 - m(L)) \qquad i = f, c$$

The long-term coefficient on relative price rises in the exchange rate equation (equation 5.4) is important in determining the dynamic properties of the inflation spiral. If this coefficient is equal to unity then the long-term values, $\phi_f(1)$ and $\phi_c(1)$, in equation 5.8 are zero. In this case, for given levels of policy variables, the rate of change of the domestic currency price of imported finished goods, Δp_f, will not be affected by changes in the world price, Δp_f^w (once the lags have fed through the system). This is because the property of dynamic homogeneity, specified in this way, ensures that the exchange rate moves to offset any differential between domestic and foreign finished goods price inflation, other things being equal. Thus, however finished goods' prices in foreign currencies are moving, when $m(1)$ is unity the rate of change of the domestic currency prices of imported finished goods will reflect domestic producer price inflation, Δp, once the lags have worked through the system rather than reflecting world price inflation. Of course, they will also respond to the paths of the variables included in X_4.

It is apparent from the theory underlying the exchange rate equation (Chapter 4) that it is the way in which expectations are formed that determines whether the exchange rate exhibits this property of dynamic homogeneity. More precisely, it depends on whether expectations are formed about the real rather than the nominal exchange rate. Unlike the cases of prices and wages, there is no clear *a priori* reason why a full dynamic adjustment should be assumed to take place. This will depend on whether speculators find it helpful to make the assumption that rates will converge to parity when they predict the future path of exchange rates. It will therefore depend on the policy stance. In general it can only be assumed that $0 \leq m(1) \leq 1$.

The question of whether there is dynamic homogeneity in the foreign exchange market is thus a matter to be decided by the data, and is subject to debate. The likely determinants of the degree of dynamic homogeneity in the exchange rate equation are discussed in more detail in Chapter 6.

5.2.4 The Inflation Spiral Equation

Equations 5.5 and 5.8 can be combined to give an explanation of the domestic rate of price inflation in terms of lagged values of itself, world price inflation in world currencies, the productivity differential and the variables that have been incorporated into the X_j:

$$\Delta p = \psi(L)\Delta p + \phi(L)\Delta p_f^w + \theta(L)\{\Delta p_c^w - \Delta p_f^w\} + G(L, X) \qquad (5.9)$$

where $G(L, X)$ is written for $G(L, X_1, X_{2f}, X_{2c}, X_3, X_4, \Delta prt - \Delta pr)$ and $\psi(L)$, $\phi(L)$ and $\theta(L)$ are combinations of the lag distributions in equations 5.1 to 5.4 with $\phi(1) = 0$ if $m(1) = 1$. The dynamic homogeneity conditions for the goods and labour markets ensure that:

$$\psi(1) + \phi(1) = 1 \qquad (5.10)$$

in equation 5.9. Given that $\psi(1) < 1$ (that is $m(1) < 1$ so $\phi(1) > 0$), equation 5.9 can be solved for Δp and written:

$$\Delta p = (1 - \psi(L))^{-1}[\phi(L)\Delta p_f^w + \theta(L)\{\Delta p_c^w - \Delta p_f^w\} + G(L, X)] \qquad (5.11)$$

The two representations of the Inflation Spiral Equation (ISE) illustrated in equations 5.9 and 5.11 show that, given $m(1) < 1$ and given the assumptions underlying equations 5.1 to 5.4, domestic inflation is determined by world price inflation and by the factors incorporated into the X-variables. The variables included in the X's are 'real': in general they do not vary with the price level or the rate of inflation.[2] These, along with world price inflation in world currencies, are the influences that impinge on the domestic inflation spiral, with long and complicated lag structures reflecting the self-perpetuating nature of the inflation process, to cause accelerations and decelerations in price rises.

To complete the model, equations describing the paths of world finished goods and primary commodity price changes in world currencies are needed (this is discussed in Appendix 5A). We assume that the first, the increase in world finished goods' prices (in world currencies), are determined in a process similar to that described by the ISE. For the second, the change in world primary commodity prices (in world currencies), it is convenient to use an equation of the form (see equation 5A.1):

$$\Delta p_c^w = \mu(L)\Delta p_f^w + X_5 \qquad (5.12)$$

Here, p_f^w is the finished goods price in the same currency basket as that in which p_c^w is measured, and X_5 represents the other factors that influence the path of primary commodity prices, including excess demand or supply.

The result of combining this equation with the model for domestic inflation (equation 5.11, assumed to apply in other countries) is an equation for the weighted average inflation rate for finished goods in developed countries of the form:

$$\Delta p_f^w = [\Omega(L) + \Phi(L)\mu(L)]\Delta p_f^w + G(L, X^w) \qquad (5.13)$$

where X^w is the world counterpart of X and includes X_5, see equation 5A.2.

Equation 5.13 gives us an expression for Δp_f^w determined only by the real variables included in $G(L, X^w)$. Substituting equations 5.12 and 5.13 into equation 5.11 then shows that Δp depends only on $G(L, X)$, $G(L, X^w)$ and X_5. Since these contain only real variables it is clear that, according to our structural model, there is no direct causal 'nominal' link running from the rise in any domestic variable exogenous to the inflation spiral (such as the money supply) to price inflation. Instead the following proposition holds.

Proposition 1: price inflation is the result of a cumulation of 'real' influences on the inflation spiral operating over time, in markets for goods and services, for labour and for foreign exchange, at home and overseas.

In any one country the rate of increase of the prices feeding into the economy (import prices) is relevant. But taking the world as a whole, real pressures on the inflation spiral will cumulate over time, given the inertia of the process, and may result in a substantial rate of inflation.

5.3 DYNAMIC PROPERTIES OF THE SPIRAL

5.3.1 Introduction

The implications of the assumptions relating to money illusion and dynamic homogeneity for the dynamic properties of the inflation spiral are examined in this section. A number of propositions are derived from the fact that the reduced form inflation process in equation 5.5 has the property of dynamic homogeneity (embodied in equation 5.6).[3] This is an important element of our story, for, combined with the assumption that international competitiveness is determined in the long run by fundamental factors relating to market clearing, we find that these propositions describe price behaviour that is potentially explosive or, at the very least, highly unstable.

5.3.2 Role of world prices in domestic currency

Assuming no policy changes and assuming equilibrium in all domestic goods and labour markets (that is, that $X_1 = 0$ and $X_3 = 0$), then equation 5.5 implies that the domestic inflation rate will simply be a long distributed lag of a combination of rises in imported finished goods prices and primary commodity prices in domestic currency. For, if equation 5.5 is rewritten in the following form:

$$\Delta p = \psi_1(L)\Delta p + \{\psi_2(L) + \psi_3(L)\}\Delta p_f + \psi_3(L)(\Delta p_c - \Delta p_f) + F_1(L, X_1, X_3) \quad (5.14)$$

it is clear that if $\psi_2(1) + \psi_3(1) > 0$ and if there is no inflationary pressure in domestic markets ($F_1(L, X_1, X_3) = 0$), then domestic finished goods price inflation will be determined by the rate of increase of finished goods' prices and primary commodity prices in the rest of the world in domestic currency.

Further, if the assumption of no money illusion in domestic goods and labour markets is valid, then equation 5.6 holds:

$$\psi_1(1) + \psi_2(1) + \psi_3(1) = 1 \qquad (5.6)$$

Given this, it is clear from equation 5.14 that, in the absence of any domestic inflationary pressures, the domestic rate of inflation will simply be equal to the rate of increase of the country's import prices in domestic currency in the long term (when the lags have fed through).

It is commonly assumed that the 'core' rate of inflation, the rate to which inflation will return when there are no domestic inflationary pressures, is something that comes out of the labour market (as we shall see, the labour market plays an important role in determining the domestic rate of inflation). Equation 5.14 seems to suggest, however, that when there are no domestic pressures, domestic price inflation will become equal to a weighted average of the rates that pertain in the economies with which a country trades.[4] However, the rate of change of import prices in domestic currency will depend crucially on the behaviour of the exchange rate and, in particular, on the feed-back onto the exchange rate path from domestic price inflation. This result therefore begs the question of how the exchange rate reacts to differential rates of domestic and foreign inflation. This is addressed below.

5.3.3 Domestic pressure and competitiveness

Before examining the role of the exchange rate, we return to equation 5.14, this time to examine the effect of inflationary pressures in domestic labour or goods and services markets on international competitiveness. We first examine the situation when the exchange rate does not fully respond ($m(1) < 1$).

Given that equation 5.6 holds with $\psi_2(1) + \psi_3(1) > 0$, and assuming that $\Delta p = \Delta p_f$ initially, then it is immediately apparent that if $\Delta p_c = \Delta p_f$ but $F_1(L, X_1, X_3) > 0$

for a while, then domestic prices will rise faster than imported finished goods prices in domestic currency as the effect of this feeds through the system. If $F_1(L, X_1, X_3)$ were zero thereafter, the level of domestic prices would then remain higher than the level of comparable prices overseas when converted into sterling. International competitiveness would have deteriorated.

According to equation 5.14, therefore, given $m(1) < 1$ and given that there is dynamic homogeneity in domestic goods and services markets and in labour markets (that is, equation 5.6 holds) the following proposition is true.

Proposition 2a: inflationary pressures in domestic markets lead to persisting changes in a country's international competitiveness.

The question that arises next concerns the role of the exchange rate in determining competitiveness. The foreign exchange market has an impact on competitiveness, through the influence of a change in the exchange rate on the domestic currency values of import prices. But according to equation 5.14, given our assumptions regarding homogeneity, this effect is merely temporary. Any increase in import prices, be it caused by a rise in the world price level or a fall in the exchange rate, will eventually be reflected *in toto* in a rise in the domestic price level, after the lags have all fed through.

Equation 5.14 thus indicates that, given only the homogeneity assumptions in the domestic wage and price equations, the following proposition is true.

Proposition 2b: a change in the exchange rate will have no effect on competitiveness once the lags have worked through the system.

The **only** way to produce a persisting improvement in competitiveness, given goods and labour market dynamic homogeneity and given $m(1) < 1$, is therefore to manipulate downward pressure on domestic prices so they rise by less (or fall by more) than foreign prices in domestic currency during some period. An attempt to achieve the same result by a devaluation, perhaps by reducing domestic interest rates relative to those abroad, will have only a temporary effect on competitiveness; the effect of the increased import prices on the domestic price-setting spiral means that the devaluation will lead to a higher domestic inflation rate than would otherwise have been the case.

5.3.4 Role of exchange rate response

We now incorporate into the reduced form model (equation 5.14) the effects of pressures in the foreign exchange market on the prices of imported goods. The equations for import prices in sterling are given in equations 5.8, reproduced below:

$$\Delta p_c = \phi_c(L)\Delta p_c^w + (1 - \phi_c(L))\Delta p + \xi_c(L)(\Delta p_c^w - \Delta p_f^w) + F_{2c}(L, X_{2c}, X_4)$$

$$\Delta p_f = \phi_f(L)\Delta p_f^w + (1 - \phi_f(L))\Delta p + F_{2f}(L, X_{2f}, X_4) \tag{5.8}$$

Here, $\phi_f(1)$ and $\phi_c(1)$ are both products of the factor $(1 - m(1))$ so if the exchange rate elasticity with respect to relative price inflation is unity $(m(1) = 1)$, then for a given level of policy variables the rate of change of the domestic currency price of imported goods will be decoupled from that of the world currency price of imported finished goods (once the lags have fed through the system). If the exchange rate's reaction to differential inflation rates is less than unity $(m(1) < 1)$, however, world inflation rates will affect the domestic rate (unless there is, eventually, a feed-back through some other variables). The degree of dynamic homogeneity in the exchange rate equation is therefore potentially a very important determinant of the properties of the domestic inflation spiral. This has consequences for the effect of domestic inflationary pressure on both competitiveness and the domestic inflation rate.

We now proceed to examine in more detail the effect of full and partial dynamic homogeneity in the exchange rate equation in the case where the policy variables in X_4 are not manipulated to offset inflationary pressures.

(a) Full dynamic homogeneity

If there is full homogeneity $(m(1) = 1)$, so that when X_4 is equal to zero the exchange rate adjusts fully to any differential between foreign and domestic price inflation, then any increase in domestic prices above world prices (following domestic inflationary pressure) will result in a fully offsetting depreciation once the lags have fed through, other things being equal. This, in due course, will cause equal increases in the sterling values of the prices of imported goods. These will then cause a further rise in domestic prices. And the process will continue indefinitely.

Clearly, with the exchange rate behaving in this way, competitiveness will be unaffected by the disparity between domestic and foreign inflation rates (caused by domestic inflationary pressure) once the lags have fed through.

Here we have two propositions which, on the face of it, contradict each other. First we maintain that competitiveness is determined by domestic inflationary pressure and that the exchange rate has no effect on it (once the lags have fed through); then we assert that, if the exchange rate behaves in a certain way (responds fully to differential inflation rates) then competitiveness is independent of domestic inflationary pressure (once the lags have fed through). The resolution of this conundrum lies in the qualification concerning the lags. The effect of a transitory pressure in domestic markets chases itself around the inflation spiral (including the exchange rate) in these circumstances, and inflation will be higher than it would otherwise have been for ever. Given a persisting pressure, the magnitude of the effect that is being transmitted around the spiral becomes larger in each period: it cumulates. So long as the domestic pressure persists there will be a continuous increase in domestic inflation.

Thus, given dynamic homogeneity in goods and services markets, in labour markets and in the foreign exchange market, we can conclude the following:

Proposition 3a: a temporary bout of inflationary pressure in domestic markets will cause a persisting higher level of domestic inflation.

The same line of reasoning implies the following proposition.

Proposition 3b: a persisting pressure in domestic markets will cause accelerating domestic price inflation.

In terms of the ISE this result can be jusified in the following way. If the exchange rate has full dynamic homogeneity, then equation 5.9 does not define a unique long-term domestic inflation rate for given rates of world price inflation. For if $\psi(1) = 1$, the distributed lag function $\psi(L)$ can be written $\psi(L) = L + \psi^*(L)$ with $\psi^*(1) = 0$, and equation 5.9 becomes:

$$\Delta^2 p = \psi^*(L)\Delta p + \phi(L)\Delta p_f^w + \theta(L)(\Delta p_c^w - \Delta p_f^w) + G(L, X) \qquad (5.15)$$

with $\psi^*(1) = 0$ and $\phi(1) = 0$. It follows that in a long run with constant real primary commodity prices $(\Delta p_c^w = \Delta p_f^w)$ this becomes:

$$\Delta^2 p = G(1, X) \qquad (5.16)$$

This equation says that the rate of change of domestic price inflation is independent of world price inflation once the lags have fed through; it is determined solely by the values taken by the 'real' pressure variables incorporated into the X variables.

If the domestic economy is in equilibrium with $G(1, X) = 0$ then, although a temporary effect from world finished goods price inflation may be visible on domestic price inflation, the rate of inflation will be given by the cumulation of past values of $G(1, X)$ after the lags have had full effect. For abstracting from lags, the inflation rate will be given by:

$$\Delta p_T = \Delta p_0 + \sum_{t=0}^{T} G(1, X(t)) \qquad (5.17)$$

The rate of inflation at time T, Δp_T, will therefore differ from the rate of inflation at time 0, Δp_0, by the cumulated effect of the past path of $G(1, X)$ between time $t = 0$ and $t = T$.

If the X variables were persistently different from zero, $G(1, X) = \tau > 0$ say, then $\Delta^2 p = \tau > 0$ and the domestic inflation rate would continually accelerate (or decelerate if $\tau < 0$). It is in these circumstances, that is, persistent domestic inflationary pressure combined with full adjustment of the exchange rate to differential inflation rates, that extreme price instability, or possibly hyperinflation, becomes a possibility.

(b) Less than full homogeneity

If the process generating the path of the exchange rate lacks dynamic homogeneity so that $0 \leq m(1) < 1$ in equation 5.4, then with no policy influence on X_4, pressure in domestic markets will produce a discrepancy between domestic price inflation and the rate at which import prices in sterling are rising. The effect of this on relative price levels will then persist unless there is an offsetting shock. If $m(1) > 0$, part of the effect of the pressure on domestic prices will be fed back onto domestic prices, through exchange rate movements and their effect on import prices, to increase the rise in domestic prices next time around. But given that $m(1) < 1$, the complete effect of domestic pressure will not be seen on the exchange rate and the deterioration in domestic competitiveness will persist.

In terms of equation 5.9 this means that the domestic inflation rate is determined by the rate operating in the country's main trading partners, for with $\psi(1) < 1$, equation 5.11 holds:

$$\Delta p = (1 - \psi(L))^{-1}[\phi(L)\Delta p_f^w + \theta(L)\{\Delta p_c^w - \Delta p_f^w\} + G(L, X)] \qquad (5.11)$$

and in a long run situation in which $\Delta p_c^w = \Delta p_f^w$ and $G(1, X) = 0$ we have:

$$\Delta p = (1 - \psi(1))^{-1}\phi(1)\Delta p_f^w \qquad (5.18)$$

However, the story does not end there. For in this case, only part of the full effect of domestic inflationary pressure will impact on inflation. The rest will be absorbed in a deterioration in international competitiveness and will be exported, that is, it will put upward pressure on inflation in other countries. The deviation of competitiveness from its equilibrium level will cause a balance of trade deficit (other things being equal) and an offsetting rise in foreign holdings of sterling assets. The exported inflation will cause a higher rate of inflation in the rest of the world; in due course this may feed back through higher rises in import prices. One day the imbalance in international portfolios will presumably unwind, and when this happens (unless there has been offsetting downward domestic pressure) there will be a depreciation of the exchange rate; this will affect the value of import prices in domestic currency and will give a delayed boost to the domestic inflation rate.

It follows that the full effect of the domestic pressure will, eventually, come through on to the domestic inflation rate (given dynamic homogeneity in the relevant markets in the rest of the world), but only after international financial asset equilibrium is reinstated.

The difference between the cases of unit and less than unit dynamic homogeneity in the exchange rate process is therefore in the timing with which the effect of inflationary pressure feeds through on to the domestic inflation rate. In the one case the consequences for inflation feed through fast and unacceptably high inflation may develop before there is time for offsetting policy initiatives. In the other, the consequences develop more slowly and there is plenty of time for offsetting factors to be instigated by the authorities or to happen by chance before the full effect is seen.

5.4 DETERMINANTS OF INFLATION

Now that the model has been described in full it can be used to identify the factors most likely to be important in determining the path of the inflation rate. These can be separated into three main classes. The first concerns the extent to which inflation in one period feeds through to become inflation in the next period. The second concerns the domestic inflationary pressures which are incorporated into the X-variables. Some of these are likely to be more serious as potential creators of inflation than others because they persist over time and their effect cumulates. The others have a transitory effect: by their nature they influence the spiral for a very brief period only. Third, it is clear from the ISE that primary commodity price rises can have a very important impact on the domestic inflation rate.

Here we examine the likely importance of the last two of these classes of factors. The first was dealt with in section 5.3.

(a) Persisting influences on the spiral

There are two types of influence on inflation that are likely to persist and to create a cumulating effect.

The first relates to the aggregate level of activity in the economy. If demand is expanded or contracted, either as a result of policy or for some exogenous reason (activity abroad or a change in the savings ratio, for example) then this will influence the inflation spiral through each of the three main equations, as a result of both the levels and difference terms that relate to activity. Thus, while output is expanding, the prices of goods and services will rise by more than they otherwise would have done because of the output growth term in the price equation. Also, the fall in unemployment associated with the expansion in activity will cause wage settlements to be higher than they would otherwise have been.

Further, if output is higher than 'trend', or 'full capacity' output, capacity utilization will be high, and this will put upward pressure on prices for as long as the situation persists. Moreover, unemployment is likely to be below its market clearing level in these circumstances, and this will put upward pressure on wage settlements; and profits will be above trend, leading firms to grant higher wage settlements to their employees than would otherwise have been the case. Finally, the balance on overseas trade will be further in deficit (less in surplus) than it would otherwise have been in these circumstances, causing a fall in the exchange rate and faster increases in the domestic currency prices of imported goods (other things being equal). All these combine to create higher inflation whenever activity grows faster than trend, or if it remains at a high level for a period.

The second source of persisting inflationary pressure relates to the intercepts on the dynamic equations that describe price-setting in the markets. If the labour market operates in such a way that there is a real wage premium, this will show up in the form of a non-zero intercept in the wage equation. This means that, in order to avoid high or accelerating inflation, some other variable in the wages equation (unemployment?) will have be higher (or lower) to offset the effect of this on the wage bargaining outcome.

Similarly, if the foreign exchange market suffers from pessimistic expectations, this will affect the intercept on the equation describing the exchange rate path. Again, a non-zero intercept means that another variable (the domestic interest rate?) has to be higher (lower) than it would otherwise have been to offset the effect of the intercept on the path of the exchange rate.[5]

(b) Temporary effects on inflation

Some of the remaining factors incorporated into the X-variables of the equations are changes in the real values of policy instruments. The direct effect of these on price-setting operates for only a brief period. They may be changes in the real level of tax instruments, or changes in the real values of public sector prices and so on. Of course, the effect of these on the inflation rate may persist as a result of the dynamics of the spiral, as explained in the previous section.

Another influence which, although temporary in nature, may be longer lasting than these, is the deviation of expected or trend productivity growth (postulated here to be the measure relevant to wage settlements) from its actual rate (taken to be the variable that affects price-setting).

(c) World prices

It is clear from the ISE (equation 5.9) that when real commodity prices rise, this will cause domestic prices to rise faster than they would otherwise have done, and when real commodity prices fall, domestic price inflation will decline (other things being equal). Thus we might, perhaps, have expected one of the findings reported in Chapter 7, that the turning points in domestic inflation reflect, with a lag, the booms and slumps in world commodity markets, other things being equal.

5.5 POLICY IMPLICATIONS

5.5.1 Introduction

Before examining the implications of this model for the policies that might prevent or alleviate inflation, we note, once again, the factors identified as likely to be important in determining the rate of inflation. These fall into three classes: first, the degree of inflation inertia; second, the paths of the variables impinging on the inflation spiral; third, price inflation in the rest of the world (in particular, primary commodity price rises).

This suggests that there may be a number of alternative policy options for preventing high inflation from developing or for dealing with it after it has occurred. In this section the parameters and variables which have implications for policy are identified. Chapter 8 discusses the policy options in more detail.

5.5.2 Preventing inflation developing

The model we have developed has a number of implications for the prevention of inflation.

(a) Preventing automatic exchange rate indexation

One of the features of the inflation spiral which has been given some prominence in our analysis is the degree to which inflation is passed through from one year to the next: the extent of inertia in the inflation spiral. It is clear that, given no money illusion in the goods and services market and in the labour market, there is little scope for restructuring these areas to achieve a lasting reduction in inflation inertia without intervention (section 6.2 has a discussion of this). In the foreign exchange market, however, the situation is different. According to the model, the degree of inflation pass-through in the short term depends on the way in which exchange market operators form their expectations and this, in turn, may well depend on the extent of the differential between the rate of inflation at home and abroad.

In order to prevent the effective indexation of the exchange rate (to stop $m(1)$ from becoming equal to unity) it is therefore important that the authorities prevent the country's inflation rate from deviating too far from that of its main trading partners. If relative inflation rates become important in determining the path of the exchange rate, then speculators will come to expect the rate to move to reflect the inflation rate differential. Automatic full inflation indexation of the exchange rate in equilibrium will follow, with the implications of high inflation volatility and the associated danger of unacceptably high inflation, or even hyperinflation, given a period with a persisting inflationary pressure.

(b) Bottlenecks

We have assumed that it is profit maximization that motivates price setting in the goods and services markets, for if it is far removed from this the firm is unlikely to survive. This being so, the main causes of inflationary behaviour in this market arise when capacity is constrained (the value of the variable 'cu' is large and negative) and demand cannot be met by domestic production: that is, when bottlenecks occur and a non-linear relationship develops between demand and price rises.

To prevent inflationary pricing in the markets for goods and services, the authorities must therefore aim to avoid a situation in which the demand for domestic output expands beyond the level which can be met from the resources and capacity available. This means that whenever possible the rate of increase of demand (Δy) needs to be held to a level that can be met by domestic production without excessive imports; and the level of demand (Y) should not exceed that which can be met by the available capacity ($\bar{Y}$) so the capacity utilization term in the price equation (cu) does not become excessively large.

(c) Labour market pressures

In the absence of capacity constraints in production (bottlenecks), the main thrust of domestic inflationary pressures seems to originate in the labour market (Chapter 7). Indeed, one of the findings of the empirical analysis is that unrealistic[6] wage settlements seem to have been one of the main causes of domestic inflationary pressure during the period studied. This is seen in the model in the non-zero intercept in the wages equation.

It seems that a labour market may quite easily develop a structure that makes unrealistic real wage outcomes likely. That is, for a given set of conventions and institutions in the labour market, the real wage 'acceptable' to the unions (labelled 'WACC' in our empirical work) may not be soundly based on achievable economic factors (this may be because of 'leapfrogging', where each union demands and achieves a wage rise as large or larger than the last published settlement); further, the strength of the unions in the wage bargaining process may be too great compared to that of the firms. Clearly this needs to be avoided if there is not to be a tendency to rising inflation. It is a challenging task to design a labour market structure in which the real wage outcome of wage bargaining does not tend to put upward pressure on inflation (so the intercept on the wage equation falls to zero).

The remaining policy implications of our labour market model for preventing a rise in inflation involve manipulating the paths of the explanatory variables. If unemployment is reduced too fast or too far, or if profits are too high, then according to our model there will be upward pressure on inflation. If taxes are increased and there is no offsetting fall in some other tax or price then, again, there will be upward pressure on inflation.

(d) Exchange rate policy

We have seen (sections 5.2 and 5.3) that the role of exchange rate policy in influencing inflation may owe more to the structure of price-setting in the goods and services and labour markets than to behaviour in the foreign exchange markets. Thus, given dynamic homogeneity in both the goods and services market and in the labour market, devaluation to improve international competitiveness will only create upward pressure on inflation once the lags have fed through: it will have no lasting effect on competitiveness.

Indeed, to prevent too great a rise in inflation, in the face of domestic inflationary pressure, the authorities could hold the exchange rate up by raising the short-term domestic interest rate. In this case some of the effect of the pressure will be seen on international competitiveness instead of on inflation. Meanwhile, a countervailing deflationary pressure could be created to deal with the problem.

5.5.3 Curing inflation

It is often inevitable that inflation becomes unacceptably high. This may be because of inadvertent overheating of the economy, because there have been excessive rises in primary commodity prices in real terms, or because of unrealistic expectations on the part of wage bargainers or undue power on the union side of the wage bargaining process. If this happens, the choice of policy prescriptions is rather limited, according to our model. There are only two main approaches: deflation and incomes policy.

(a) Deflation

The authorities can deflate the economy using either fiscal or monetary policy or a combination of both. The policy stance may be informed by the path of some so-called intermediate targets or target ranges, involving the money supply, or the ERM. According to the model, this will affect price setting in all the markets that make up the inflation spiral. It will affect the goods market through the capacity utilization term as well as through the reversible output growth term. Wage setting will be influenced through the unemployment terms (this may have a lasting effect but it equally may be wholly reversible) as well as through profits. The effect will be seen in the foreign exchange market because the higher interest rate and the larger balance on trade will cause the exchange rate to remain higher, other things being equal, leading to lower increases in import prices.

It is not clear, however, whether this policy will lead to a sustained reduction in inflation. This is because, according to the data, if there is a non-reversible effect the main part of it comes through the wage equation. The data are not at all clear about the significance of the functional form in this respect; it may be wholly reversible.

(b) Incomes policy

Given the UK experience of incomes policies, they appear unpromising. Incomes policies in the UK have generally persisted for only a short period, the beneficial effect on inflation has often been reversed in the catch up that has followed its end, and the effect on pay relativities has caused much aggravation. In the case of the 'Social Contract', which lasted long enough to have a substantial effect on inflation, the benefits were swamped by the 'Winter of Discontent', the effect of the Clegg awards and the rise in inflation associated with the second sharp rise in oil prices.

Indeed, our model suggests that the incomes policy of the late 1970s had a substantial and beneficial lasting effect on the rate of inflation in the UK. It seems, therefore, that it would be worth investigating whether there is some form of incomes policy which might have a good chance of being more successful, and less painful, than the recessions that are currently used to deal with unacceptably high inflation.

APPENDIX 5A: WORLD PRICE INFLATION

5A.1 Introduction

This Appendix looks at two issues relating to the inflation spiral that are not dealt with elsewhere but are needed in order to complete the analysis: it provides a simple equation for the path of primary commodity prices so the model can be completed; it uses this to provide an analysis of the determinants of the world rate of inflation.

5A.2 World commodity prices

There are various theories concerning the determinants of world commodity prices.[7] In the long run they are determined, in real terms, by the level of demand and the cost of supplying at that level. As a result, some have modelled them using a Phillips curve type of approach (Chapter 3 has a discussion of the Phillips curve). On a shorter time-scale they may be affected by speculative factors in a manner similar to that of financial instruments (e.g., the model of foreign exchange markets in Chapter 4). Indeed, there have recently been a number of models of primary commodity prices (in particular, Moutos and Vines 1988) that have used an approach often thought more appropriate for exchange rate equations.

Here we simply assume that the expected real price of primary commodities is affected by market disequilibrium, in the same way as the real wage in a conventional expectations augmented Phillips curve. A convenient form for the equation explaining the (logarithmic) change in commodity prices in world currencies, Δp_c^w, is then:

$$\Delta p_c^w = \mu(L)\Delta p_f^w + \eta(L)[(D_c - S_c)/S_c]$$
$$= \mu(L)\Delta p_f^w + X_5 \qquad (5A.1)$$

where p_f^w is the (expected) price of finished goods in the same currency basket as that in which p_c^w is measured (proxied here by the actual price), D_c and S_c represent commodity demand and supply, and X_5 could, in principle, include other factors affecting the path of primary commodity prices as well as excess demand or supply. The functions $\mu(L)$ and $\eta(L)$ are distributed lags of parameters.

There is little feed-back from disequilibrium in a primary commodity market onto the demand for the commodity (the share of primary commodities in the total value of finished goods is only about 10 to 15 per cent), or on to the full capacity supply. As a result, such disequilibria tend to be large and to persist, and large variations in the relation between commodity prices and finished goods prices are observed. The inflationary (or disinflationary) effects of such disequilibria tend to cumulate.

It follows that the international primary commodity markets can have a substantial effect on inflation rates throughout the world.

5A.3 Determinants of world inflation

Our analysis would not be complete without an examination of the implications of our model for the mechanism by which world price inflation is determined. The rate at which the prices of finished goods are rising in world currencies can have a crucial influence on domestic price inflation.

If the foreign exchange market has less than full dynamic homogeneity, $(m(1) < 1)$, the world rate of price inflation is relevant to domestic price inflation. The rate of increase of a weighted average of price indices for the developed world can be analysed by considering a set of equations like equation 5.9, with one for each country.

The result of combining equation 5A.1 with our inflation spiral equation (equation 5.9) is an equation for the weighted average inflation rate in developed countries (using a superscript w to indicate world variables) of the form:

$$\Delta p_f^w = [\Omega(L) + \Phi(L)\mu(L)]\Delta p_f^w + G(L, X^w) \qquad (5A.2)$$

where $\Omega(1) + \Phi(1) = 1$ and $G(L, X^w)$ is the world counterpart of $G(L, X)$.

It follows that if $\mu(1) < 1$, world price inflation would tend to decline towards zero over time in the absence of positive inflationary pressure. However, to assume that $\mu(1) < 1$ is to assume that the prices of primary commodities tend to fall in real terms (that is, in relation to world finished good prices) when there is inflation in the developed world so long as world primary commodity markets were in equilibrium. It seems implausible that the terms of trade should depend on the rate of inflation in the long term.

If $\mu(1) = 1$ on the other hand, then $\Omega(1) + \Phi(1)\mu(1) = 1$ and the long-run version of this equation can be written:

$$\Delta^2 p_f^w = g\{1, X^w\} \qquad (5A.3)$$

In this case the rate of inflation that operates in the world in the long term is determined by the cumulated effects of the inflationary and deflationary influences in all world labour, goods and primary commodity markets. Our model suggests that world inflation has remained broadly constant in recent years because any net inflationary pressure there may have been in goods and labour markets has been offset by the decline in real commodity prices. An alternative explanation is examined in the next chapter. This involves the assumption that there is less than full dynamic homogeneity in goods and labour markets, that is, that price-setting in these markets is, indeed, subject to money illusion.

REFERENCES

Moutos, T. and Vines, D. (1988) *Output, Inflation and Commodity Prices*, Centre for Economic Policy Research, Discussion Paper No. 271.

Winters, L. A. and Sapsford, D. (1990) *Primary Commodity Prices: Economic Models and Policy*, Cambridge University Press, Cambridge.

ENDNOTES

1. Once again, L is used to represent the lag operator and $\Delta \equiv 1 - L$. The symbol $a(L)$ represents $\sum a_i L^i$ so $a(1)$ indicates the long-term effect an explanatory variable has on the dependent variable in any relevant structural equation.

2. Of course, the policy reaction to inflation may be such that these factors are correlated with the level of inflation.
3. In this context, refer to section 1.3 on the exogeneity of the factors impinging on the spiral.
4. Figure 7.5 shows the path predicted for UK price inflation during the period 1971 to 1985 given only the world price effects, that is, the path inflation would have taken if $G(L, X)$ in equation 5.11 had been zero throughout.
5. A non-zero intercept in the price-setting equation is likely to arise only if monopoly or the existence of cartels, allowing 'unrealistic' price levels, is sufficiently widespread.
6. That is, wage settlements that are larger than implied by the fundamentals, productivity, the terms of trade and so on.
7. Winters and Sapsford (1990) have brought together a collection of the latest work in this area.

6

The dynamics of the inflation spiral

6.1 INTRODUCTION

This chapter examines the implications for inflation of the dynamic properties of the equation for the inflation spiral (the ISE) in more detail. In particular, it takes the factors identified as important in Chapter 5 and examines their effect in more detail.

Section 6.2 examines the likelihood of there being automatic full inflation indexation (dynamic homogeneity of unity) when the goods and services market, the labour market and the market for foreign exchange are all in equilibrium. Section 6.3 notes the implications of the extent of inflation indexation in the goods and services market and the labour market. In section 6.4 we examine the effect the level of dynamic homogeneity in the exchange rate equation would have on the dynamics of the inflation spiral if policy were inflation neutral.

Finally, section 6.5 notes some of the implications of our results concerning the dynamics of the inflation spiral for the interpretation of the path of inflation in the recent past and the prognosis for the future.

6.2 INFLATION INDEXATION

6.2.1 Introduction

The assumption of no money illusion implies that there should be full dynamic homogeneity (referred to here as 'inflation indexation') in both the goods and services market and the labour market. In the market for goods and services this means that price setting will ensure that the profit margin is independent of the rate of inflation, other things being equal: prices will rise at the same rate as unit costs when markets are in equilibrium (as discussed in section 2.4.4). In the labour market it means that the real wage will be independent of the rate of inflation when the labour market is in equilibrium. This is because the real wage will rise at the same rate as labour productivity, so nominal wages rise at the sum of the going rate of price rises and productivity growth (section 3.5.3).

This no money illusion assumption turns out to be of considerable importance to our understanding of the factors underlying the path of inflation. Further, it is critical to the determination of the policy prescriptions for preventing and for curing inflation: if there were less than full inflation indexation in either the goods and services market or the labour market, then one policy option in the face of high inflation would be simply to wait for it to die away. Since this assumption is so important, we examine the basis for it in more depth.

It is less clear whether there is full inflation indexation in the foreign currency market. Both theory and data are unclear on this. The reasons for this are summarized in this section. Later in this chapter the implications for inflation of both full and less than full inflation indexation of the exchange rate are examined for the case in which policy variables are inflation neutral.

6.2.2 The goods and services market

Dynamic homogeneity in the domestic goods and services market implies that when all unit input costs and all competitors' prices are increasing at the same rate, and output is at its full capacity level, then prices rise at the same rate as costs. This means that the profit margin is independent of the rate of inflation. If, in times of high inflation, industries did not adjust prices to offset fully the increases in unit costs and/or competitors' prices, thereby allowing their rates of profit to be squeezed, then the assumption of dynamic homogeneity would be violated. There are two reasons why this might be so.

First, the fact that prices are adjusted at discrete intervals could result in a small degree of money illusion in price-setting in the goods and services market. The administrative cost of changing menu prices means that manufacturers tend to make infrequent adjustments to their prices, changing them, perhaps, only once a year. This means that price rises often lag cost increases. Given a fixed interval between price adjustments, the effect of this on the variation of profits over the period will clearly be greater when inflation is high than when it is low.

However, it seems likely that firms will compensate for any effect arising from delay when they readjust their prices. Thus, they may take a forward looking view of cost increases (though we have been unable to detect any evidence in support of an effect from expected future cost rises). A reluctance on the part of firms to adjust in this way for increasing (or decreasing) costs and changing competitors' prices when inflation is high would imply the existence of some element of money illusion in the goods and services market.

Second, casual empiricism suggests that profits are lower when inflation is high than when it is low. Does this imply money illusion on the part of entrepreneurs, or is there some other explanation? In fact, it seems that this can be explained by the reduction in aggregate demand in the economy that follows the Government's policy reaction to high inflation. This puts downward pressure on firms' price setting decisions through a reduction in the demand for their output, and through a fall in the level of utilization of their capacity.

In conclusion, it seems likely that the assumption of dynamic homogeneity in the goods market is pretty well founded. Certainly, the statistical analysis in Chapter 2 suggests that it is not obviously inconsistent with the data.

6.2.3 The labour market

It is easier to imagine that there may be circumstances in which the level of dynamic homogeneity is less than unity in the domestic labour market than it is to produce a convincing argument for this in the market for goods and services. Dynamic homogeneity in the labour market implies that in equilibrium (all prices rising at the same rate and the other factors that impinge on the wage bargaining process all neutral) the rate of increase of wages is equal to the rate of increase in prices combined with the appropriate measure of productivity growth. In this case the real wage will increase at the same rate as expected labour productivity.

However, there are two reasons why the institutional structure of the labour market may mean that the real wage is affected by the rate of inflation. If this were the case it would certainly be relevant to the dynamics of the inflation process.

First, the price level facing any individual rises relatively smoothly over time: the individual faces many different prices each of which will be increased, perhaps once a year, leading to a continuously increasing aggregate price level.[1] However, most individuals' pay jumps in nominal terms once a year and remains fixed at the resulting nominal level until the next annual settlement day. It follows that between each wage settlement people's real incomes slowly erode. This could have an effect on the path of real wages over the years.

If the real wage is always brought back to the level appropriate in the labour market at the start of each wage round, without reflecting the likely degree of erosion as a result of inflation in the following period, then the average real wage during the wage round will be depressed to a greater extent when inflation is high than when it is low. The higher the rate of inflation, the further the annual average real wage will fall behind during the period between settlements. This phenomenon was noted in 1940 by Keynes in his book *How to Pay for the War* (Keynes 1940). It is exactly the same, in principle, as assuming that price-setters fail to take account of expected rises in unit costs when making their annual adjustment to prices.

There is a second reason for supposing that there may be a lack of inflation indexation in the labour market. Wage bargainers do not necessarily negotiate wage rises solely on the basis of price rises. Instead there is evidence (from surveys conducted by the CBI, for example) that wage bargainers are concerned with relative wages; that is, they are concerned that the earnings of their group should match, or better, the earnings of those in comparable groups.

As a result of the effect of one group's wage rise on those of another group, the price rise between wage settlements may not be precisely compensated in the way that has been assumed. For 'instead of a perfect wage–price–wage spiral we have an imperfect one, with a wage–wage effect helping to drive it' (Tylecote 1981, p. 23). If this is so, the simple form of dynamic homogeneity in the labour market may be partially lost. In particular, the wage–wage element may result in considerable lags, leading to upward pressure on the real wage during the part of a cycle in which inflation is low and a squeezing of the real wage at a time of high inflation.

Although the data do not reject full wage–price dynamic homogeneity, the possibility that the form of the homogeneity condition is more complex because of discrete price-setting cannot be ruled out.

6.2.4 The foreign exchange market

The exchange rate path would possess the property of full inflation indexation if, in the absence of a policy response, the nominal exchange rate were to respond directly to any differential between domestic and world inflation rates, adjusting to offset it fully.

From the analysis in Chapter 4 it is apparent that the price of foreign currency is determined in the short term by a combination of the net underlying position on demand and supply, the authorities' policy regarding interest rates and the behaviour of international currency speculators. The discussion in Chapter 4 suggests that although such principles as the Law of One Price and international commodity price arbitrage are likely to cause the exchange rate to move to restore the equilibrium level of competitiveness in the long run (when the international asset allocation will be in equilibrium), they are most unlikely to perform the task of maintaining a constant real exchange rate level from one year to the next. The price will therefore be keenly sensitive to speculators' expectations regarding the future path of the exchange rate, since this is an important factor in the determination of their investment decisions. Inflation indexation will result if the way in which speculators form expectations about the future level of the exchange rate takes account of relative inflation rates; that is, if they form expectations in real rather than in nominal terms.

In countries with inflation rates broadly similar to those of their trading partners it seems unlikely that it would pay exchange market operators to assume that the future path of the exchange rate will reflect relative inflation rates. It would be unlikely to help them make correct predictions. This is because other factors, such as the authorities' policy stance or the volatility of expectations, dominate the exchange rate path.

The situation might be very different, however, if the country's inflation rate were substantially different from that of its main trading partners, particularly if policy were such as to accommodate the differential, or to 'index' fully the exchange rate. In these circumstances the exchange rate would tend to move continuously, adjusting for the differential inflation rates from one month to the next as well as reflecting the effects of other factors. It would undoubtedly pay operators to take this into account when forming expectations about its future level.

We conclude that the extent of inflation indexation in the foreign exchange rate path is likely to vary between countries and over time. There is little that can be said about it, on the basis of theory, with confidence. It is a matter for the data.

Statistical analysis of actual exchange rate paths suggests that whereas there may be a weak or intermittent effect on nominal exchange rates from relative price inflation in countries with inflation rates broadly similar to those of their trading partners, it is also quite possible that there is none.[2] Further, given the discussion in section 6.3, the comparative stability of inflation in such countries suggests that their exchange rates do not have full dynamic homogeneity. Thus it certainly appears plausible to assume a lack of full indexation of the reaction of sterling to differential inflation rates at home and overseas

Insofar as the UK is concerned, the data do not permit an accurate estimate of the relevant coefficient. Estimates vary hugely with the precise specification of the price variables and the time period used. Standard errors are large. As a result, this coefficient cannot be determined empirically with any confidence at the present time.

6.3 SIGNIFICANCE OF GOODS AND LABOUR MARKET INDEXATION

We have assumed that behaviour in domestic markets for goods and services and for labour is not subject to money illusion: that last period's inflation is fed through in full, by these markets, onto this period's price rises. This assumption has important implications for the dynamics of the inflation spiral.

It is clearly possible that there is some lack of dynamic homogeneity in either the domestic goods and services market or the domestic labour market, or both, at least in some circumstances. Suppose, for example, that when inflation is high prices rise by less than the rise in unit costs, squeezing profits to an extent not explained by the (expected) path of activity. Or suppose that when price rises are large, wage rises do not take account of this so real wages are squeezed and unit costs rise less fast than they otherwise would have done. In either case prices can then rise by a smaller amount than they would otherwise have done next time around. In these circumstances, with equilibrium in both domestic and commodity markets (the X-variables equal to zero), a temporary bout of exogenous domestic inflationary pressure would not lead to a permanent rise in domestic inflation – instead the inflation would be temporary and would die away, perhaps quite rapidly, as it passes around the system. A persisting differential between domestic and world inflation would then arise only if there were sustained domestic inflationary pressure.

The speed with which inflation would die away in these circumstances would depend on the extent to which prices or wages failed to take full account of the going rate of inflation. If, for example, wage setting and price setting took no account of the rate at which prices were rising then, with domestic markets in equilibrium (X_1 and X_3 equal to zero), inflation would disappear almost instantly.

There would be no spiral and inflation would have no inertia. This is clearly contrary to experience. More plausibly, if there were a slight downward pressure on either wage-setting or price-setting (or both) when inflation is above some given, acceptable level, then the effect would be to put a downward, stabilizing influence on price rises so that high inflation would eventually work its way out of the system. Of course, this might take a considerable time. Nevertheless, this would be enough to remove any threat of gross price instability, even in the presence of a continuing inflationary pressure in some aspect of the domestic economy.

6.4 SIGNIFICANCE OF EXCHANGE RATE INDEXATION

6.4.1 Introduction

In sections 5.2 and 5.3, where the Inflation Spiral Equation (ISE) was derived and analysed, it became apparent that the degree of automatic inflation indexation in the exchange rate market (the extent to which the exchange rate responds directly to differential international inflation rates) can be an important factor in determining the extent of inertia in the spiral. This governs the magnitude of the effect price rises in world currencies have on the rate of increase of the domestic currency price of imported goods in the absence of policy constraints, and so can have a substantial influence on the path of the domestic inflation rate. This section considers these results in greater depth and explores their implications for the dynamics of the inflation spiral.

6.4.2 Full inflation indexation

Consider the case in which the path of the exchange rate exhibits full inflation indexation so that, with no other influences impinging upon it, the exchange rate adjusts fully to any differential between foreign and domestic price inflation.

Suppose there is a temporary bout of domestic inflationary pressure arising from, say, a temporary aspirations gap in the labour market, but for all the rest of the time domestic markets are in equilibrium. There will be a once off increase in nominal wages large enough to take the real wage temporarily above its warranted level. From then on the real wage level will be consistent with productivity, the terms of trade and other relevant fundamentals. In terms of the ISE there is a single period during which the term $G(L, X)$ in equation 5.11 is greater than zero, its value returning to zero for all subsequent periods.

Initially, the result of this will be an unwarranted increase in real domestic labour costs; and this will lead to a larger rise in domestic prices than would otherwise have taken place. The size will reflect (among other things) the share of wage costs in total costs. The result of this is that domestic prices rise by more than world prices. However, dynamic homogeneity in the foreign exchange market means that the exchange rate will respond to this differential, and there will be a fully offsetting depreciation. This causes the increase in the sterling value of import prices to be the same as the rise in domestic prices (after the lags have worked through). This then causes a further rise in domestic prices. And this rise in domestic prices, which is larger than it would have been in the absence of the originating aspirations gap, results in a subsequent wage rise consistent with the fundamentals but, also, larger than it would have been in the absence of the initiating aspirations gap.

Thus the temporary pressure in the labour market marks the start of a process of rising wages, rising prices and exchange rate depreciations leading to further wage and price rises and depreciations which will continue, indefinitely, at a higher rate than would otherwise have been the case.

A temporary bout of inflationary pressure, therefore, leads to an increase in domestic inflation which lasts not only for the period during which the pressure occurs, but for all future periods; unless a deflationary pressure occurs to cancel it out. The alarming corollary of this result is that a persisting inflationary pressure will lead to accelerating domestic inflation and price instability.[3]

6.4.3 Partial inflation indexation

Now consider the scenario of a one-period domestic inflationary pressure in the case in which the exchange rate exhibits less than unit homogeneity. In this case there is less than full indexation of the exchange rate to differential international rates of price inflation, so in the absence of other influences the pressure in the domestic market produces a discrepancy between domestic price inflation and the rate at which import prices (in domestic currency) are rising which is not then cancelled out by the movement of the exchange rate.

As long as there is some direct effect of relative inflation rates on the exchange rate it will adjust partially to the differential rates of world and domestic price inflation and there will be some depreciation. This will cause an increase in import prices, but it will be smaller than the original rise in domestic prices. This increase in import prices will feed through onto domestic inflation and back round the system. Because the effect is proportionately smaller each time it goes around the system, it will eventually die away. However, while the level of domestic prices will be significantly higher as a result of the initiating inflationary pressure (Chapter 7 proposes an estimate of the magnitude of this effect in the UK) the domestic currency prices of imported goods will have increased by less.

The failure of the exchange rate to offset totally the relative inflation differential means that the country's international competitiveness will deteriorate. Other things being equal, this will lead to a balance of trade deficit and this, in itself, will put downward pressure on the exchange rate. If, as a result, the exchange rate indeed declines, then the inflationary pressure will, after all, feed back onto price inflation, albeit by a different route.

However, exchange rate depreciation is not the only means of dealing with a balance of trade deficit. A rise in domestic interest rates in comparison to overseas rates will attract an *ex ante* inflow on capital account that will fund the deficit and can restore the exchange market to equilibrium. This policy stance will also have an indirect beneficial effect on the balance of trade since, by reducing domestic output, it will decrease domestic demand for imports and therefore reduce the demand for foreign currency. Further, the contraction in domestic activity that follows a rise in domestic interest rates will provide a disinflationary pressure in domestic markets. This may go some way towards cancelling the effects of the initiating domestic pressure, albeit painfully.

A contractionary fiscal policy will also produce some of these benefits. It will have a favourable effect on the current balance, since domestic demand for foreign imports will be reduced. It also will provide a downward pressure on inflation in the domestic markets.

Even if the postulated inflationary pressure were temporary, the loss of competitiveness that occurs in the less than unit homogeneity case would persist, other things being equal. In order to maintain equilibrium in the foreign exchange markets, therefore, interest rates must be kept higher (and/or activity lower) than in competitor countries indefinitely, or at least until such time as some dis-inflationary pressure cancels the earlier inflationary pressure.[4]

All the time the exchange rate is being prevented from depreciation by high interest rates there will be a cumulation of foreign balances in domestic currency. The currency outflow on invisibles will increasingly reflect the foreigners' earnings on these assets. This will create a need for higher earnings on trade account or for gradually increasing policy initiatives to counteract the pressure from the basic balance if the foreign exchange market is to be maintained in equilibrium. In the long term, if the distortion to international financial portfolios is unwound, this will require an offsetting trade surplus (a period in which competitiveness is favourable) in order to generate the required outflow on capital account, other things being equal.

There is, also, another route by which the exported pressure may be fed back on to the initiating economy. During the period in which the exchange rate does not pass through the inflationary pressure onto domestic price inflation, the price rises imported into other economies from the UK will be higher than they would otherwise have been. The inflationary pressure that is not absorbed within the domestic economy will therefore impinge on price inflation in the rest of the world. Given eventual full inflation indexation (dynamic homogeneity) in all goods and services and labour markets, throughout the world, this would in the end be seen in the import prices in world currency facing the UK.

The difference between the two cases (full and partial inflation indexation) therefore lies in the dynamic mechanism through which the adjustment takes place. The speed with which inflationary pressure feeds through onto the rate of price inflation is quite different in the two cases.

6.4.4 Dynamic adjustment

This section explores the dynamics of the adjustment of the inflation rate to inflationary pressure in the two cases of full and partial inflation indexation of the foreign exchange rate in the absence of a policy response.

If there is only a partial direct indexation of the exchange rate, as seems likely in the UK, the adjustment of the exchange rate to differential inflation rates will take place partly through its reaction to the *ex ante* balance of payments disequilibrium that follows the implied change in competitiveness. Since it is possible to accommodate balance of trade disequilibria for extended periods of time before resorting to exchange rate depreciation, the dynamics of the path of adjustment towards long-run equilibrium are more relevant to the inflation process than the characteristics of the final equilibrium. In an economy in which the exchange rate shows little or no direct reaction to relative inflation rates, then long before an offsetting depreciation becomes urgently required, a compensating deflationary shock may have removed the need for it.

The dynamics of the adjustment towards long-run equilibrium in the foreign exchanges are therefore very important to the understanding of the inflation spiral. Figures 6.1 and 6.2 are predicated on the assumption that some exogenous change, perhaps in the terms of trade, offsets the predicted trade deficit eventually and so prevents this from causing the fall in the exchange rate that would, eventually, be inevitable otherwise.

Figure 6.1 shows the effect of a temporary exogenous domestic inflationary pressure (perhaps caused by a brief period in which capacity constraints restricted output in the domestic production process) in the cases of full and partial inflation indexation. This is derived using our model along with appropriate coefficient adjustments. The slight overshoot is the result of the coefficient values incorporated

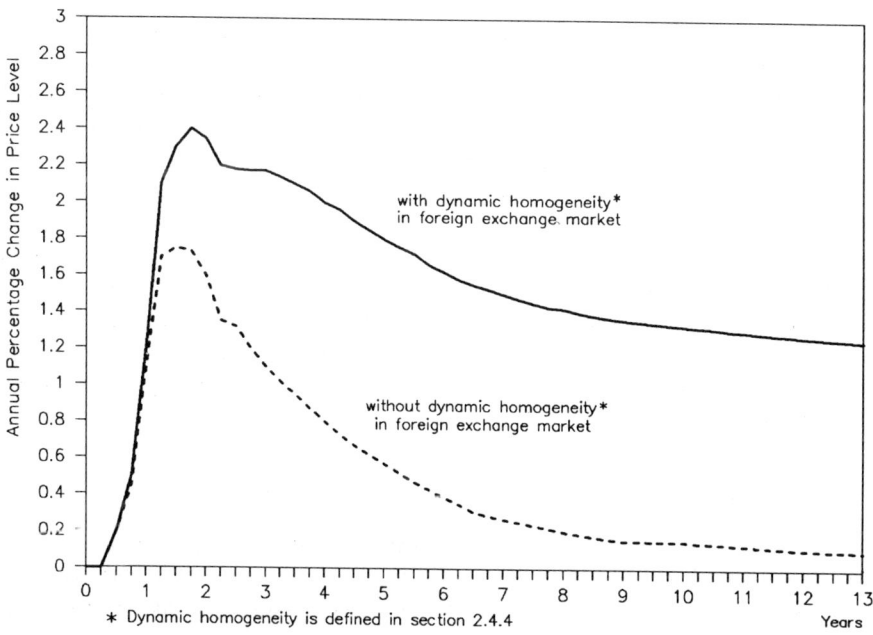

Fig. 6.1 Effect on inflation of an inflationary shock.

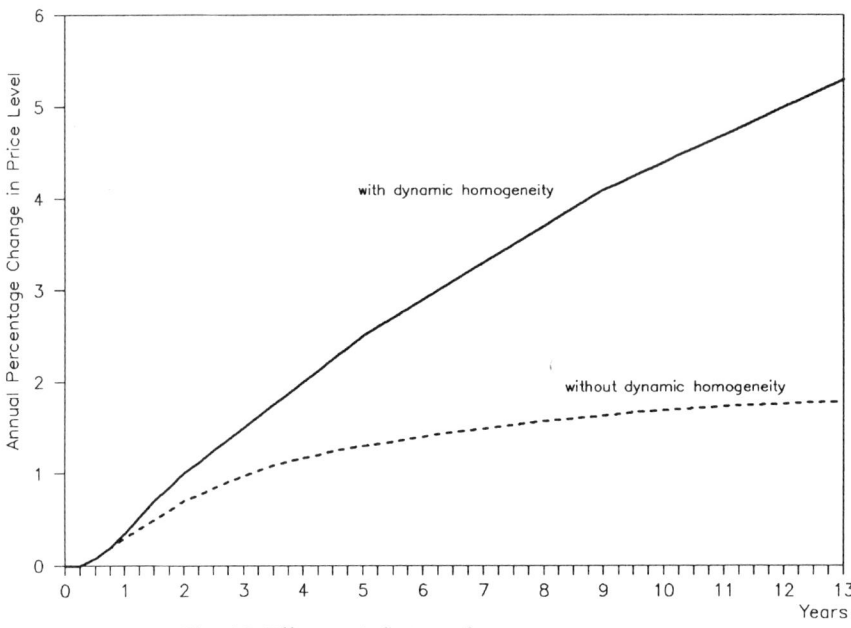

Fig. 6.2 Effect on inflation of persistent pressure.

in the model. It is clear that in the one case the rate of inflation is subject to a permanent shift upwards, while in the other the effect on inflation dies away.

Figure 6.2 shows the effect of a persisting pressure on inflation (perhaps originating in the labour market) in the two cases under the same assumptions. This shows the instability of the inflation rate that arises if the exchange rate is fully indexed, against the relative stability when there is less than full pass-through of the relative inflation effect.

In the case of less than total pass-through, a continuously varying degree of domestic inflationary and disinflationary pressure will lead to variations in international competitiveness. However, varying the domestic interest rate to provide *ex ante* capital account financing of the current account deficit or surplus can delay any realignment indefinitely, if there is the expectation that compensating shocks will occur.

6.4.5 Conclusions

Given the assumption of full inflation indexation in all goods and services markets and labour markets and a unique allocation of international financial assets in equilibrium, the effect of domestic inflationary pressure should be the same eventually, regardless of the direct reaction of the exchange rate to differential inflation rates. The difference between the cases of full and partial inflation indexation of the exchange rate is in the timing with which the effects feed through and the mechanics of the adjustment process. An economy in which the feed-through is fast is likely to suffer from price instability and to be prone to unacceptably high levels of inflation. The Latin American economies are examples of this. If the feed through is slow there is time for random exogenous downward pressures to take place and for the authorities to take action, possibly to engineer a recession, before high inflation becomes a major problem. On the other hand, if offsetting deflationary measures are not taken, the eventual devaluation would cause a sharp increase in inflation.

Viewed from another angle, without full exchange rate inflation indexation then, given a bout of inflationary pressure, there is a policy choice. The pressure could be taken on competitiveness by holding up the exchange rate (raising interest rates) and building up balances on which a return must be paid. Alternatively, it could be taken directly on the rate of inflation by allowing or engineering a compensating fall in the exchange rate. Finally, a countervailing (temporary) disinflationary pressure could be arranged, which might (depending on the form in which activity impinges on the inflation spiral) cancel it out. With full inflation indexation there is no choice: the pressure will immediately feed through onto inflation.

6.5 IMPLICATIONS OF INFLATION DYNAMICS

6.5.1 Introduction

Given the argument put forward in this chapter it seems likely that although the reduced form equation describing the UK inflation spiral has dynamic homogeneity (because of no money illusion on the domestic labour market and goods and services market) it does not exhibit full dynamic homogeneity with respect to domestic price inflation. Instead, because of behaviour in the foreign exchange market, domestic inflation is also affected by world inflation rates. However, as we have seen, this does not alter the fact that continuous domestic inflationary pressure would ultimately generate an unacceptably high domestic inflation rate.

This section explores the implications of this, both for the past, when there appears to have been a good deal of pressure generated in the labour market but inflation has generally remained in single figures, and for the future.

6.5.2 Potential price instability

We have seen that if the exchange rate path is not fully indexed for relative inflation rates, then the effect of domestic inflationary pressure operates on the exchange rate indirectly, through the effect of the loss of international competitiveness. Given this, and given the possible eventual feed-back of any exported price inflation, the inflation spiral can, indeed, be viewed as being fully inflation indexed in the very long term, when all these effects have fully worked their way through. The question that arises next is why, in the face of what appears to have been sustained labour market pressure during large parts of the 1970s and 1980s, the acceleration in inflation this predicts has failed to arise.

One possible explanation is the systematic decline in real commodity prices that has taken place during this period. This will have had a cumulating downward impact, which may have been sufficient to offset the continual upward labour market pressure. Put another way, there may have been a continuing transfer of real spending power from the primary commodity producing countries to the inhabitants of developed countries such as the UK. If this is the true explanation, another question arises: what would be the effect of the persisting inflationary pressure in the labour market if this trend in real commodity prices were to cease? Would the economy enter a period of sustained net inflationary pressure? Or would the labour market pressure end? If there is, indeed, no money illusion in domestic markets as we assume here (and this is supported by the data), then the consequences for inflation look serious.

An alternative explanation of the fact that inflation has remained relatively stable in the face of seemingly continuous labour market pressure, would be that the inflation indexation of the domestic goods and services market and/or labour market is incomplete when inflation is high (section 6.2).

6.5.3 Likely sources of disinflationary pressure

There is a number of possible sources of exogenous disinflationary pressure of which the most important has probably been the decline in the level of real commodity prices referred to above. The rapid rise in real commodity prices in the early 1970s was preceded by fifteen years of decline in the relative cost of primary commodity inputs to manufacturing (averaging around 1 per cent a year); and the underlying downward trend has since reasserted itself. It is possible that this, feeding through the international inflation spiral, has been sufficient to compensate for all of the inflationary pressure which has been generated in the labour markets of the developed world during this time.

The find of a previously unknown stock of a valuable resource, such as oil, is an obvious alternative source of disinflationary pressure for any particular economy, and is clearly of relevance to the UK in the 1970s and 1980s. This will allow a rise in the exchange rate consistent with no change in the trade balance, and therefore will put downward pressure on the domestic inflation rate.

A broadly similar situation arises if a domestic technological advance gives the domestic economy a competitive advantage, albeit temporary, over its main international competitors. This is likely to have a downward effect on inflation through other routes as well as the exchange rate, as the implied rise in actual productivity is likely to reduce the real wage pressure in the labour market for a while.

Government policy may also have beneficial disinflationary effects. A deliberate contraction of the public sector, involving reductions in public expenditure and in overall taxation (defence spending), would put downward pressure on inflation, other things being equal. However, if the services that were no longer provided by the public sector had to be purchased from the private sector (medical services, say), then there would be an offsetting upward pressure on wage settlements (discussed in section 8.5).

REFERENCES

Dornbusch, R. (1985) *Purchasing Power Parity*, National Bureau of Economic Research Working Paper No. 1590.

Keynes, J. M. (1940) *How to Pay for the War*, Macmillan, London.

Tylecote, A. (1981) *The Causes of the Present Inflation*, Macmillan, London and Basingstoke.

ENDNOTES

1. In practice there may be some discrete jumps due to the tendency for prices of many goods to be increased on the same day (1 January, for example) or when a price that represents a substantial component of the individual's disposable income is increased (mortgage interest payments, for example).
2. Dornbusch (1985).
3. It is also true that persisting deflationary pressure would lead to a downward inflation spiral. But on one interpretation, inflationary pressure is caused by the labour market attempting to obtain an inequitable share of a national cake that varies in size with productivity, the terms of trade and so on. This being so, consistent downward pressure is less likely to occur than consistent upward pressure.
4. If the inflationary pressure were a continuing situation then competitiveness would deteriorate progressively and, in order to hold the foreign exchange market in equilibrium the policy measures taken would have to increase in intensity continuously.

7

Determinants of inflation in the UK

7.1 INTRODUCTION

The empirical model listed in Chapter 5, derived from the analysis described in the earlier chapters, has been used to allocate the path of producer output price inflation between the factors identified as affecting the inflation spiral. This chapter reports the results.

Section 7.2 describes the methodology used. In section 7.3 an overview of the main results is given, along with a discussion of the allocation to domestic and foreign influences. Sections 7.4, 7.5 and 7.6 examine what can be said with reasonable confidence regarding the contributions of the markets for goods and services, for labour and for foreign exchange, and about the contributions given by the influences operating in each market. Section 7.7 presents the main conclusions.

Appendix 7A contains an update of the analysis, based on the same equations and using data to 1991Q2, but using only readily available data series.

7.2 ALLOCATION OF UK INFLATION TO SOURCES

7.2.1 Introduction

The allocation of the path of UK inflation to exogenous influences has taken the form of two related exercises, both using the Inflation Spiral Equation. The first, which for convenience has been called the 'direct reduced form analysis', looks at the contribution to domestic price inflation (Δp, the dependent variable of the ISE) from each of the variables that appear on the right-hand side of the equation (exogenous variables such as world price inflation in world currencies, Δp_f^w and Δp_c^w, and the factors incorporated into the variables labelled X, and lagged domestic price inflation). The second, which has been called the 'indirect reduced form analysis', is exactly the same except that each occurrence of lagged domestic price inflation on the right-hand side of the equation has been substituted out using a lagged version of the ISE. This leaves the equation explaining domestic price

Table 7.1 The reduced form* (variable reference numbers in parenthesis)

I Domestic price equation	II Unit labour costs	III Wage equation	IV RPI equation	V Import prices equation	VI Exchange rate equation
Price inflation ------> unit lab costs ------>	earnings ------>	RPI (lagged) ------>	lag dom prices (23)		
	productivity† (8)	retention ratio (11)	real admin prices (24)		
	labour taxes (9)	productivity (12)	VAT rate (25)		
	discrepancy (10)	import costs ⎫	real inc tax (26)		
		compet prices ⎬	interest rate (27)		
		lag dom prices (13)	discrepancy** (28)		
		labour tax rate (14)		real commod prices (29)	
		unemploy level (15)		world prices (30)	
		unemploy change (16)		exchange rate - - - - ->	lag dom prices (37)
		profit level (17)		domestic price (31)	world prices (38)
		real wage diseq (18)		residual (32)	rel int rate (dir) (39)
		lab mkt premium (19)			underlying flows (40)
		IP dummies (20)			real oil price (41)
		Clegg dummy etc (21)			rel int rate (ind) (42)
		residual (22)			remainder# (43)
import costs ⎫				real commod prices (33)	
compet prices ⎬				world prices (34)	
lag dom prices (1)				exchange rate - - - - ->	lag dom prices (44)
real admin prices (2)				domestic price (35)	world prices (45)
real unit tax (3)				residual (36)	rel int rate (dir) (46)
activity (4)					underlying flows (47)
cap util level (5)					real oil price (48)
price diseq (6)					rel int rate (ind) (49)
residual (7)					remainder# (50)

* Arrows indicate columns containing the variables in the equations substituted for endogenous variables in the price equation.

† The unit labour cost term is a linear combination of whole economy and manufacturing sector unit labour costs. This variable is therefore a weighted average of whole economy and manufacturing sector productivity.

** This discrepancy incorporates the difference between the rate of increase of producer output prices and four components of the RPI: food prices; "other" housing costs; non-food, non-housing private sector prices; the mortgage debt outstanding.

Includes disequilibrium term and residual.

inflation in terms of long lags on the exogenous variables only (world price inflation and real variables).

7.2.2 The 'direct' reduced form

The ISE was derived in Chapter 5 from equations 5.1, 5.2, 5.3 and 5.4. The result, equation 5.9, is reproduced here:

$$\Delta p = \psi(L)\Delta p + \phi(L)\Delta p_f^w + \theta(L)\{\Delta p_c^w - \Delta p_f^w\} + g(L, X) \qquad (7.1)$$

The detailed form of the substitution that led to this equation, and its implications for the variables which are included in the ISE and modelled as impinging on the inflation spiral, is summarized in Table 7.1, described below.

- In Column I of Table 7.1 the variables in the structural equation for price inflation (equation 5.1, derived in Chapter 2) are listed. In deriving the direct reduced form we have substituted for three of the terms in this equation: those in changes in unit labour costs, changes in import costs and changes in competitors' prices.
- Column II shows the variables that are combined to make up the term in the change in unit labour costs which occurs in the structural equation for price inflation (section 2.4.3). Only one of these variables is endogenous to the spiral, and substituted out in the reduced form equation: average earnings growth.
- Column III lists the determinants of average earnings increases given the model equation (equation 5.3) derived in Chapter 3. In the ISE these variables are substituted for the average earnings growth variable in the term in unit labour costs changes. Three of the variables in this equation are endogenous to the spiral: the (lagged) change in the RPI, import cost inflation and the change in competitors' prices.
- The determinants of the (lagged) change in the RPI (see Appendix 2A), which are substituted into the equation for average earnings, are listed in Column IV. The rise in the producer output price (the lagged domestic price rise variable) is, of course, an important explanatory variable, so this introduces into the ISE a substantial contribution from the lagged dependent variable.
- Column V shows that the determinants of changes in the sterling value of world prices (which occur both as input costs and as competitors' prices and are relevant to both the price equation and the earnings equation) are changes in the exchange rate (which is endogenous to the spiral) and changes in world prices (exogenous). There is also a slight effect from lagged changes in domestic prices (see Appendix 2B).
- Column VI lists the variables that replace the change in the exchange rate in the ISE, given the equation derived in Chapter 4 (equation 5.4). This again contains a contribution from the lagged dependent variable of the ISE (the lagged increase in the producer output price index).

In the 'direct reduced form analysis' we look at the contribution to price inflation (the dependent variable) from each term in the ISE, the equation that results after

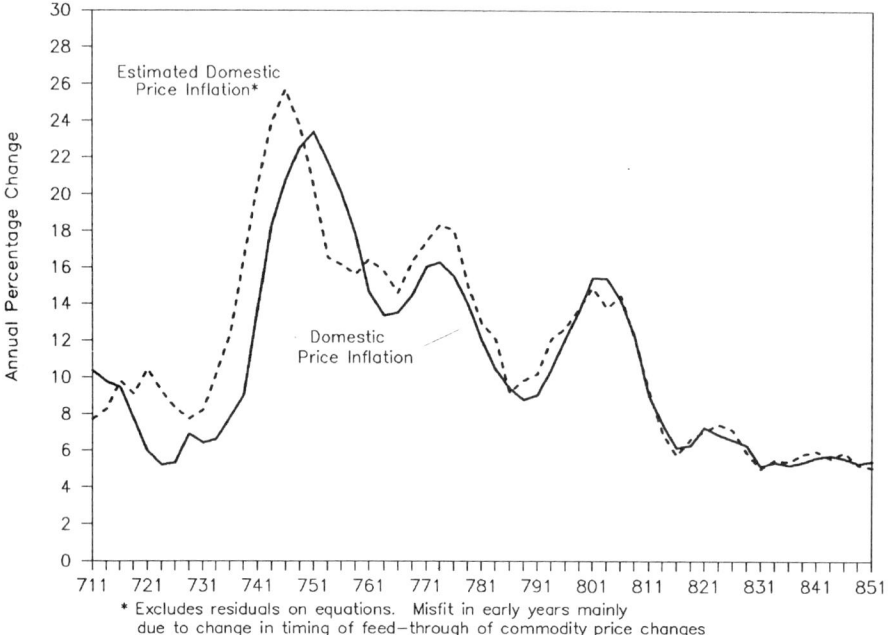

Fig. 7.1 Track of inflation spiral equation.

substitution for all the variables endogenous to the spiral, as in Table 7.1. As shown in Table 7.1, there are 50 terms in the ISE, and many of these are weighted sums of lags of an exogenous explanatory variable. In some cases one explanatory variable occurs in more than one of the terms in the equation; thus the real commodity price variable occurs twice, in term 29 and in term 33. This arises when a variable operates on price setting through more than one channel. Real commodity prices operate on price-setting indirectly, affecting unit labour costs through their influence on wage bargaining (because of their effect on profits), and more directly, as a cost to the productive process. In both cases they operate through the filter of the exchange rate.

The terms cited in the table can be collected together in different ways in order to answer different questions about the path of inflation. For example, the contribution of lagged domestic inflation can be separated from the contributions of all the other factors in order to examine the extent of inertia in the spiral, or the net effect of productivity changes can be looked at.

Figure 7.1 shows the contributions of all the terms except the residuals on the estimated equations. The misfit in the early years is largely due to the change in the timing of the feed-through of a rise in real commodity prices; this has shortened during the period investigated.

7.2.3 The 'indirect' reduced form

The indirect reduced form analysis is based on equation 5.11. This is derived from equation 5.9 (listed above as equation 7.1) by transforming it in the following way:

$$\Delta p = (1 - \psi(L))^{-1}[\phi(L)\Delta p_f^w + \theta(L)\{\Delta p_c^w - \Delta p_f^w\} + g(L, X)]$$
$$= \sum_j \beta_j L^j [\phi(L)\Delta p_f^w + \theta(L)(\Delta p_c^w - \Delta p_f^w) + g(L, X)] \qquad (7.2)$$

The indirect reduced form analysis thus allocates the contribution of the sum of all the lagged domestic price inflation terms in equation 7.1 to the exogenous factors that, according to the model, have determined it. This allows us to calculate the long-term contributions to price inflation of each of the exogenous factors that affect the domestic inflation spiral, world price inflation and the real exogenous pressures.

The sum on the right hand side of equation 7.2 has, in fact, an infinite number of terms. It follows that with only a finite number of lags of data included, the equality will not hold exactly. The degree of inertia in the spiral is so great[1] that it was found necessary to include over 70 values of the β_j's in equation 7.2 in order to get within about 5 per cent of equality between the two sides of equation 7.2 by the end of the period considered (1986). Allowing, also, for the lags in the

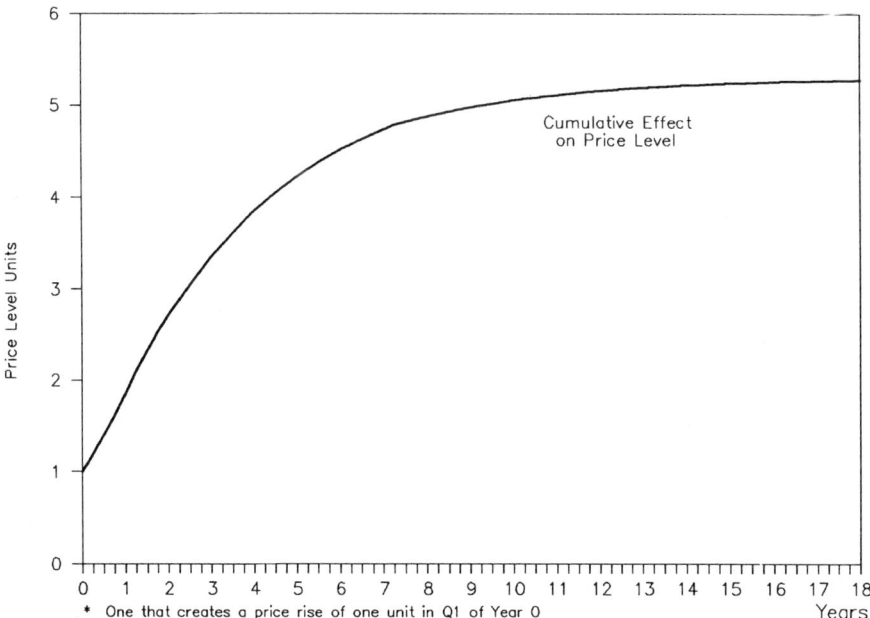

* One that creates a price rise of one unit in Q1 of Year 0

Fig. 7.2 Effect of an inflationary shock.

structural model, reasonably reliable back data were obtained for all the explanatory variables so as to allow predictions of price inflation to be analysed from 1969Q4 using equation 7.2. The inaccuracies resulting from this approach are indicated at the bottom of Table 7.3.

The results of the calculations underlying this indirect reduced form analysis indicate that, with the model developed here (which has a coefficient of 0.5 on the relative price effect in the exchange rate equation) the sum of the β_j parameters in equation 7.2 is $5\frac{1}{2}$ (it is equal to $1/(1-0.82)$, where 0.82 is the sum of the coefficients on lagged price inflation):

$$\sum_j \beta_j = 5.5 \tag{7.3}$$

That is, the long-term effect of an inflationary shock on the domestic price level is to raise it by about $5\frac{1}{2}$ times the size of the direct, first round, effect (ignoring any feed-back from inflation exported to the rest of the world). This results from the inertia associated with the inflation spiral. Further, according to this model it takes about $2\frac{1}{2}$ years for half of the full effect of an inflationary shock to come through. Figure 7.2 indicates the cumulated effect of the β parameters on the price level.

7.3 OVERVIEW OF RESULTS

An important conclusion that can be drawn from both the direct and the indirect reduced form analysis of the ISE is that the profile of domestic price inflation has been heavily influenced by changes in real commodity prices.

Figures 7.3 and 7.4 show the contributions to domestic price inflation from all of the factors listed in Table 7.1 using the direct reduced form analysis. For the purpose of these charts these factors have been collected into four groups:

(i) all the factors involving lagged domestic inflation: this is the variable $\psi(L)\Delta p$ in equation 7.1, and consists of the sum of the variables 1, 13, 23, 31, 35, 37 and 44 of Table 7.1;

(ii) all the terms in world finished goods price inflation in overseas currencies: this is the term $\phi(L)\Delta p_f^w$ in equation 7.1 and consists of the sum of variables 30, 34, 38, and 45 of Table 7.1;

(iii) all the terms in changes in real primary commodity prices: this is the term $\theta(L)(\Delta p_c^w - \Delta p_f^w)$ in equation 7.1. It consists of the sum of variables 29 and 33 of Table 7.1; and,

(iv) the rest: this is the sum of all the real pressures that operate on the inflation rate and cumulate over time, that is, the term $g(L, X)$ in equation 7.1. It is therefore the sum of all the remaining variables in Table 7.1, including the residuals on the price, wage, import price and exchange rate equations (variables 7, 22, 32, 36, 43, 50) and the small discrepancies (variables 10 and 28) as well as the terms reflecting economic variables such as activity or changes in real unit taxes.

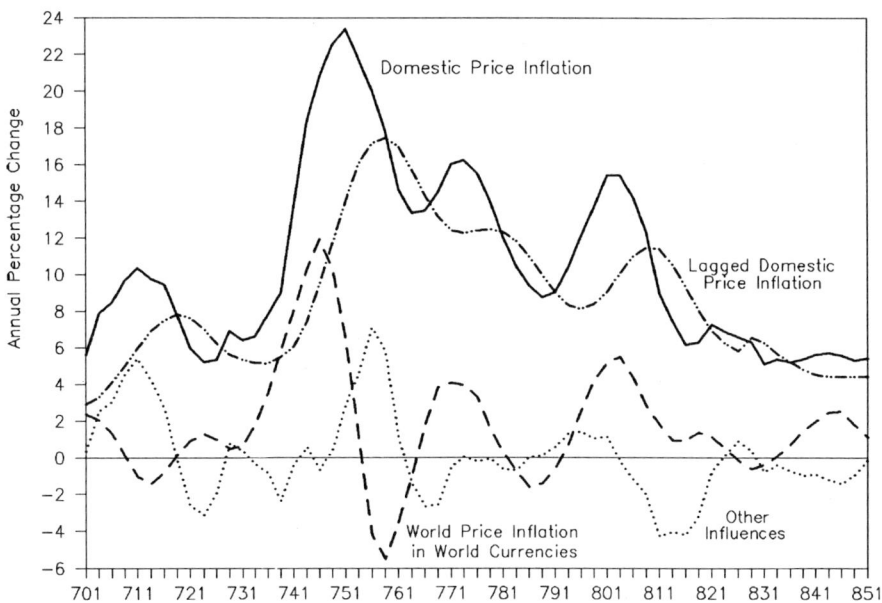

Fig. 7.3 Contributions to domestic price inflation.

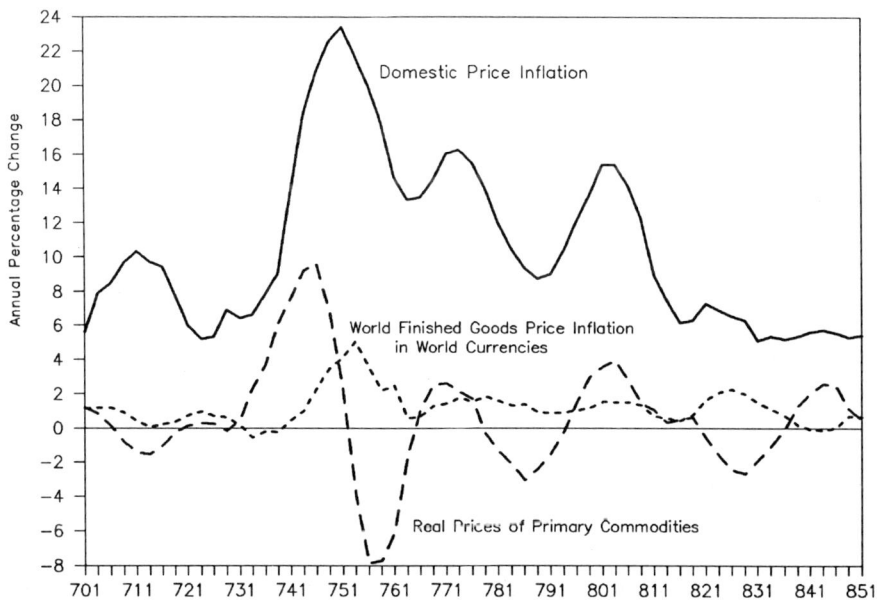

Fig. 7.4 Influence of world prices in world currencies.

The factors included in the fourth category are mainly domestic in origin. But influences on the sterling exchange rate other than the relative price terms are included, and so are the residuals on the import price equations. These obviously may, to some extent, reflect factors that have their origins in the rest of the world.

Figure 7.3 shows the path of producer output price inflation over the period from 1970Q1 to 1985Q1 alongside the paths of the factors listed in Table 7.1 collected into three groups. In this case the groups are: lagged domestic inflation (the inertia effect) group (i) above, world price inflation in world currencies groups (ii) and (iii) (in this chart these are not separated into the component parts), and the rest, group (iv).

It is clear from this chart that the turning points of domestic price inflation during the period under consideration relate closely to the path of world price rises in world currencies, and are therefore largely determined by events in the rest of the world. It is also clear that throughout the period the level of inflation in the UK has been heavily influenced by the level of past price inflation feeding through the spiral.

In Figure 7.4 the contribution to domestic price inflation from world price rises in world currencies is divided between real commodity price changes (commodity price rises in world currencies minus the rate of increase of finished goods prices in world currencies) and the rate of increase of world finished goods' prices in world currencies. It is clear from this that it is the changes in real commodity prices that have been driving the turning points in UK domestic price inflation. Further, the chart suggests that price inflation in other countries responds to commodity prices in a manner broadly similar to that of UK prices. The UK is both importing and exporting this effect, which is travelling around the world inflation spiral.

Figure 7.3 also shows the path of net (mainly) domestic inflationary pressure over the period. It is interesting to note that, whereas this tended to be positive on average through the 1970s, it became negative around 1980 and remained so for most of the time until around the middle of the decade. This changing domestic pressure is allocated among the individual markets (and insofar as it is reasonable, the individual factors involved in each market) in the later sections of this chapter.

The question that arises next is: how is this allocation of inflationary influences between world inflation, real commodity prices and domestic pressures affected when we abstract from the role of lagged domestic inflation by substituting its determinants according to the model?

Figure 7.5 shows the cumulated contributions of world price rises in world currencies and of the other factors (mainly domestic) to the path of domestic price inflation according to the analysis summarized in equation 7.2. That is, the 'indirect' reduced form approach has been used and distributed lags of Δp_f^w, Δp_c^w and the X_i have been substituted for the terms in lagged domestic inflation $\psi(L)\Delta p$ in equation 7.1. It suggests that world price inflation in world currencies has been of far greater importance than domestic factors over the period considered.

Figure 7.6 shows the cumulated contribution of world price rises in world

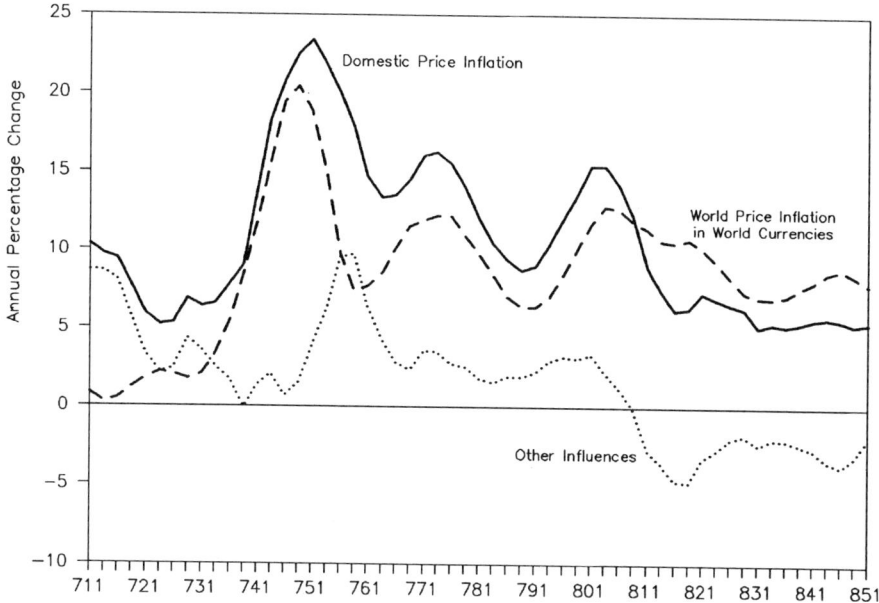

Fig. 7.5 Cumulated contributions to price inflation.

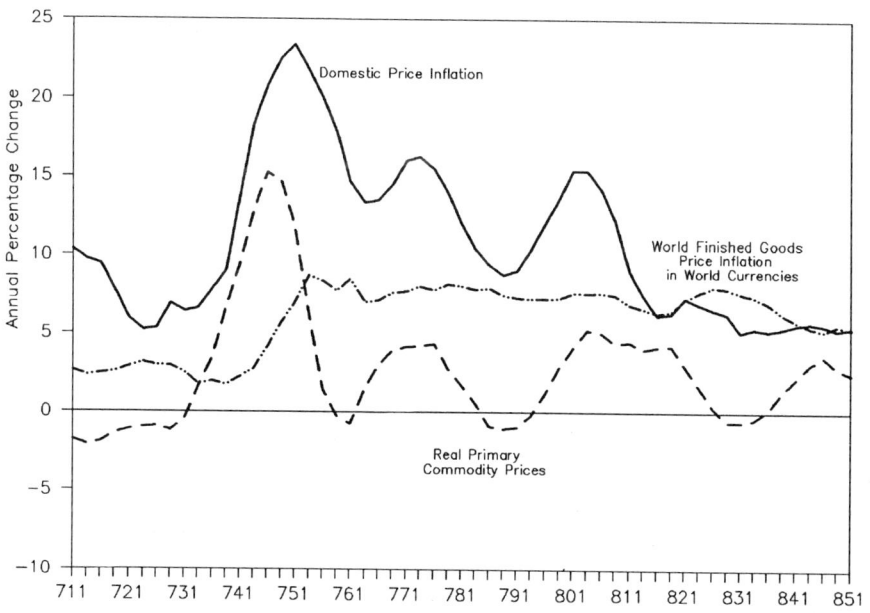

Fig. 7.6 Cumulated effect of world prices.

currencies split between the contributions of changes in real commodity prices and changes in world finished goods prices in world currencies. These figures, like Figures 7.3 and 7.4, demonstrate clearly the influence of changes in real commodity prices on the profile of domestic inflation. Further, they also suggest that the main effect of world finished goods price inflation has been to determine the underlying level of the domestic inflation rate. Like Figure 7.3, Figure 7.5 also suggests that domestic pressures augmented inflation in the 1970s but have exerted downward pressure in the early 1980s.

The next question concerns the robustness of these results. To what extent do the coefficient values and lags depend on well-determined estimates or acceptable priors and to what extent are they subject to estimation uncertainty and so to the vagaries of the data series involved and to the inevitable measurement errors affecting economic data? We would argue that these results, unlike some of those presented later in this chapter, are pretty robust. First, in estimating the price equation the split between the contributions of labour costs and world prices in domestic currencies is determined by input–output coefficients, rather than by the 'best' estimate provided by the particular manifestation of the data used. Further, these input–output shares are easily accepted by the data. Although the input–output constraints imposed are undoubtedly inappropriate, to some extent at least, over some parts of the period, the fact that these constraints have been imposed lends more credibility to the allocation in the charts than if they had depended on 'best' estimates from one sample of data.

Second, because the allocation depends on the modelling of the spiral's inertia it depends on the assumption of no money illusion that underlies the dynamic homogeneity constraints that were analysed in Chapter 6.

The allocation of inflationary pressures shown in the charts, and the conclusions that follow concerning the sources of UK inflation, depend mainly on this assumption and the input–output constraint. There are two further assumptions involved. One relates to the coefficient imposed on competitors' prices in the price equation. This affects the size of the total allocation to labour costs and material costs, but not the relative allocation which is determined by the input–output coefficients. The other concerns the arbitrarily chosen coefficient on relative price inflation in the equation for the exchange rate set at 0.5. The effect of these is investigated in Figures 7.7 and 7.8.

In Figure 7.7 the coefficient on relative price inflation in the exchange rate equation is varied between zero and one (the value in the model used for the analysis in the rest of this chapter is 0.5).[2] This shows that this coefficient affects the level of the contribution of world price inflation to the domestic inflation rate. If the coefficient on relative price inflation should, in fact, have been set at zero, then the effect of the domestic inflationary factors has been overestimated by our analysis.

Figure 7.8 shows the effect on the contribution of world prices in the 'direct' analysis of varying the long-term coefficient on competitors' prices in the price equation between 0 and 0.2 (its size in the version of the model used for the analysis

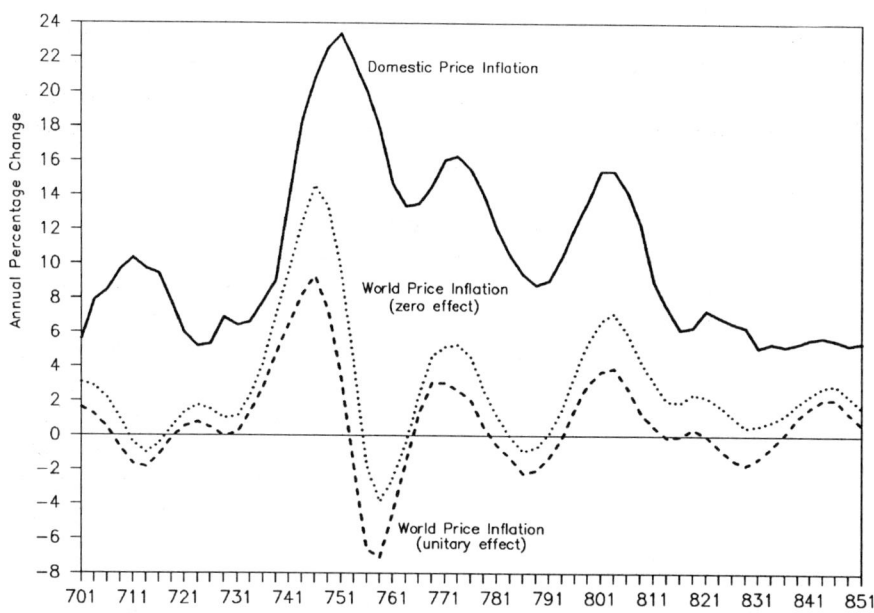

Fig. 7.7 Varying effect of relative prices on exchange rate.

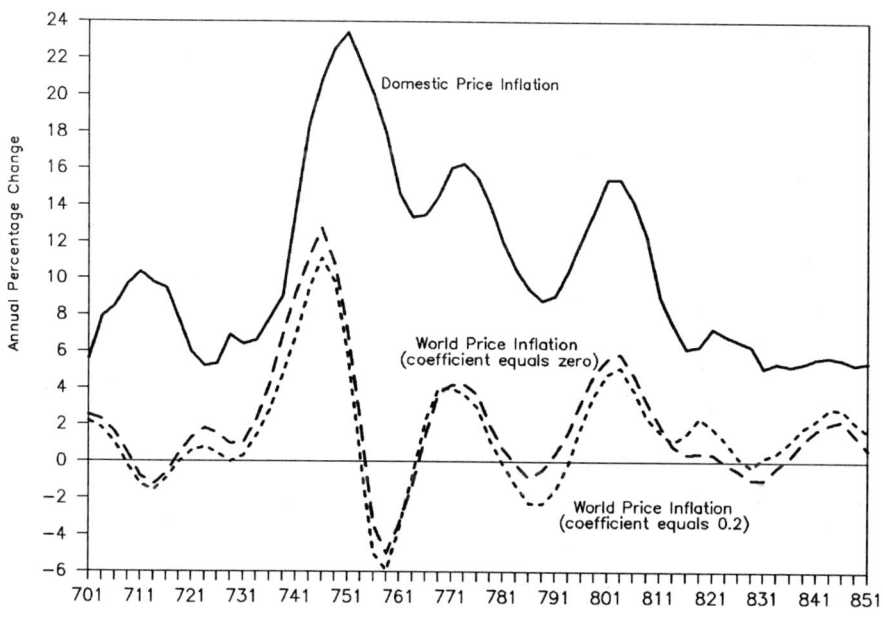

Fig. 7.8 Varying effect of competitors' prices.

in the rest of this chapter is 0.1). The allocation of domestic price inflation between world prices and the other determining factors is not much affected in this case.

We conclude that the finding that most of the turning points in domestic price inflation have been related to those in world commodity price inflation during the period examined (with the timing affected by domestic policy initiatives) is remarkably robust.

Tables 7.2 and 7.3 present the data underlying Figures 7.3, 7.4 and 7.5 in a different way. They summarize the contributions of the various markets to the rise in domestic prices over a number of periods. These have been chosen to relate to the cycle of inflation in recent years.

Table 7.2 shows that the main determinant of price inflation through most of the period has been lagged domestic inflation. This has an aggregate weight of 0.82 in the ISE as a result of the assumptions concerning dynamic homogeneity. There is a small upward pressure added from world price inflation, which picks up the remaining weight of 0.18. Not surprisingly we find that in the two periods 1973–75 and 1979–81 rapid rises in real primary commodity prices added significantly to the domestic inflation rate.

The contribution of the domestic market for goods and services has generally been small but variable. However, during the period 1979–81 it seems to have exerted a significant counter-inflationary influence.

The import price residuals are treated separately in this table because their contribution is not negligible and it is not clear where they belong. Their magnitude is partly attributable to the rigidity of a model such as this. We believe they may be picking up the effect of variations in the lag with which overseas prices affect sterling prices (it appears to have become shorter). If so, they indicate uncertainties in the timing of the overseas price effects.

Table 7.2 Summary of contributions to domestic inflation from 'direct' analysis

| | percentage rise in price levels between final quarters of years shown | | | | |
	1969–73	1973–75	1975–79	1979–81	1981–85
Lagged domestic inflation	21.9	20.1	50.9	20.5	21.3
World price inflation	2.7	5.1	4.9	2.5	4.0
Real commodity price changes	0.3	9.4	−4.7	4.6	−0.1
Labour market influences*	2.9	4.1	−6.6	6.9	−5.6
(of which incomes policy)	(0.5)	(−0.8)	(−8.0)	(1.2)	(0.0)
Foreign exchange market*	−0.3	3.9	3.8	−6.5	6.1
Domestic goods market*	0.3	−1.9	1.6	−2.3	0.2
Import price residuals	0.6	−3.6	1.9	−1.2	−1.9
Total	28.4	37.1	51.8	24.4	24.0
(Period)	(4 yrs)	(2 yrs)	(4 yrs)	(2 yrs)	(4 yrs)

*In each case the residual on the relevant equation is included.

Table 7.3 Summary of contribution to domestic inflation from 'indirect' analysis

	percentage rise in price levels between final quarters of years shown				
	1969–73	1973–75	1975–79	1979–81	1981–85
World price inflation	9.2	12.0	28.6	14.3	25.4
Real commodity price changes	−2.5	18.4	7.0	8.8	7.8
Labour market influences*	7.0	5.3	−4.6	6.7	−3.7
Foreign exchange market*	8.9	10.7	24.1	−5.5	4.0
Domestic goods market*	−4.8	−2.6	−4.7	2.4	−4.5
Import price residuals	7.0	−7.9	−0.7	−3.0	−6.1
Column sum**	24.8	35.8	49.7	23.7	22.9
Total	28.4	37.1	51.8	24.4	24.0
(Period)	(4 yrs)	(2 yrs)	(4 yrs)	(2 yrs)	(4 yrs)

*In each case the residual on the equation is included.
**The domestic price inflation figure, labelled 'Total', differs from the column sum because only a finite number of terms is included, see section 7.2.3.

If the effect of incomes policies (as represented in our model) is netted off the labour market contribution, then the labour market has increased inflation in all the periods cited except the most recent. The estimated effect of the 'social contract' of the late 1970s is considerable.

The foreign exchange market created significant upward pressure on inflation in the period 1973 to 1980 and has had a powerful influence on the profile of inflation in the early 1980s, beneficial at the beginning of the 1980s and inflationary thereafter.

Table 7.3 presents the same data as in Table 7.2 but using the 'indirect' analysis. Among other things it indicates the cumulative effect that changes in real commodity prices seem to have on the prices of finished goods in the rest of the world. A substantial role in influencing UK inflation is allocated to factors affecting the exchange rate (other than the relative price inflation variable which is, of course, excluded from the foreign exchange market allocation with a coefficient of 0.5). These include the effect of the stance of fiscal and monetary policy on foreign exchange market operators' expectations.

7.4 CONTRIBUTIONS FROM LABOUR MARKET

7.4.1 Methodology

Figure 7.9 shows the effect on inflation of labour market influences using the direct reduced form analysis summarized in equation 7.1. That is, it presents the effect on producer price inflation of the factors subsumed into 'X_3' of equation 5.3

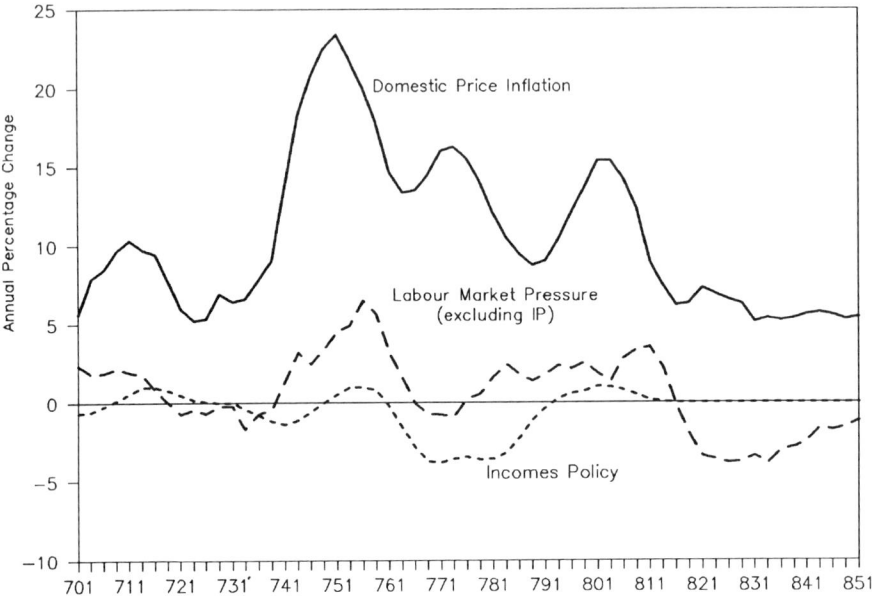

Fig. 7.9 Effect of labour market pressure.

along with the effect labour productivity and labour taxes have as a consequence of their role in the unit labour cost term.

Two points should be noted about the construction of the series shown in the figure. First, in practice it is the RPI that influences the employees' side of wage increases, not the producer output price index (the path of which we are attempting to explain). It follows that if the RPI rises at a slower (or faster) rate than producer output prices this will result in downward (or upward) pressure on producer price inflation operating as a result of the labour market influences. This has not been treated as a labour market influence in this figure; its effect is shown in Figure 7.11.

Second, in the steady state wages will rise faster than prices by the trend rate of productivity growth; indeed, a series for trend productivity growth is included in the wage equation. As a result it seems appropriate to include in the series plotted in Figure 7.9 the downward influence on price inflation that comes through productivity rises reducing unit labour costs in the price equation. As we shall see below, the variable used here is a weighted average of actual productivity growth in manufacturing and in the economy taken as a whole. The variable plotted in Figures 7.9 and 7.10 as representing 'labour market pressure' is therefore the sum of variable 8 and variables 11 to 22 in Table 7.1 excluding variable 20; it includes the residual on the wage equation. The variable labelled 'incomes policy' (variable 20 of Table 7.1) includes the effect of both policy and catch-up as estimated in the wage equation.

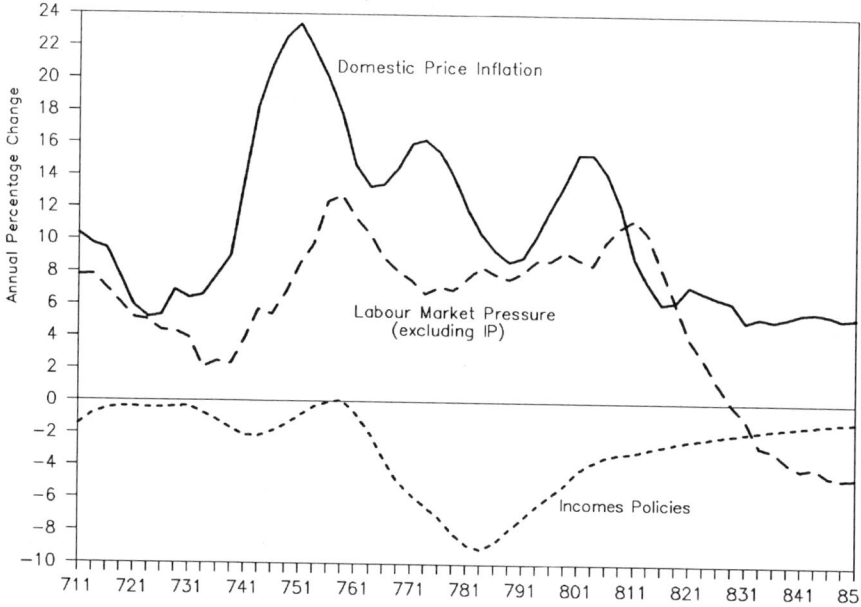

Fig. 7.10 Cumulated labour market pressure.

Figure 7.10 shows the cumulated contributions of the labour market (including the productivity term, variable 8, and excluding the estimated effect of incomes policy, variable 20) according to the indirect reduced form analysis summarized in equation 7.2. That is, it shows the cumulated sums of lags of these variables weighted by the β_i values.

7.4.2 Limitations of the analysis

Table 7.4 shows the breakdown of the contribution of the labour market influences on inflation in the direct reduced form analysis, given the estimated version of the wage equation, in the same periods as were used in Tables 7.2 and 7.3. Clearly this breakdown within the labour market is far less robust than the allocation of the influences on inflation between the markets. (The latter depends on input–output coefficients, on the assumption of dynamic homogeneity in labour and goods markets and on the values of the coefficients which are investigated in Figures 7.7 and 7.8.)

If this breakdown into factors within the labour market had been considered robust then it might have been possible to carry the analysis further. For example, an attempt could have been made to take the effect on inflation which this analysis attributes to domestic market disequilibria and allocate it back to the domestic policy variables that created the disequilibrium in the first place. In fact, we took

Table 7.4 Contributions of labour market to domestic inflation using 'direct' reduced form analysis*

	percentage rise in price levels between final quarters of years shown				
	1969–73	1973–75	1975–79	1979–81	1981–85
Deviation of productivity from trend (V8 + V12)	−0.9	0.8	0.0	2.8	−6.3
Level of unemployment** (V15)	6.7	4.1	2.1	0.6	−5.8
Change in unemployment** (V16)	0.2	1.0	−1.0	−0.7	0.1
Level of profits (V17)	5.1	3.1	0.6	1.6	−3.7
Real wage disequilibrium (V18)	−1.0	−2.2	1.2	0.3	2.8
Tax rate (V11 + V14)	0.9	0.4	0.9	−0.8	1.2
Labour market premium (V19)	2.0	1.0	2.0	1.0	2.0
Incomes policies (V20)	0.5	−0.8	−8.0	1.2	0.0
Residual and dummies (V21 + V22)	−10.8	−2.9	−3.2	0.1	1.9
Total	2.7	4.3	−5.4	6.1	−7.7
Total *excluding* incomes policies (row 10 − row 8)	2.2	5.1	2.6	4.9	−7.7
RPI effect	0.3	−0.2	−1.1	0.8	2.2
Total including RPI effect [+] (row 10 + row 12)	3.0	4.1	−6.5	6.9	−5.5

*Variable numbers in parentheses refer to Table 7.1.
**Percentage of labour force unemployed for 12 months or less.
[+]Included in Table 7.2 as 'labour market influence' apart from rounding.

the view that, because of the inevitable uncertainty in the allocation of the labour market pressure between the explanatory variables, the results of such an analysis would be of little value.

7.4.3 Profile of total labour market pressure

The series plotted in Figure 7.9 indicate that whereas the labour market exerted upward pressure on price inflation almost continuously through the 1970s, partially offset by the successful incomes policies of the 1975 to 1978 period, there was a sharp change in 1981. From 1981 to the mid-1980s the labour market exerted a downward influence which progressively declined in intensity.

7.4.4 Effect of incomes policies

Figures 7.9 and 7.10 indicate the importance, given the model presented here, of maintaining an incomes policy for more than one year. This means that its effect on the inflation spiral cumulates, and is not cancelled out by the catch-up effects that tend to occur at the end of a period of incomes policy.

According to our model the earlier, shorter, incomes policies only had a temporary effect on inflation; each time their effect was almost totally reversed by the catch-up. However, with a sustained incomes policy, reductions in wage inflation lead falls in price inflation with the real wage depressed below the level it would otherwise have taken throughout the period during which the policy is operative. The catch-up restores the real wage to around the level it would have been without the policy, and in doing so gives the economy an inflationary boost. However, we estimate that it only cancels out the inflationary effect of one round of the policy. The remaining effect of the policy feeds through the spiral, putting a cumulating downward pressure on inflation.

7.4.5 Role of unemployment

The second and fourth rows of Table 7.4 are derived as deviations of data from the average value during the period 1973Q1 to 1985Q4 (Chapter 5). Little else can be done in the absence of a reasonably acceptable model of the 'non-accelerating inflation' levels of short-term unemployment and profits. The effect of this arbitrary and rather mechanical transformation can be seen in the path of the residual in the table, particularly for the period 1969–73. Indeed, without a robust model for the 'non-accelerating inflation' level of these variables it is not possible to say much about the role the levels of unemployment and profits have played in generating domestic inflation over this period.

7.4.6 Labour market premium

The value attributed to the 'real wage premium' (the average by which wage settlements have exceeded the level implied by the fundamentals) is 0.5 per cent per annum. This is derived from the intercept on the estimated equation by subtracting the average levels of short-term unemployment and profits during the period 1973Q1 to 1985Q4. As an indicator of exogenous labour market pressure, this estimate cannot, therefore, be viewed as being robust. We conclude that during this period there has, on average, been an underlying inflationary pressure in the labour market of about 0.5 per cent per annum.

After feeding through the spiral, the effect of this labour market premium would be to add just over $2\frac{1}{2}$ percentage points to the annual inflation rate. This premium, therefore, appears to have had an important upward influence on the total effect that labour market factors, net of the estimated incomes policy effect, might otherwise have had on inflation.

7.4.7 Role of productivity

Given the modelling of the effects of incomes policy, the eleventh row of Table 7.4 shows the underlying effect of the labour market on inflation during the period shown. It suggests that there was a dramatic turn-around in 1981. The analysis allocates this to a combination of the rapid growth in productivity, the high level of short-term unemployment and the low level of profits.

As noted above, the model used to generate these figures assumes that wage settlements depend on trend productivity growth (variable 12 of Table 7.1) with a unit coefficient, constrained and not rejected by the data. The data for trend productivity growth is simply a smoothed interpolation derived from the path of actual productivity. The effect of earnings growth on price-setting is offset by the actual rate of increase in productivity (variable 8 of Table 1), with a coefficient equal and opposite to that on wages growth. Actual productivity is derived as a weighted average of productivity in manufacturing and in the economy as a whole, with the weights derived from input–output analysis. The model therefore suggests that deviations of actual from trend productivity can have an influence on inflation. This will presumably be short-lived, since expectations of trend productivity growth will reflect the historical path of actual productivity growth.

7.4.8 Relative price effect

The downward influence of the RPI shown in Table 7.4 for 1975–79 (see also Figure 7.11) was mainly the result of prices that are included in the RPI but do not affect the producer price index. For example, the producer price index excludes food, drink and tobacco; food prices are included in the RPI and they have been rising less fast than prices generally during this period. The upward pressure from the RPI in 1981–85 reflects real rises in nationalized industry prices.

7.4.9 Conclusion

It is clear from the above discussion that the allocation of the contribution to inflation from the labour market between alternative sources is not robust. The contribution attributed to the terms in unemployment and in profits depends on the assumption about their non-accelerating inflation levels; the striking role of productivity growth depends on the assumption that trend productivity affects wage settlements while actual productivity influences price setting; the value taken by the labour market premium is highly uncertain and constrained to be constant by the mechanical nature of the exercise undertaken.

Whereas the estimate of the total influence of the labour market on inflation seems quite robust, little can be said with any confidence about the role of individual terms. It is difficult, therefore, to be confident about the effect of fiscal or monetary policy on inflation. The effect of incomes policy, on the other hand, seems rather more robust.

7.5 CONTRIBUTIONS FROM GOODS MARKET

Figure 7.11 shows the contribution of the goods market to the rate of inflation according to the 'direct' approach. It shows the sum of the contributions from

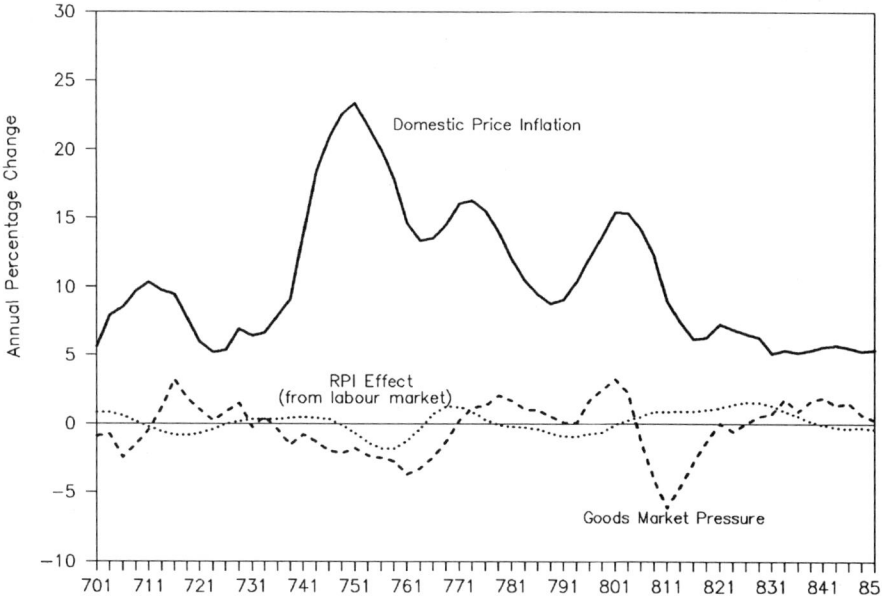

Fig. 7.11 Effect of goods market pressure.

variables 2 to 7 and variable 9 of Table 7.1. This includes the effect of changes in real unit taxes and administered prices and the effect of changes in the margin. This figure also shows the effect of the fact that the RPI often rises at a slightly different rate from that of producer output prices (the RPI effect in the chart is the sum of variables 24 to 28 in Table 7.1). The RPI effect varies in direction and has no long-term influence.

Figure 7.11 indicates that during the period examined, after netting off the effect of costs and of competitors' prices, the goods market has exerted a slight downward pressure on inflation. Figure 7.12 shows the cumulated effect on inflation of the pressures operating through the goods market, and confirms this. Table 7.5 provides a more detailed breakdown. It shows the analysis of the contribution of the goods market to domestic inflation in the 'direct' analysis, given the price equation incorporated into the ISE.

The contribution of the goods market to domestic inflation over this period has not been large and the allocation shown in Table 7.5 is not robust, as is evidenced by the relatively large contribution of the residual. (The 'residual' in this table incorporates the deviation of the lagged price level from the weighted average of lagged costs and competitors' prices; the residual on the estimated equation is the larger of the two components.)

The most striking features of the table are the apparently large influence of the fall in manufacturing output in the 1979–81 period, the downward influence of

Table 7.5 Contributions of goods market to domestic inflation using 'direct' reduced form analysis*

	percentage rise in price levels between final quarters of years shown				
	1969–73	1973–75	1975–79	1979–81	1981–85
Change in activity (V4)	1.6	0.2	−0.1	−3.1	1.6
Capacity utilization (V5)	2.9	1.8	−1.8	0.1	−3.5
Real administered prices (V2)	−0.4	0.4	1.2	0.3	−0.1
Tax rate (V3 + V9)	−0.9	−0.7	2.6	1.1	−1.1
Disequilibrium and residual (V6 + V7)	−2.9	−3.5	−0.2	−0.7	3.3
Total	0.3	−1.9	1.6	−2.3	0.2
(Period)	(4 yrs)	(2 yrs)	(4 yrs)	(2 yrs)	(4 yrs)

*Variable numbers in parenthesis refer to Table 7.1.

capacity utilization between 1981 and 1985, and the inflationary influence attributed to the rise in company taxes in the 1975–79 period.

7.6 CONTRIBUTIONS FROM FOREIGN EXCHANGE MARKET

Figure 7.13 shows the contribution of the foreign exchange market to the rate of inflation after netting off the contribution of relative price inflation with a coefficient of 0.5. It shows separately the estimated contributions from different terms in the equation although the breakdown is not robust.

Table 7.6 gives more detail concerning the results illustrated in Figure 7.13. The figures in the table for the effect of expectations suggest that it may have been lack of confidence that caused the depreciation of sterling in the mid-1970s; possibly this was related to a belief that the authorities wanted to see a lower real exchange rate. According to the model, this influenced the actual path of the exchange rate and led to a rise in inflation. During 1973 to 1976 the increasing effect of North Sea oil on the underlying flows is estimated to have created an offsetting downward pressure, but our model of the foreign exchange market is not sufficiently robust (given the data series that pertain) to allow an accurate assessment of the effect of this on inflation.

In the 1979–81 period the exchange rate path exerted downward pressure on inflation, ameliorating the effect of the second sharp rise in oil prices. The model suggests that the rise in the real exchange rate during this period was largely due to market sentiment driving the rate up. Indeed, this process is itself attributed partly to the oil price rise by our model. However, it may well be that the market expected the rise in oil prices to be accommodated by policy, or the market may

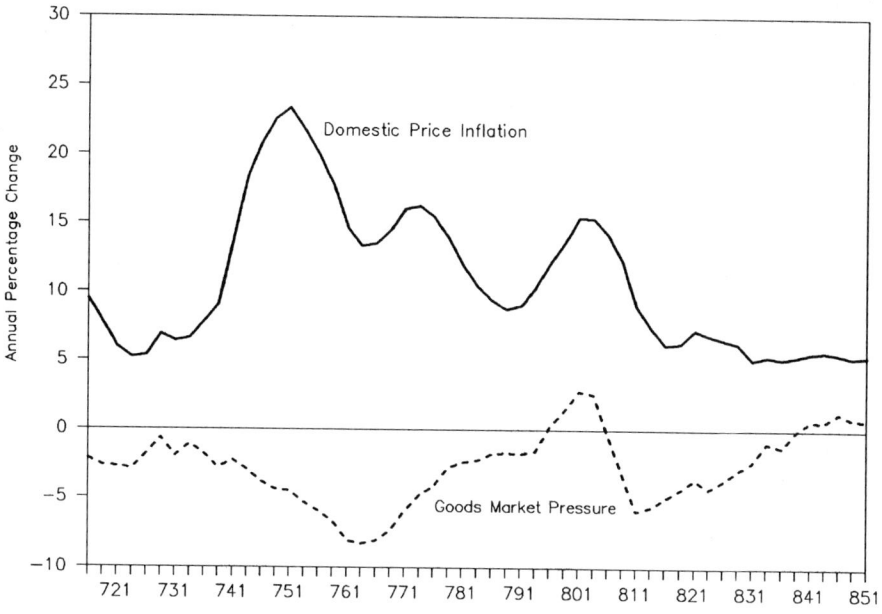

Fig. 7.12 Cumulated goods market pressure.

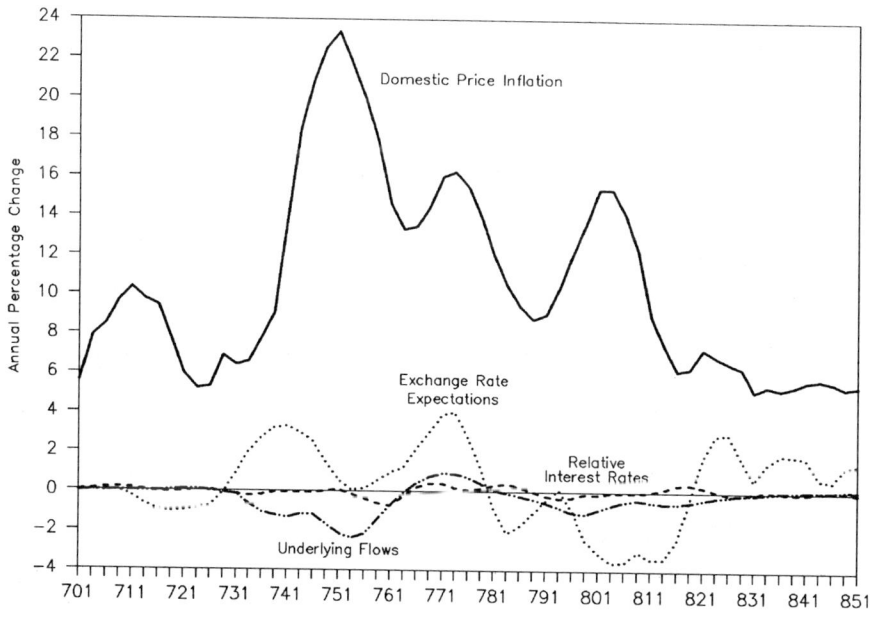

Fig. 7.13 Effect of foreign exchange market pressure.

Table 7.6 Contributions of foreign market to domestic inflation using 'direct' reduced form analysis*

	percentage rise in price levels between final quarters of years shown				
	1969–73	1973–75	1975–79	1979–81	1981–85
Relative interest rates (V39 + V46)	0.0	0.1	−0.1	−0.1	0.3
Underlying flows (V40 + V47)	−0.1	−0.6	−1.4	−0.9	−0.2
Expectations of which:					
change in real oil price (V41 + V48)	0.0	0.0	−1.2	−1.6	−0.8
relative interest rates (V42 + V49)	0.0	0.3	−0.3	−0.3	0.8
remainder (incl. residual) (V43 + V50)	−0.2	4.1	6.8	−3.6	6.0
Total	−0.3	3.9	3.8	−6.5	6.1
Relative price effect* (V37 + V38 + V44 + V45)	1.8	−0.5	4.9	2.0	0.6
Total (including relative price effect)	1.5	3.4	8.7	−4.5	6.7
(Period)	(4 yrs)	(2 yrs)	(4 yrs)	(2 yrs)	(4 yrs)

*Included in rows 1 and 2 of Table 7.2.

have envisaged oil revenues driving up the rate. Again these pressures affected the actual path of the exchange rate, which rose putting downward pressure on inflation. But in the following years there was a renewal of the upward pressure.

7.7 CONCLUSIONS

This chapter reports the results of the empirical analysis of inflation using the model described in the earlier chapters. The main conclusions drawn from this are the following (illustrated in Figures 7.3, 7.4, 7.5 and 7.6 and Tables 7.2 and 7.3):

- The turning points in domestic inflation are mainly attributed to changes in the real cost of primary commodities feeding through with a lag.
- One of the main influences on the level of inflation in the UK has been the effect of increases in the export prices of other countries' finished goods, in their own currencies, feeding into the UK domestic inflation spiral through the exchange rate.
- Domestic factors, including the effects of macroeconomic policies, are estimated to have caused increased inflation in the 1970s but to have exerted a downward influence in the early 1980s.
- On average, since the early 1970s, wage rises have been significantly larger than

warranted by productivity growth, changes in the terms of trade and changes in the level of taxes.

These conclusions rely mainly on the homogeneity assumptions and on the values taken by input–output coefficients; given these assumptions, they are robust.

APPENDIX 7A: UPDATE OF EMPIRICAL ANALYSIS

7A.1 Introduction

The data on which our analysis was based finish in 1985. It is therefore of some interest to use the model to investigate what seems, according to this analysis, to have been creating upward or downward pressure on the inflation spiral during the period since the analysis was completed.

7A.2 Methodology

For this purpose we have collected, from recent editions of *Economic Trends* and *International Financial Statistics*, data roughly appropriate for the endogenous variables in our model of the inflation spiral and the world currency world price variables. These include, from *Economic Trends*: the Producer Output Price Index (all manufactured products, Table 24), average earnings (GB, whole economy, Table 23), the Retail Prices Index (all items, Table 24), import prices (unit value indices, non-oil goods, Table A3 in March, June, September and December issues), the sterling exchange rate index and the sterling rate against the dollar (Table 28) and output per person employed (whole economy and manufacturing industry, Table 20). From *International Financial Statistics* we collected the export unit value index, industrial countries, in dollars, and the world commodity price indices for agricultural raw materials (excluding food and beverages) and for metals, both in dollars.

The equations listed in detail in Chapters 2, 3 and 4, and summarized in Chapter 5, have been used to derive, as residuals, the contributions to inflation from the various markets. The model developed earlier consists of structural equations for changes in domestic prices, Δp, the prices of imported finished goods and primary commodities in domestic currencies, Δp_f and Δp_c (both approximated here by Δp_{im}), wages, Δw, and the exchange rate, Δrx (equations 2.17, 2B.2, 3.16, 4.22). Inverting these we get the equations:

$$X_1 = \Delta p - [a(L)(\Delta w - \Delta pr) + (b(L) \mid c(L))\Delta p_{im} + d(L)\Delta p] \qquad (7A.1)$$

$$X_2 = \Delta p_{im} - e(L)(\Delta p^w - \Delta rx) - f(L)\Delta p \qquad (7A.2)$$

$$X_3 = \Delta w - [\Delta prt + g(L)\Delta p + l(L)(\Delta rpi - \Delta p) + (h(L) - j(L))\Delta p_{im}] \qquad (7A.3)$$

$$X_4 = \Delta rx - m(L)(\Delta p^w - \Delta p) \qquad (7A.4)$$

In these equations p^w represents the logarithm of prices of imported finished goods or primary commodities in world currencies, *rpi* represents the logarithm of the Retail Prices Index (important in the explanation of wage settlements), while Δpr and Δprt are logarithms of the actual and trend rates of productivity growth. The terms X_1, X_2, X_3, X_4 incorporate all the (real) variables which impinge on the inflation process in each market, causing inflation to increase or decrease, but which do not play a direct, primary role in promulgating price rises around the inflation spiral.[3] They also include the residuals on the equations. The contribution from these residuals is likely to be relatively large, as these data are outside the estimation period of the equations and the data series collected are not as carefully defined and constructed as those used in the earlier work.

Once the left-hand side variables in these equations have been calculated, a substitution similar to that described in Table 7.1 allows the contributions to inflation from eight terms to be calculated. These relate to:

lagged domestic price inflation (the inertia effect);
world prices in world currencies;
goods market pressures;
labour market pressures;
foreign exchange market pressures;
import price residuals;
the effect of the path of productivity;
the discrepancy between the RPI and the producer price index.

The paths of most of these are shown in the attached figures. In order to construct the figures showing effects over a long period we have attached the new data to the earlier series.

7A.3 RESULTS

(a) Summary

Figure 7A.1 shows the summary of the results in the same form as in Figure 7.3. There are three main conclusions to be drawn. First, this again indicates the substantial effect lagged domestic inflation has on the current level (the weights on lags of domestic price inflation sum to 0.82). Second, the contribution of world price inflation over the recent period (1985 to 1991) has averaged close to zero (the weight on this is 0.18). Third, the average contribution of domestic factors has been to increase the inflation rate.

In Figure 7A.2 we look at the results of the 'indirect' reduced form analysis for the entire period from 1971 to 1991. This shows that there was a dramatic fall in the contribution from domestic factors in the early 1980s turning into upward pressure around 1987. The cumulated effect of world inflation was about 2 to 4 per cent in the late 1980s, but cumulated upward pressure from within the UK

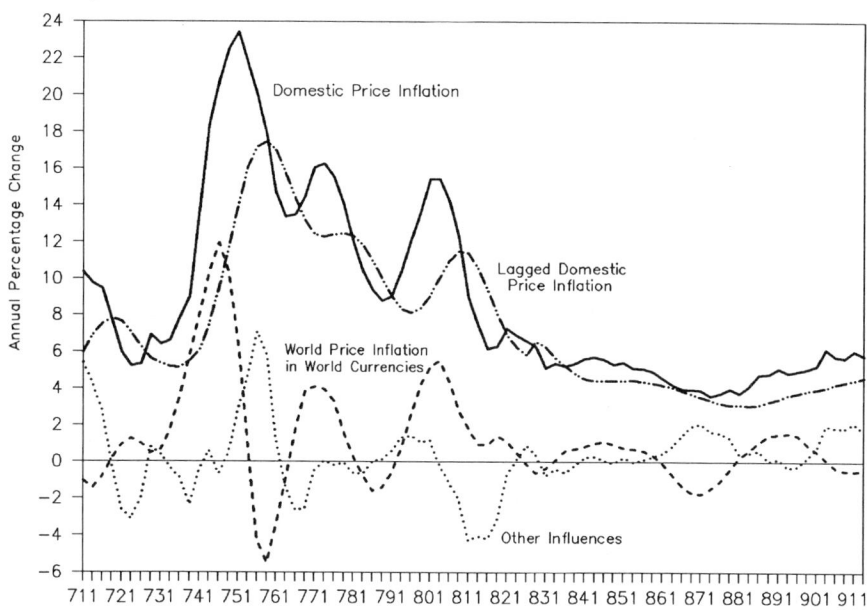

Fig. 7A.1 Contributions to domestic price inflation.

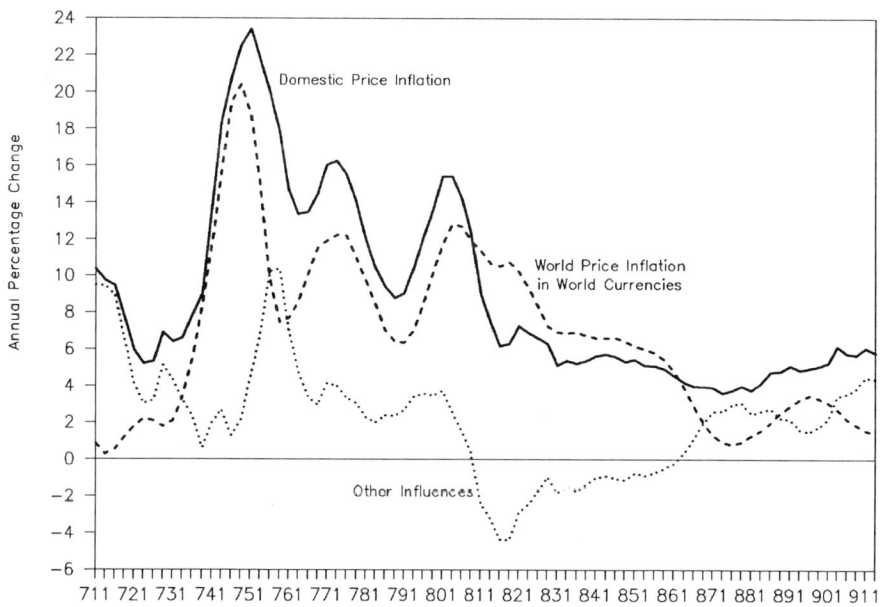

Fig. 7A.2 Cumulated contributions to price inflation.

pushed the inflation rate (as indicated by the Producer Output Price Index) up to 6 or 7 per cent.

(b) Price equation

In constructing the rate of increase in unit labour costs for the price inflation equation we have used the rise in average earnings in the whole economy (historically there has been little lasting deviation between the rise in this and the rise in manufacturing earnings). This has been adjusted for productivity changes using the simple average of the increases in whole economy and manufacturing output per employee. During this period productivity in manufacturing industry has increased at an historically high rate while whole economy productivity has risen at quite a moderate rate so the choice of the weights on these may have affected the path of our residual. The import price index used is the unit value index for imported goods excluding oil.

Figure 7A.3 shows the total contribution of all the factors in the price equation other than these costs and lagged price inflation (with a small weight corresponding to the administered price and tax terms in the price equation). It includes the residual. This is the variable X_1 in equation 7A.1 above. On average over the period this has contributed little to price inflation. Whereas this seems to have put upward pressure on price inflation during the mid-to-late 1980s (1986 to 1989), this became

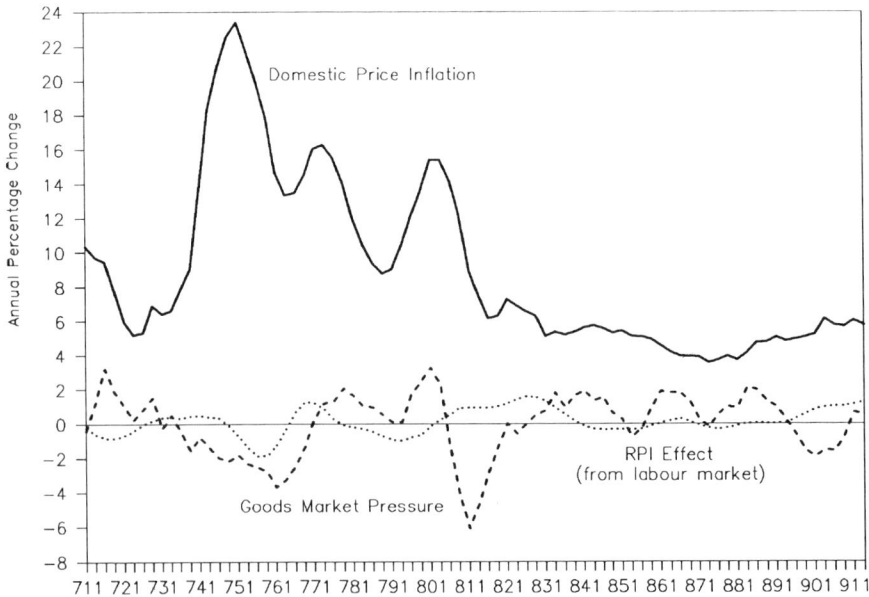

Fig. 7A.3 Effect of goods market pressure.

a downward pressure around 1990. There is support here for the conjecture that there was overheating in the goods market in the second half of the 1980s.

Figure 7A.3 also shows the effect of the small discrepancies between the Retail Prices Index and the Producer Output Price on the inflation rate, producing upward pressure around 1990/91.

(c) Labour market

The productivity variable used in the wage equation for this analysis is the whole economy one. This is because we have assumed that it is expected trend productivity that affects wage settlements and that no one expected the high rates of productivity growth that took place in the manufacturing industry during this period. Given this, the contribution of the labour market to the rate of domestic price inflation (the variable X_3 in equation 7A.3, but including the productivity term in the price equation) is shown in Figure 7A.4. In the early 1980s it put downward pressure on inflation but increasingly this turned into upward pressure as the decade progressed.

Figure 7A.4 also shows separately the contribution of productivity to inflation over the period 1983 to 1991. This arises because we have used different definitions in the two equations and there are different lags determining the effect on price inflation from the two sources. Throughout the second half of the 1980s the high

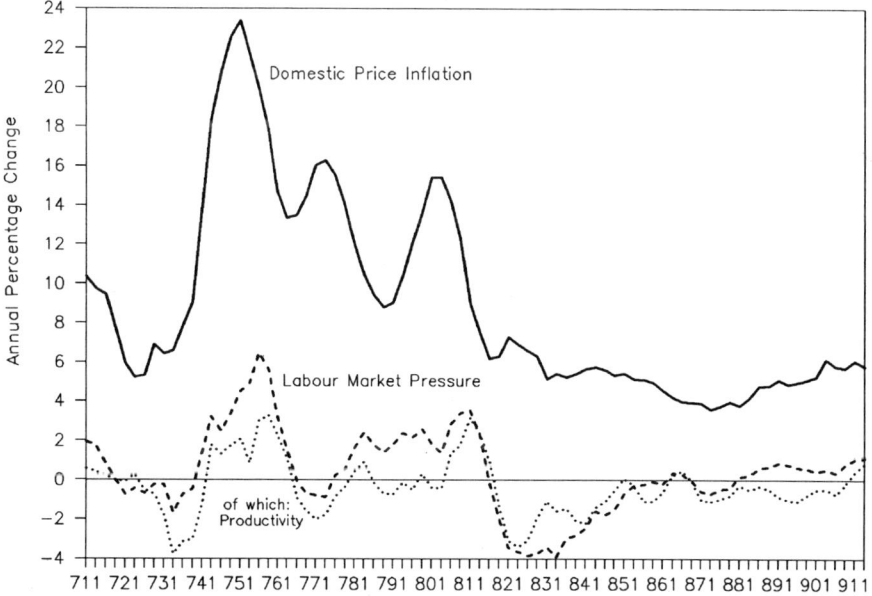

Fig. 7A.4 Effect of labour market pressure.

rate of growth of productivity in the manufacturing sector was good for inflation. Only in 1991 did this reverse.

The world price data collected from *International Financial Statistics* have been weighted and lagged in an *ad hoc* fashion that approximates the coefficients and lags used in our model of import prices. The contribution of the discrepancy between the import price data used in the equation for price inflation and these data (not shown in the figures), adjusted for the sterling/dollar exchange rate, is very small.

(e) Conclusion

From this updating exercise we draw two conclusions.

The first concerns our model. Given the fact that the variances of the 'X' factors in the update period are broadly similar to those in the estimation period, we conclude that the model is reasonably robust. The features of the model that are important and are used in this update (the homogeneity constraints, the input– output constraints and the lag distributions on the endogenous variables) seem to be giving meaningful results.

Second, this analysis of the data suggests that the cause of the recent rise in inflation lies within the domestic economy. There was upward pressure in the domestic goods and services market through most of the second half of the 1980s (although the net effect over the decade taken as a whole was close to zero). Indeed, there was increasing upward pressure in the domestic labour market through the second half of the decade. The cumulated effect of this seems to have added about 4 per cent to domestic inflation rates during the years between 1987 and 1991.

ENDNOTES

1. The coefficient on lagged domestic inflation in the ISE is 0.82, while the coefficient on world price inflation is 0.18.
2. Of course, if this coefficient took the value unity it would be impossible to perform the indirect reduced form analysis as the sum in equation 7.2 would not converge.
3. Except for the term in $(\Delta rp - \Delta p)$, which has been included explicitly in equation 7A.3.

8

Policy considerations

8.1 INTRODUCTION

In recent years the macroeconomic policy debate has centred around the assumption that the principal determinant of domestic inflation is excessive domestic aggregate demand. The key to both prevention and cure of inflation then seems to lie simply with the control of demand, using a combination of fiscal and monetary measures.

Aggregate domestic demand certainly appears, from the analysis reported in Chapter 7, to have played a role in the determination of inflation in recent years. However, the results listed there and in Chapter 6, along with the work of many other authors,[1] imply that the influence of other elements cannot be ignored. These other influences include domestic supply side factors, institutional considerations and effects arising in the foreign exchange market as well as other countries' inflation rates and imbalances in world markets for raw materials. If high or rising inflation is caused by factors other than excess domestic aggregate demand, then the use of fiscal and monetary instruments may not be the most appropriate way to control and cure it. Microeconomic policies directed at such supply side issues as creating a non-inflationary wage negotiating structure, or a direct approach to reducing nominal wage rises, may also be important aspects of the policymaker's anti-inflation armoury.

In this chapter we investigate the potential for a number of policy options to be successful in preventing or curing inflation. The macroeconomic policy options are addressed and evaluated in sections 8.2 to 8.6 and summarized in section 8.7. Section 8.8 examines the role of microeconomic policy in preventing and in curing excessive inflation. In sections 8.9, 8.10 and 8.11 we examine the potential for using micro-economic policies based on behaviour in the labour market and in the goods and services markets to reduce inflation. Section 8.12 notes the distortions that occur in the inflation rate as a result of the structure of the Retail Prices Index.

In section 8.13 we look at the potential for implementing internationally coordinated policies relating to inflationary pressure originating in world commodity markets. Section 8.14 presents the conclusions.

8.2 DEMAND MANAGEMENT

8.2.1 Introduction

This section examines the potential for fiscal and monetary policy, through the manipulation of the level of aggregate demand in the economy, to prevent inflation from rising and to reduce it when it has become unacceptably high.

Since much of the policy debate has been predicated on the hypothesis of the Expectations Augmented Phillips Curve as an explanation of the way in which inflation responds to excess demand, we begin with a brief description of its properties and implications. We then look at the implications of our model of the inflation spiral for the success of such a policy.

8.2.2 Inflation and demand

The Expectations Augmented Phillips Curve (EAPC) assumes that wage inflation is determined by expected price inflation and a factor related to excess demand/supply in the labour market (section 3.2). Excess demand/supply is proxied, in the EAPC, by the deviation of unemployment from the non-accelerating inflation unemployment rate, or NAIRU. This hypothesis is usually combined with two further assumptions: that price inflation depends on wage rises, and that price expectations are backward looking.[2]

Given these assumptions, the consequences of a policy of demand management can be deduced. If the policy stance allows the demand for labour to grow and unemployment was initially at the NAIRU, then this will push unemployment below that level. The result, according to the EAPC, will be that nominal wage rises will be larger than expected price rises. Other things being equal, this means that the rate of inflation will rise. Indeed, the inflation rate will continue to rise throughout the period during which unemployment is below the NAIRU. When the level of unemployment returns to the NAIRU, this will be associated with a higher prevailing rate of inflation than that which operated before the expansion in demand took place.

By the same token, a contraction in the demand for labour will raise unemployment above the NAIRU and this will lead to a reduction in inflation. Given the EAPC hypothesis, there will be downward pressure on inflation throughout the period during which unemployment is above the NAIRU.

It follows, given the premise of the EAPC, that judicious manipulation of the path of the unemployment level (excess demand in the labour market) can be used to control inflation. The macroeconomic policy implication of the EAPC hypothesis is, therefore, that the government can, to some extent at least, control the long-term rate of inflation by the management of aggregate demand using fiscal and/or monetary policy.

The part of the EAPC hypothesis that is crucial to this result is the assumption that the deviation of the *level* of unemployment from the NAIRU has an effect on the *change* in the rate of inflation (the difference between wage inflation and expected price inflation), rather than on the level of inflation. This being so, the long-run trade-off between the inflation rate and unemployment will be vertical: when expectations are fulfilled unemployment must be at the NAIRU and the inflation rate must be constant. But inflation can take any value at that unemployment level (section 3.2.1).

8.2.3 Relationship between inflation and demand

There are a number of differences between the EAPC and our Inflation Spiral Equation (ISE). Three of these relate to the interaction between inflation and activity. These are relevant to whether demand management can prevent and cure inflation and are discussed in this section. Other differences derive from the fact that the ISE is more complex than the EAPC and contains potential influences on inflation that are missing from the simpler approach of the EAPC (relating to the goods market, productivity, taxes, the exchange rate, primary commodity prices and so on). The implications of these for policy options are dealt with in later sections.

(a) Activity effect: level or change ?

First, the wage equation incorporated into our ISE includes an appreciable influence of the level of unemployment (as illustrated by Table 7.4). However, the statistical evidence supporting the hypothesis that this has operated during the estimation period is inconclusive. In the estimation of the wage equation the relevant coefficient is barely significantly different from zero at the 95 per cent level (Tables 3.6 and 3.7). Given the data used in the estimation of the equation, the effect of unemployment on wage rises may come about as the result of a difference term in unemployment; this is clear from Table 3.7. This would be consistent with the EAPC approach if the NAIRU were determined by lagged unemployment (the 'hysteresis' effect).[3]

If this were the case it would have significant implications for the interpretation of policy in the past and for the prognosis of its effect in the future. With no activity-related levels term in the wage equation, the level of activity effect that operates in the goods market (the capacity utilization term) would be the only one creating a persisting reduction in inflation in the case of a deflation. Further, although in these circumstances this term can be expected to produce downward pressure for a substantial period, it will cease to do so when capacity has adjusted to the new level of activity.

Indeed, if there were no activity levels terms in the ISE, only activity difference terms, then there would be no reason to expect demand management to have any lasting effect on the rate of inflation. A contractionary policy would reduce the rate of inflation when demand was falling in real terms. But while activity was held at a low level, instead of putting continuous downward pressure on inflation,

inflation would remain constant (abstracting from lags) throughout. A subsequent expansion, designed to return activity to its previous level, would result in a rise in inflation which would take it, also, back to the level it was at before the policy initiative began (other things being equal). The costs incurred by using demand management in this way would have been suffered in vain. (If the EAPC specification were correct in its assumption that short-term variations in the level of activity have a significant influence on changes in the rate of inflation, then the inflation rate would continue to fall throughout the period for which activity was below the long-run equilibrium level.)

Thus, the precise form of the dependence of wage settlements on unemployment (and price rises on output and capacity) is crucial to the success of demand management or the use of fiscal or monetary policy to control inflation; and the data are unclear about how this has operated in the past.[4]

(b) Activity effects in goods and currency markets

A second difference between the ISE and the EAPC, that is relevant to macro-economic policy, is that with the ISE the influence of domestic activity on inflation does not operate only through the unemployment term in the wage equation. An additional effect acts through the change in output and the capacity utilization terms in the price equation and, in some circumstances, through the current balance term in the exchange rate equation.

Other things being equal, the inclusion of these terms in the analysis should increase the estimate of the extent to which demand management can influence inflation. Of course, these terms would automatically be included if the estimates were based on simulations using a large macroeconomic model (Wallis 1987). The statistical analysis in Chapter 2 suggests that the capacity utilization term may be quite important.

(c) Degree of domestic inflation indexation

A third difference between the EAPC and the ISE relates to the degree of pass through of domestic inflation from one period to the next (the extent of automatic domestic inflation indexation). If the exchange rate equation does not exhibit full inflation indexation then, in spite of the assumption of no money illusion in domestic labour and goods markets, the coefficient on lagged domestic inflation in the ISE will be less than unity and there will be a term in foreign inflation rates that maintains the requirement of unit dynamic homogeneity (full inflation indexation).

The relationship between inflation and activity is then not as simple as the 'vertical' relationship of the EAPC, even when there is an activity level effect. The ISE will include an influence on domestic price inflation from foreign inflation. At any point in time, the level of activity at which domestic inflation is non-accelerating will depend on the difference between inflation at home and abroad at that time, among other things.

With international asset equilibrium restored in the long run, however, the ISE will again become vertical, like the EAPC, since then the real exchange rate would be at the long-run equilibrium level (as discussed in Chapter 6). The difference is therefore one of timing; but because the difference in timing is likely to be very substantial this is highly relevant to policy prescriptions.

8.2.4 Costs of demand management

There are two important types of cost associated with the demand management policy we have been examining in this section. The first is well known and has often been assessed (e.g., Okun 1978). This is the cost of the unemployment and the reduced output which are inevitably associated with reducing inflation by deflating the economy. This is a short-term cost, and a very significant one. As activity contracts workers become unemployed (remaining so sometimes for substantial periods of time) and firms which might have been viable become bankrupt (throwing out of work both employers and employees). The cost in terms of lost output and human suffering is considerable.

The second type of cost associated with using demand management to 'cure' inflation is longer lasting, less generally acknowledged and potentially more serious. It relates to the damage such a policy may do to the fabric of the economy: the capacity to produce at full employment without upward pressure on inflation. Every time a recession is engineered to squeeze inflation out of the system, a number of firms are driven into bankruptcy. To the extent that these are inefficient, or in sectors of the economy that are on the decline, this may be no bad thing. They are likely to be replaced by new firms when the economy recovers, or by the expansion of existing firms; they are dead wood that requires to be cut away. However, if the severity of the policy is such that whole sectors of industry that might have been viable in the longer term are demolished, then damage is being done to the fabric of the economy, potentially efficient machinery is being scrapped, and the cost could be high. When the economy is reflated bottlenecks will be reached at lower levels of activity and the trade-off between inflation and unemployment will have shifted outwards (the non-accelerating rate of unemployment will have increased). Indeed, the path of unemployment suggests that this may have happened in the UK more than once in recent decades (Figure 8.1).

Demand management to cure inflation may, therefore, create a situation in which inflation is more likely to be a problem in the future. This being so, it is doubly important to ensure, as far as possible, that this policy option has a reasonable chance of succeeding in its objective before it is implemented; that is, we need to be confident that the effect is not reversible.

8.2.5 Conclusion

Although the statistical analysis reported here does appear to lend some support to a role for fiscal and monetary policy in the control of inflation, it also raises a serious question. The effect of demand on inflation may simply be reversible: wage

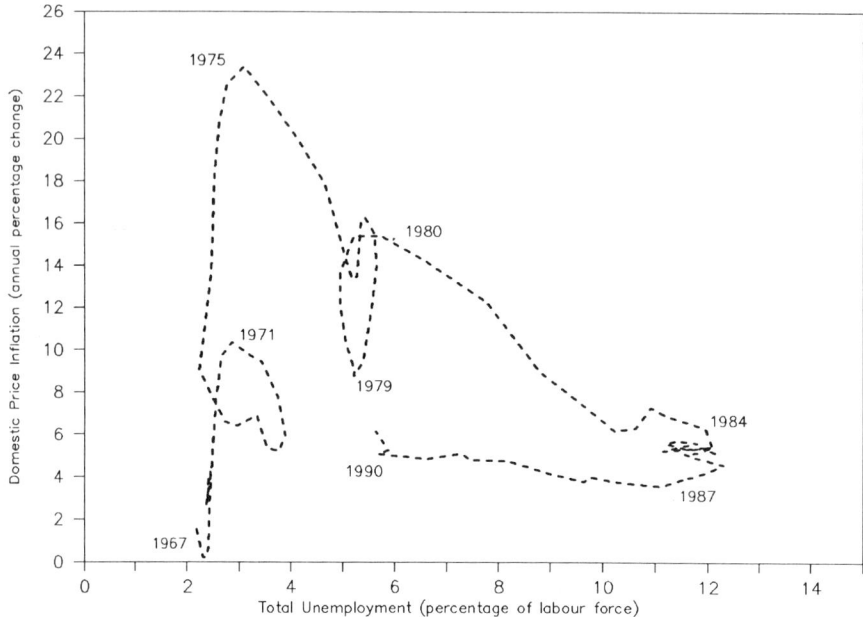

Fig. 8.1 Unemployment–inflation trade-off.

settlements (given price inflation) and price rises (given cost increases) may depend on changes in unemployment and activity rather than on their levels. In this case the effect of demand management on inflation will be merely transitory. Further, the use of fiscal and/or monetary policy to attempt a 'cure' for inflation may create a situation in which inflationary bottlenecks occur at a higher unemployment rate in the future.

8.3 GOVERNMENT INCENTIVES

8.3.1 Introduction

We have seen in the previous section that the government has an influence on the path of inflation through its decisions regarding monetary and fiscal policy. The question that arises next concerns whether or not the government has an adequate incentive to use that influence to hold inflation down.

One option that is open to a government, in the run up to an election for example, is to 'go for growth'. An expansionary stance on macroeconomic policy would generate a rise in activity, in employment and in consumer confidence; and our model supports the view that it is only later that the accompanying rise in inflation will be apparent. Carefully timed, this can be highly beneficial to those concerned primarily with the reaction of the voters in an election. The longer term political benefit rests on the presumption that if the government then wins the election there will be plenty of time to sort out inflation before the next election, while if it loses the other party will have to pick up the tab. However, it may be that an expansionary policy such as this will cause 'overheating', with supply side bottlenecks, which prevent the rise in demand from being met by increased output, leading to a larger rise in prices than would otherwise have been the case. The analysis in Chapter 2 suggests that a bottleneck can create a ratchet effect: an upward pressure on inflation that is not reversed when demand returns to its previous level. The effort to reverse this can then cause a disproportionate amount of pain.

8.3.2 A nominal framework

It is partly because the government has an incentive to expand activity in this way that it has been recommended that macroeconomic policy is operated subject to a given nominal framework. In this case the government sets, and publishes, an 'intermediate target'. It chooses an appropriate target growth rate for some nominal factor in the economy and publishes its intention to ensure the target is achieved. The implication, not wholly plausible, is that the government will lose face, and is therefore less likely to be re-elected, if the target is not met.

A further implication is that if wage rises are too great and price inflation rises, the policy stance will ensure that output must fall and a greater number of people will lose their jobs. The message to wage bargainers, therefore, is that excessive wage claims will automatically be 'punished' by increasing unemployment.

A number of different forms of nominal framework, with published targets, have been suggested in recent years. In the early 1980s the preferred framework related to the money supply, and many alternative definitions of money were debated. If all nominal values move together and the money supply were to conform with the target set for it, then price inflation would be under control. However, the link between the money supply and price inflation proved unreliable as innovations produced shifts in money demand: the monetary aggregates failed to perform in line with the government's published targets even when inflation rates were not excessive.

Another target that has been debated is nominal GDP; if there were a sufficient tendency back towards full employment then success in achieving a nominal GDP target would automatically imply the achievement of a target for inflation. (If not, the achievement of the target would also be consistent with a situation in which unacceptably high unemployment was combined with unacceptably high inflation.) Here there are information problems: the data for nominal GDP are available only a considerable time after the event and revisions continue to affect the data for some years.

The latest nominal target chosen by the government involves the entry into the Exchange Rate Mechanism (ERM). It consists of holding a specific indicator of the level of the sterling exchange rate constant in nominal terms: if domestic price inflation gets too far out of line with overseas price inflation then the government will have to take measures to bring it down. Otherwise, loss of competitiveness would eventually drive sterling out of the permitted range.

According to our model none of these is truly an intermediate target in the sense that it comes between government policy and inflation in a simple causal chain. Instead, the causal relationship is forked: if government policy succeeds in holding inflation down to acceptable levels then the government's target is also likely to be met, other things being equal. The institution of the target is therefore not, in itself, a policy for the reduction or control of inflation. Instead, its purpose is twofold: to strengthen the government's resolve to pursue some other, effective, anti-inflation policy in the face of the temptation to 'go for growth'; and, to influence the expectations of those involved in wage bargaining in the hope that this, in itself, is an effective policy for controlling inflation (section 8.5).

8.3.3 An independent central bank

One way in which it might be possible to achieve the same end, that of preventing government from creating inflationary pressure for short-term political benefits, is to institute an independent central bank. This would be given the objective of operating monetary policy (in particular, setting short-term interest rates) in such a way as to hold price inflation at an acceptable level.

This option is popular at present. There seems to be widespread agreement that, as European monetary union progresses and there is a need for a European Central Bank, it should be independent of political control. The main argument in favour of this is empirical: the countries with the lowest inflation rates in recent years have been those with a central bank which is independent of political influence and charged with the task of maintaining price stability. The case most often cited is that of the Bundesbank,[5] which is independent from government instructions in law (all the government can do is hold up decisions for two weeks, but it has never used this power) and is committed to 'safeguarding the currency'.

Opponents question the direction of causality between low inflation and an independent central bank.[6] Whereas an independent central bank may be successful in a country with a built-in tendency to low inflation, it may be less so in a country in which some inflationary pressure is endemic. They also suggest that, if monetary policy is used solely to control inflation and pays no regard to the level of unemployment or the economic cycle, it could well lead to higher unemployment and/or a more volatile cycle. The empirical evidence currently available suggests that, whereas an independent central bank is associated with a lower inflation rate, it implies neither more unstable growth nor higher unemployment than the case of a politically dependent central bank (ibid.).

Our conclusions on this aspect of monetary policy, summarized in section 8.2 and derived from our model, are twofold: that it is not clear whether or not it is an effective way of controlling inflation; and that, if too sharp a deflation is initiated so the fabric of the economy is damaged, this would lower the level of unemployment at which inflation begins to accelerate. This suggests that a structure in which monetary policy is implemented with no regard to the implications for unemployment or the productive potential of the economy may lead to a seriously suboptimal outcome. In an economy which does not have a built-in tendency to low inflation this could be a serious problem.

8.4 EXCHANGE RATE MANAGEMENT

8.4.1 Introduction

In the context of our model two quite distinct approaches to controlling or influencing the rate of inflation by means of managing the exchange rate can be identified. The first involves the day to day running of the economy. The paths of variables that affect the exchange rate are chosen, or influenced, by the authorities to have the desired effect given the exchange rate regime (and therefore **given** the manner in which expectations are formed, the extent of capital mobility and so on). The other involves a change of approach. The government changes the exchange rate regime. The intention here is to affect the manner in which exchange rate expectations are formed (rather than the level of expectations **given** the manner of forming them), to change the way exchange market operators act and, perhaps, to change the way in which domestic entrepreneurs who are dependent upon international competitiveness for their livelihood behave in the domestic labour market.

Thus whereas the first approach operates within the existing framework by changing the values taken by the variables feeding into the exchange rate equation (interest rates or the level of activity, for example), the second attempts, insofar as it is possible (perhaps by changing the manner in which expectations are formed), to change the way in which the nominal exchange rate and, possibly, the nominal wage are determined. The second, therefore, could alter the form of the exchange rate equation in our model (Chapter 4), and affect the values of the coefficients in it. Further, it could also affect some of the coefficient values, and in an extreme case the structure, in the wage equation (increasing the importance of competitors' prices, for example).

8.4.2 Influencing the exchange rate path

The authorities can influence the path of the exchange rate, given the exchange rate regime, in any of three ways: by direct influence on demand or supply, buying or selling domestic currency in the market (sterilizing to ensure no effect on domestic interest rates); by influencing others' demands indirectly by changing the relative costs of holding different currencies (changing domestic interest rates and causing substitution); or by changing the level of activity in the economy, which will have an indirect effect on the total need for foreign currency (income effect). The first of these is of little use in the battle to control inflation; the second and third both have a role to play.

(a) Direct intervention

The authorities can influence the path of the exchange rate by direct intervention in the foreign exchange market, buying and selling sterling in exchange for foreign currencies and thereby generating an exogenous demand or supply. However, such a policy is more appropriate for exchange rate smoothing than for influencing the rate of inflation.

The speculative element in foreign exchange market behaviour means that exchange rates tend to be volatile, swinging around their long-term trend. The uncertainty which this creates imposes substantial costs on domestic industry. Some degree of short-term stabilization can be achieved by direct central bank intervention in the foreign exchange market. The extent to which the Bank can use this to reach stable rates depends on the magnitude and volatility of the capital flows and the quantity of foreign reserves it holds.

According to our model, the temporary injections of demand that a central bank can afford out of its reserves have little effect on the longer term path of the exchange rate so this policy option is not relevant to the control of inflation.

(b) The price mechanism

Use of the price mechanism to influence the path of the exchange rate can have an effect on the rate of inflation. A way of exporting inflation from the domestic economy to trading partners involves creating a differential between domestic and foreign interest rates to induce an appreciation of the exchange rate. The result will be a reduction in the domestic currency prices of both imported finished goods and raw materials, reducing the domestic inflation rate. On the other hand, export prices in foreign currencies will rise faster than they otherwise would have done, putting upward pressure on the inflation rate in the economies of trading partners.

The cost of this policy will be a reduction in international competitiveness, with domestic manufacturers having increasing difficulty in selling into foreign markets and, indeed, in maintaining their share of domestic markets. The loss in competitiveness thus results in current account deterioration which will continue for as long as the currency is held above its long-run equilibrium value (with the current account deficit being financed by the surplus on capital account that is induced by the interest rate differential).

Further, if there is a persisting differential between the rates of inflation at home and abroad and if the authorities succeed in maintaining a constant **nominal** exchange rate, then there will be an increasing loss of competitiveness and an increasing deterioration in the trade balance. Moreover, given that the exchange rate path is determined by the maintenance of risk-adjusted uncovered interest parity (risk averse speculators equalizing the returns from alternative currencies), the deteriorating trade balance means that an **increasing** interest rate differential will be required to hold the exchange rate fixed in nominal terms (Chapters 5 and 6). The rising domestic real interest rates will have implications for the level of activity in the domestic economy. In the absence of an offsetting counter-inflationary pressure there will eventually be no option but to allow the domestic currency to depreciate in order to restore competitiveness. The inevitable consequence of this will be to trigger the long delayed rise in the domestic rate of inflation.

Thus, the use of interest rates to manipulate the exchange rate and modulate the effect of inflationary pressure on price rises can at best be only temporary; it can buy time between the experience of domestic inflationary pressure in an economy and its outcome on price rises, and during this period a counter-inflationary effect may be induced (or may occur of its own accord, perhaps as a result of the higher domestic interest rate) which cancels the effect of the initiating inflationary pressure. It is worth noting, also, that this exchange rate policy is a beggar-thy-neighbour instrument which, because of the relative nature of exchange rates, cannot be used by all members of a trading group at the same time.

(c) Reducing domestic demand

Finally, if fiscal or monetary policy is used with the intention of reducing demand in the economy, it will also have the effect of causing a reduction in the demand for foreign currency and, therefore, a rise in the exchange rate and a consequential reduction in inflation, other things being equal. However, our model suggests that when demand once again returns to the full employment level the exchange rate also will return to its earlier level. This is, therefore, not an effect that can be used to contain or reduce inflation in the long term.

8.4.3 Changing the exchange rate regime: the ERM

Many variations in exchange rate regime are possible. Real life examples include the institution of the Bretton Woods system in 1945, the move to floating rates in 1973 and joining the Exchange Rate Mechanism (ERM) in 1990.

(a) General issues

Exchange rate regimes are chosen with the intention that they serve a number of different purposes. For example, the volatility of exchange rates causes considerable difficulties to entrepreneurs involved in trading. If these entrepreneurs can be confident about the future value of the exchange rate, in either nominal or real terms, their operations are less risky and there is a benefit to be shared. An exchange rate regime may be chosen with this in mind. On the other hand it may be chosen because of its potential to reduce the volatility of the interest rate path consistent with the achievement of some policy objective or to impose a discipline on the way in which traders behave in, say, the labour market. Here we are concerned with the potential for an exchange rate regime to affect a country's inflation rate.

(b) The European Exchange Rate Mechanism

Joining the Exchange Rate Mechanism in late 1990 was intended to create an environment in the UK in which there would be 'convergence': inflation rates and interest rates in the UK would reduce to the level that pertains in Europe. Does our model suggest that this will take place? Are there likely to be costs associated with this policy?

First, given a period of successful membership of the ERM, continuing membership will become credible and exchange market operators will change the way in which they form expectations about the future path of the exchange rate. They will expect the nominal rate at which sterling is exchanged with European currencies to remain within the required band. This should allow the nominal exchange rate to be held within the band at a lower cost in terms of interest rate volatility than would have been the case outside the ERM. Convergence of interest rates therefore seems likely.

Second, any discrepancies between price rises in the UK and in Europe that lead to higher prices in the UK will result in lost UK sales as domestic goods are priced out of both European and UK domestic markets. UK firms manufacturing tradable goods, who depend on price competitiveness for their livelihood, will therefore be critically concerned to keep their costs down. Wage settlements in this sector of the domestic economy are therefore likely to contract relative to those in other sectors, producing downward pressure on inflation. Some pressure towards convergence of inflation rates is therefore likely to arise. However, there is an obvious potential cost arising from this in terms of the quality of the employees the export sector can attract compared to those choosing to work in non-trading sectors, if a pay differential opens up between the sectors as a result of this. Further, it is not clear that this will be enough to bring about the convergence of inflation rates on which continued membership of the ERM, without realignments, must depend.

'Convergence' in areas other than interest rates and inflation rates is not on the ERM agenda and is more doubtful. Fixing the exchange rate within a narrow band will reduce the extent to which an individual economy can respond to shocks. Given a shock that originates outside the block signed up to the tied exchange rates, the need for individual countries to respond in different ways arises because of differences in their economies. These may be due to differences in their natural resources (reserves of oil or minerals, for example) or to differing institutions (wage negotiating conventions).

If the differences between the economies are substantial, with some labour markets adding a real wage premium in each wage round while other labour markets take a trim in real wages, then this may involve a far higher rate of unemployment for some than for others. The question that arises then is whether there will be a structural change in the labour market on joining the Mechanism such that these institutional arrangements become aligned.

Barrell, in his 1990 paper,[7] reports a statistical analysis of the wage and price behaviour in France and Italy in which he searches for a break in behaviour associated with joining the ERM. In each case there has been an impressive reduction in inflation and in each case this has been associated with a substantial rise in unemployment. The inflation differential between France and Germany fell from 6.5 per cent in 1983 to 1.5 per cent in 1988, a fall of 5 per cent; meanwhile the unemployment rate differential increased by 2.5 per cent. On the basis of his statistical analysis Barrell concludes that there was no structural change. The differential between Italian and German inflation fell by 8.5 per cent and the unemployment rate differential increased by over 3 per cent. Barrell found significant statistical evidence of a change and cites the dismantling of the wage indexation system (the *Scala Mobile*) as being a likely cause of this break.

Since 1988 the inflation gap between France and Germany has closed further, to only 0.7 per cent, while the unemployment differential has widened by a further 0.5 per cent. The inflation gap between Italy and Germany has remained broadly constant, but unemployment in Italy has worsened by 0.5 per cent more than in Germany.

This suggests the following answer to our question. Membership of the ERM may leave the position of the (short-term) inflation–unemployment trade-off unchanged, as seems to have been the case for France, merely changing the point at which the country lies on it.[8] If this point was previously suboptimal, with higher inflation combined with lower unemployment than was considered ideal for the country concerned (given the choice set available) then joining the Mechanism will have led to a preferred situation. However, the question that arises then is: why was the position that obtained previously suboptimal?

On the other hand, membership of the ERM may lead to a shift in the trade-off, as seems to have been the case for Italy. The question then concerns the change in institutional structure associated with the shift, why it was necessary and whether there are costs associated with it. In Italy the structural change seems to be associated with the abolishing of the *Scala Mobile* (section 8.8 has a discussion of the likely effects of wage indexation). What institutional changes are likely to take place in the UK that will bring about a shift in the inflation–unemployment trade-off? The answer to this question is beyond the scope of our model.

8.4.4 A single European currency

A single European currency is the final objective of the move to ever closer union in Europe. What will be the effect of this, given our model?

With a single European currency, and different institutional arrangements for setting prices and wages in different countries, the UK may find itself with a progressive worsening of price competitiveness, similar to the situation described in section 6.4. The differences that result from the single currency are that there would be no need for total revenue from net exports from the UK to balance net capital flows, and there would be no role for domestic interest rates to differ from those in Europe in order to hold the rate at parity. However, high wage rises in the UK would mean high prices compared to other parts of Europe and low sales, perhaps in some industries none.

There are three possible labour market responses: there might be no change in wage setting institutions in the UK, instead the UK might suffer persistent high unemployment; the wage setting mechanism might change of its own accord, coming into line with those in the other countries using the same currency; or the government might intervene either to create an environment in which wage settlements take place at a lower level (section 8.9) or to hold wage settlements at a lower level in real terms (section 8.10). It could also control the areas in which price setting puts upward pressure on inflation (section 8.11). Our model cannot distinguish which of these is most likely to take place.

8.5 ROLE OF EXPECTATIONS

8.5.1 Introduction

In this section we identify the ways in which expectations may be relevant to policy regarding inflation and examine what the model has to say about them.

Conventional wisdom maintains that the most important influence of expectations on inflation arises from the effect expectations of future price rises have on the level of wage settlements. If this is the case, then the manner in which these expectations are formed matters to the determination of inflation. First, this would affect the extent to which demand management, designed to influence the inflation rate, results in lost output; it is therefore relevant to the cost of this anti-inflation policy. Second, if the government can influence price expectations then, through this, it may be able to have a direct effect on the rate of inflation.

According to our model there are other points at which expectations may affect the inflation spiral. Two, in particular, are important. First, expectations of the future level of the exchange rate are relevant to its current level, and the way in which these are formed may be of great importance to the dynamics of the spiral. Second, expectations of productivity growth may have an influence on both wage and price rises and the net effect seems to be a nontrivial factor in the determination of the path of inflation. The possible policy implications of these are also addressed in this section.

8.5.2 How price expectations are formed

There are a number of hypotheses available in the literature concerning the manner in which expectations are formed. If expectations are relevant to price-setting in, say, the labour market, the effect of demand management on inflation will depend upon which one of these hypotheses, if any, is correct.

(a) Adaptive expectations

Consider adaptive expectations first. The hypothesis of adaptive expectations has individuals forming their expectations by updating last period's expectations in the light of last period's outcome; effectively this means that they base their expectations of inflation on the whole history of past rates, giving greatest weight to the more recent inflation experience.[9]

If the adaptive expectations hypothesis is true, then inflation expectations will be backward looking. Given that price expectations are relevant to the spiral, it then follows from our model that whenever the government uses a deflationary monetary or fiscal policy to constrain nominal demand in order to bring about a fall in inflation, a painful reduction in output will be needed in order to induce a reduction in price rises.

The assumption of adaptive expectations was used in much of the early Expectations Augmented Phillips Curve work.[10] It has since to a large extent been supplanted by the rational expectations hypothesis. Now, economic agents are generally assumed by economists to form their expectations 'rationally': they are assumed to take into account all available information when forming their expectations.

(b) Rational expectations combined with the EAPC

The rational expectations paradigm assumes that individuals learn from experience. This means that they will not make systematic forecasting errors. In this case, given access to all the relevant information, including the policy stance of the government, the expected future rate of inflation will not vary in a systematic way from the actual future inflation rate (the idea is that if it did, agents would learn and make an adjustment).[11] Of course, this is not to preclude **any** differences between expected and actual inflation rates, in a world of uncertainty perfect foresight is not possible, rather these differences will be unsystematic and random in nature.

In the context of the EAPC the assumption of rational expectations means that the possibility of a short-term trade-off between output and inflation noted in section 8.2.2 is removed. According to the EAPC the outcome on inflation can be different from that expected only if unemployment is different from the non-accelerating inflation rate. It follows that if expectations are rational, so that there is never a systematic deviation of expected from actual price inflation, then there can never be a systematic deviation of unemployment from the non-accelerating inflation rate.

Suppose that there is an unacceptably high prevailing (and fully anticipated) rate of inflation, and the government decides on a tight monetary policy as its favoured policy option. As soon as this is announced, given that the government announcement carries credibility, economic agents would adjust their expectations regarding price inflation to the level implied by the new policy stance. Given that these expectations are then realized, the EAPC implies that unemployment must be at the NAIRU. In the conventional language, the short-run Expectations Augmented Phillips Curve would shift downwards. The government would thus have achieved a lower level of inflation without having to endure any recession whatsoever. There would be no output or unemployment costs to tighter fiscal control. Clearly, this theory also predicts that an expansion in aggregate nominal demand would not stimulate employment but would simply lead to higher inflation expectations and hence higher inflation.

This hypothesis does not carry much credibility generally as it allows no role for an employment level different from the NAIRU, making it difficult to explain the observed variations in the unemployment level.

(c) Managing expectations as a policy option

The insight that rational expectations combined with the EAPC would allow costless reductions in inflation has implications for the general case in which expectations are not rational.

We have seen that, abstracting from the inevitable lags in adjustment, there might be no unemployment cost to reducing inflation if price expectations rather than lagged price rises determine wage and price setting behaviour. This would be the case if the reductions in price expectations were in line with the level of inflation implied by a successful policy outcome. In this case, a policy of persuading decision-takers that inflation would fall in the future could be used in conjunction with monetary or fiscal measures to reduce the output cost of an anti-inflationary policy. In order to continue to be successful in implementing such a policy, the government must, of course, take care to preserve its credibility.

8.5.3 Role of price expectations

It is unfortunate, given the above, that we have found so little empirical support for an influence of price expectations on the inflation spiral.

Price expectations could, in theory, play a substantial role in each of the three main markets addressed in our model. However, it is only in the exchange rate equation that the role played by expectations cannot be proxied by lagged actual values of the variable; and there it is the future level of the exchange rate, not prices, about which expectations are formed. In each of the other main equations an *a priori* case can be made for lagged data playing the role sometimes ascribed to expectations (decision-taking could be backward looking, e.g., Chapters 2 and 3).

It may, of course, be the case that wage settlements are based on the expected future rate of price inflation. This would maintain expected real purchasing power over the coming months, but would risk the possibility of *ex post* discrepancies and a need to negotiate 'corrections' when expectations proved to have been inaccurate. They also could, alternatively, be based on published figures for past price inflation. This would allow employees to catch up after the event, without the problem of dealing *ex post* with discrepancies. It may be that they depend on a mixture of both.

In our econometric analysis of the data on wage increases we experimented with survey data on both consumers' and companies' price expectations along with published data for price (RPI) inflation and the rise in traded goods' prices. This work suggests that past RPI inflation provides a far better explanation of wage settlements than the results of surveys of price expectations (Table 3.4). It does, however, support a minor role for companies' price expectations, along with lagged values of the rise in traded goods' prices. Although this appears to present powerful evidence against a substantive role for price expectations, it cannot be considered conclusive evidence that expectations play virtually no role in wage settlements, since a more satisfactory time-series for consumers' price expectations could give a different result. Descriptions of wage negotiations in the press generally refer to published RPI figures and so support these findings.

Equations explaining price rises usually contain lagged or current actual values of cost variables rather than data for expectations. Indeed, surveys of price-setting seem to suggest that actual costs, rather than expected future costs, are relevant to price-setting (Chapter 2). When an expected wage settlement series and a series for the expected future output price were included in our price equation we found that the lagged cost data gave a better explanation (these experiments are not reported in Chapter 2).

The conclusion to be drawn is that there is little empirical support at present for the proposition that price expectations play any role, let alone an important one, in propagating inflation around the spiral. This does not augur well for the success of policies that depend on the manipulation of expectations to reduce inflation (the nominal target approaches described in section 8.3). Nor does it offer encouragement to those who believe that the pain of inflation control by demand management can be reduced by the government making announcements about its intentions regarding the money supply.

8.5.4 Exchange rate expectations

Given the theory on which our exchange rate equation is based, with speculative flows moving to clear the market, it is impossible to escape the need to model the way in which expectations of the future exchange rate level are formed. We have explained these exchange rate expectations explicitly in terms of lagged economic variables rather than by using a full rational expectations approach (section 4.4.3).

The view we have taken on this is reminiscent of the 1964 paper by Baumol and Quandt (section 2.2.5). Inevitably there are uncertainties associated with economic modelling and, more fundamentally, there is no consensus regarding the working of the macroeconomy. It follows that, when attempting any sort of a full rational expectations solution to the modelling of expectations in the foreign exchange market, even implicitly, the marginal return is likely to be less than the marginal cost of performing it. Consider the difficulty economists have in modelling and forecasting the path of the economy. We have therefore assumed an *ad hoc* approach to modelling exchange rate expectations, in which they depend on lagged economic variables of various sorts (Chapter 4).

According to our model, the aspect of exchange rate expectations that matters most to policy is their degree of inflation indexation. This is central to the dynamics of the inflation spiral (Chapter 6). We note here the importance of operating an anti-inflation policy in such a way that, as with the ERM, exchange rate expectations continue to be based on the nominal rather than the real exchange rate.

If the cumulated effect of domestic inflationary pressures is such that a country's inflation rate becomes significantly higher than that of its main trading partners, there is a danger that the exchange rate path becomes indexed to inflation. This may be because operators in the exchange markets come to expect this to be the case (expectations are self-fulfilling in this area) or it may be the result of government policy. Either way, it will create a situation in which inflation becomes very volatile, as every variation in inflationary pressure shows up in the inflation rate in the short term, and in which there is a tendency for inflation to become extremely high (Chapter 6) if there is a period of excess demand in the economy.

Finally, as reported in Chapter 4, there appears to be no definitive statistical evidence either for or against a role for exchange rate expectations influencing the path of the exchange rate. However, since the *a priori* proposition that expectations about the future level of the exchange rate are relevant to its current level is convincing, there is a clear possibility that 'talking' the exchange rate up or down will have an effect, albeit temporary, on the path of inflation.

8.5.5 Expectations of productivity growth

The empirical breakdown of the factors contributing to the inflation process in Chapter 7 reveals that quite an important role seems to have been played by productivity growth in recent domestic inflation experience. The growth of labour productivity, or expectations concerning it, enter the inflation spiral in two different ways as it affects both wage bargaining and price setting. In our model wage settlements depend on expected **trend** productivity growth while the unit labour cost variable that affects price-setting depends on **actual** productivity growth. Any discrepancy between the two therefore ends up affecting the rate of inflation. This section explains how this arises, describes the effect it has on inflation and notes the policy implications.

First, in our wage equation wage rises are negotiated in a bargaining process in which the data suggest that the union, or employee side, has more influence over the outcome than the firm, or employer side. The real wage agreed can be viewed as reflecting a compromise between the employees expectations regarding the trend growth of labour productivity in the economy taken as a whole and the employers' expectations of productivity in the particular firm (as well as all the other things that determine the potential to be shared out).

Second, for any given level of nominal wages, increased *actual* productivity growth reduces the unit labour costs faced by manufacturers and so, according to the model, has a direct effect on the prices charged.

It follows that any discrepancy between actual productivity growth (assumed to influence price-setting) and trend expected productivity growth (which is taken to affect wage-setting) will have an effect on inflation. If actual productivity growth is greater than that expected, inflation will be lower than it would otherwise have been. Put another way, for a given wage rise the subsequent price rise will be smaller. If actual productivity growth is smaller than expected, inflation will be higher.

This is a factor that needs to be taken into account when assessing the likely success of a contractionary policy to deal with a high rate of inflation. A typical example arose when the UK, along with almost all other OECD countries, experienced a sharp decline in the rate of growth of labour productivity following the 1973 oil shock. This slowdown was not a direct result of the oil and primary commodity price increase, instead it was a consequence of the contractionary policies which were adopted thereafter. Firms tended to hoard labour in the hope of a rapid recovery and the drop in actual productivity added to the upward pressure on inflation. In the early-1980s the opposite effect can be seen in Table 7.4 of Chapter 7.

To the extent that it is true that price setting reflects actual productivity growth while wage setting depends on its expected rate, there may be potential for the authorities to talk down the expected rate and, by doing so, exert a downward pressure on inflation. This is known as 'exhortation' and, as an anti-inflation policy, is apt to attract some ridicule.

8.6 OTHER INFLUENCES BY THE AUTHORITIES

8.6.1 Introduction

One of the ways in which the government can influence inflation is by manipulation of the price variables which are under its own control and which, one way or another, affect the inflation spiral. These include tax rates, the prices of services provided by government, such as local authority rents, prices charged by nationalized industries (rail fares, postage and so on, many now privatized) and the wages of those employed in the public sector such as civil service employees and those employed in the health service, education and the armed services.

8.6.2 Taxes, prices and wages

(a) Taxes

A number of different tax variables occur in the equations that make up the model of the inflation spiral. At first sight this appears to give the government an opportunity to manipulate the paths of these variables in such a way as to have a beneficial effect on inflation. In fact, of course, for a given fiscal stance and given the level of public sector involvement in the economy, this is not the case. Under these assumptions, if one tax is reduced another must be increased. Abstracting from the possibility of money illusion, the net result on inflation would be zero.[12] In practice there may be a small amount of money illusion in the way in which people react to tax increases, so there may be a small, probably unpredictable, effect on inflation when one tax is reduced and another increased.

A further question concerns the inflationary effect of an expansion or contraction of the public sector. If goods or services that have been provided free, or subsidized, by the public sector are switched to the private sector, and taxes are reduced below the level they would otherwise have been as a result, are there likely to be effects on inflation? Again, the answer is that there will not. In the absence of money illusion, real earnings will rise sufficiently to allow the goods or services to be bought out of the increase in net earnings. In fact, again, there is likely to be a small effect that varies with the particular change made reflecting its potential for engendering money illusion. There may also be benefits relating to an increase in efficiency following the move into the private sector.

If, however, the public sector ceases to provide goods and services which are not directly consumed by the private sector (cuts in defence expenditure), then taxes can be cut with no offsetting increases in other taxes or in real earnings. This will result in a once-off downward pressure on domestic inflation.

(b) Public sector prices

There is always the temptation for the public sector to delay increasing prices for public sector goods and services. This delays the effect these price rises will inevitably have on the inflation spiral. However, in general, delayed or reduced rises in public sector prices will have no long-term effect on price inflation. Either the price will need to be raised by more later, or the shortfall in revenue will have to come out of higher taxes which will have inflationary effects of their own. Either way the effect on inflation will be the same in the long term (unless there is some degree of money illusion).

Further, this policy also has a cost. It leads to relative prices that do not reflect the cost of resources and production; it is not efficient in the economic sense of leading to an efficient allocation of resources. But since the demand elasticities of goods and services provided by the public sector are often quite low, the economic cost of such inefficiency may not be great.

(c) Public sector wages

A form of incomes policy that was used in the UK in the late 1970s and on and off through most of the 1980s involves holding public sector wage increases below the likely settlement level in the private sector. The idea is that this will put downward pressure on private sector settlements as a result of the well-known 'leapfrogging' effect. There is evidence, econometric as well as circumstantial, suggesting that private sector settlements do reflect, to some extent, the size of the settlements in the public sector (Foster *et al.* 1984). This has implications for the inflationary potential of public sector pay rises, as well as for the potential costs of holding them down.

However, one effect of this policy is that public sector pay falls behind that in the private sector. In the longer term this is likely to create problems. Either there will be a substantial 'catch-up', such as the Clegg awards in the late 1970s (discussed in Chapter 3), or the quality of the workforce in the public sector will eventually decline.

8.7 CONCLUSIONS ON MACROECONOMIC POLICIES

Macroeconomic policy, as one of the most frequent causes of inflation, has a clear role to play in its prevention. If an expansionary policy is pursued and this extends the economy beyond the level that can be met by the capacity available in the short run, then more of the demand expansion will be met by price rises than would otherwise have been the case. (In our model this is picked up by the capacity utilization term in the price equation and the term in excess demand in the wage equation.) An inflationary surge will then be injected into the spiral. Given the inertia of the inflation spiral (with current price rises reflecting the rate of past price increases, Chapters 2 and 3) the resulting inflation can be difficult to eradicate.

The output and employment effects of a policy induced expansion come through before the inflation associated with it; this means that the government has a (short-term) incentive to over-inflate the economy. Because of this there have been a number of experiments with nominal targets. These are imposed by the government on itself to encourage and facilitate the achievement of low inflation. According to our model none of these will, of itself, bring about low inflation (although, of course, it is possible they have an effect on expectations and influence the inflation spiral through this route). It is necessary, instead, to espouse a policy that will anyway achieve low inflation in order to achieve any of these so-called 'intermediate targets'.

Most macroeconomic policies designed to cure high inflation involve an indirect influence by the government on activity, and therefore on the activity-related variables that impinge upon the inflation spiral. We have seen (Chapter 5) that if the **level** of activity has a significant effect on the **change** in inflation (put another way, if the NAIRU exists), then correcting high inflation by following a contractionary macroeconomic policy is a feasible policy option. It may be painful and costly in terms of output and unemployment; it could do longer term damage to the economy by causing viable capacity to be wasted; but it should work. If, however, the activity effect that influences the change in inflation depends on

changes in activity rather than upon its level (if there is no NAIRU), then the suffering incurred by the use of demand management to alleviate high inflation will be to no purpose. When activity expands again, inflation will simply return to the level it would have taken in the absence of the painful deflationary policy, other things being equal. We have found the data ambiguous on this 'functional form' issue, arguably the most important one for policy (Chapter 3).

It is often maintained that the damage caused by a restrictive fiscal or monetary policy designed to control inflation can be alleviated if inflation expectations rather than past actual price rises are relevant to wage setting. For in this case an attempt can be made, by the authorities, to reduce expectations concerning inflation. If this were successful it would, indeed, reduce the pain of the correction period, for the reduction in nominal demand below the level it would otherwise have been would be taken on wages and so on prices, rather than on activity. However, we have found little support from the data for the proposition that expectations matter to the rate of wage inflation (Chapter 3). Of course, if expectations do affect wage rises, if expectations are 'rational', and if the EAPC equation holds, then inflation could be reduced with no pain; and some economists have subscribed to all three propositions. But our analysis lends no support to this thesis.

It is clearly important to run macroeconomic policy in a way that does not damage the ability of the economy to reach full employment without incurring inflationary pressures. In terms of our model this means both that the capacity to produce, implicit in the capacity utilization term in the price equation, should not be reduced, and that the NAIRU implicit in the wage equation should not rise. If either of these were to happen, then the term in capacity utilization in the price equation, or the term in excess demand in the wage equation, would bite at a level of activity below that corresponding to an acceptable level of unemployment. In this case price rises and/or wage rises would begin to accelerate while unemployment was still unacceptably high. That is, given that there seems to be a necessity to deflate the economy in order to prevent inflation becoming unacceptably high, it is important that the recession induced is neither too sharp nor too deep. Otherwise there may be unnecessary damage to the long-term industrial base or to the pool of skilled workers. Wherever possible the capacity to produce at a level consistent with full employment without inflationary pressures being triggered needs to be maintained.

Finally, according to our model (Chapters 5 and 6), the effect on price inflation of a bout of domestic inflationary pressure can be offset, to some extent, by holding the exchange rate at a higher level than it would otherwise have taken using the domestic interest rate as an instrument, as is consistent with membership of the ERM. However, unless an effective downward pressure on inflation is induced by this policy stance, or occurs of its own accord, this can have only a temporary effect. The disequilibrium on trade account that follows this policy means that unless price inflation falls for some other reason the exchange rate will eventually decline towards its long-run equilibrium level. And when it does so, the dammed-up inflation will run through the system.

8.8 THE CASE FOR MICROECONOMIC AND INTERNATIONAL POLICIES

A number of potentially effective remedies for a tendency to high inflation originate on the supply side of the economy and relate to microeconomic policies. The results of our model suggest that many of the 'causes' of domestic inflation are not associated with excess domestic demand (too much money chasing too few goods) but instead originate from institutional factors or from exogenous supply side or international shocks. In particular, there is evidence (presented in Chapter 7) that inflationary pressure in the UK arises from institutional aspects of the labour market, and also that unacceptably high domestic inflation has been caused by excess demand in world markets for primary commodities. Further, an important characteristic of the process of inflation is the 'inertia' evident in the spiral process, with the current inflation rate largely a perpetuation of the past inflation rate. A policy question that arises, therefore, concerns the role of microeconomic policy. The following sections consider the institutional and supply side measures that might be implemented to reduce a tendency to high inflation or to deal with a high rate of inflation once it has arisen.

Four ways in which inflationary pressure is generated within the labour market can be identified. First, the results reported in Chapter 7 suggest that the target real wage implicit in labour market behaviour has been a continuing source of inflationary pressure in the UK in recent years; indeed, that work suggests that it has, on average, accounted for some 2.5 per cent of the annual inflation rate (after taking account of feedbacks) during the period 1970–1985. Clearly, an important policy objective is to relieve the pressure on inflation through this channel. The scope for this is discussed in section 8.9. This would involve changing the intercept on the wage equation in our model.

Second, a related issue concerns the level of the 'market clearing' rate of unemployment and whether it can be reduced. If there is a level of unemployment below which wage settlements tend to take off, can this be reduced by increasing labour mobility or other policy strategies? In the model this issue is also inextricably entwined with the question of the target real wage since the market clearing level of unemployment also involves the intercept on the wage equation.

Third, the principal mechanism by which inflation is transmitted over time is the wage–price–wage type of spiral generated by an absence of money illusion within the labour market and the goods and services market. This is implicit in the homogeneity assumptions which are built into the wage and price setting structure of our model (supported by the data, as illustrated in Chapters 2 and 3). One approach to reducing inflation when it has become unacceptably high involves implementing some policy, perhaps an incomes policy, to break the automatic full pass through of past price rises on to wage rises. This possibility is discussed in section 8.10; in model terms it involves reducing the coefficient on lagged price inflation in the wage equation or replacing the price inflation index by one consistent with a lower inflation rate and full employment.

Fourth, there may be some scope, from time to time, to reduce inflationary pressure in the labour market by direct manipulation of the paths of some of the explanatory variables, such as employment taxes or income taxes. This has already been discussed in section 8.6.

In principle, the same four approaches also apply in the goods market. However, there seems to be less scope for influencing inflation through the goods market than through the labour market. The first possibility is to reduce the real margin pressure (this is analogous to the real wage pressure of the labour market) due to monopoly power or implicit cartel arrangements. A second would be to increase the level of activity at which the capacity utilization term in the price equation bites. Another possibility seems to be price controls, analogous to an incomes policy, but these are likely to create more damaging distortions than incomes policies. These issues are addressed in section 8.11. Again, the scope for direct intervention by the authorities to control the paths of some of the variables affecting price-setting is limited, and was dealt with in section 8.6.

8.9 INSTITUTIONAL FACTORS IN THE LABOUR MARKET

8.9.1 Introduction

In Chapter 3 it was recognized that negotiation between employers and employees is the dominant mode of wage setting, rather than wage rises simply reflecting the market pressure associated with the interaction of demand and supply in the labour market. Employers will be arguing for a low real wage and employees for a high one, often paying scant regard to the market balance. Typically this negotiation takes the form of bargaining between unions and firms, but even where business units are not highly unionized wage deals are influenced to a large extent by the results of the bargaining that takes place in the unionized sector. It follows that any policy option which reduces the extent to which unions, or other wage bargainers, can achieve real wage increases in excess of those warranted by the fundamentals (productivity improvements, changes in the terms of trade and changes in tax rates) will permanently reduce the level of labour market pressure (the intercept on the wage equation). We therefore begin with an examination of the policy options available to address directly the seemingly continuous labour market inflationary pressure of recent decades.

The most obvious approach is legislation to reduce the power of the unions; the potential for this is considered below. We then go on to discuss two examples of aspects of the institutional structure of wage bargaining that might be changed to improve the prospects for inflation. These are: the co-ordination of wage bargaining; and the duration of pay agreements.

8.9.2 The role of legislation

There still remains scope for implementing legislation that would limit the power of the unions and help to restructure the wage negotiation process in such a way as to reduce the pressure for wage rises which are larger than can be justified by the fundamentals (productivity increases, for example). Indeed, the most direct and obvious method of dealing with the problem of inflationary pressure in the labour market would be to limit and/or redesign the powers of trade unions through legislation. Both the banning of closed shops and further limitations on the scope for legal strike action (anyway under consideration at present) could reduce the effective bargaining power of trade unions if carried out successfully. Such policies might, of course, produce a political backlash and a wave of public sympathy for union ideals and this could result in a subsequent reversal of the legislation.

A political initiative of this sort has been implemented recently by the Conservative government of the mid-1980s. Along with the success with the 1984 miners' strike, which proved, indeed, to be a watershed in domestic industrial relations, the government implemented some significant changes in labour law. These included providing for secret ballots on some key issues and effectively eroding the legal basis of many forms of industrial action. There is insufficient data, at present, to enable an econometric estimate of whether or not this has had a substantial effect on the labour market premium in the UK.[13]

8.9.3 Co-ordination of wage bargaining

The extent to which bargaining takes place on a national level, between representatives of employer and union confederations and, possibly, government representatives rather than between managers and shop stewards at the local plant level, may be an important factor in determining the scope for labour market pressure on inflation. An economy with a high degree of national bargaining has been termed a 'corporatist' economy. The distinguishing feature of 'corporatism' is that it is the representatives of groups with similar interests that wield power and contribute to decision taking rather than individuals. In the labour market this means that ratification of wage agreements is not done by the rank and file of union membership. Analysis of economies with a highly corporatist orientation reveals that real wage moderation has often been achieved in the face of inflation pressure and supply shocks.[14] There is evidence, particularly from Scandinavian economies, that co-ordination of wage bargaining can have a beneficial effect on the real wage premium.

Co-ordination of wage bargaining requires a national pay strategy. The wage round would begin with the publication of a national economic assessment that sets out the potential for non-inflationary pay increases. The idea is that the current role of the RPI in wage bargaining (Chapter 3) would be filled, instead, by a 'norm' (section 3.6.2). This would be followed by a round of pay negotiations between representatives of the major economic groupings (government, unions, entrepreneurs and consumers, as considered appropriate) and these would be synchronized in order to avoid leapfrogging.[15]

A disadvantage of synchronizing pay negotiations in this way is that it may impose a going rate on firms regardless of the state of their profits and regardless of shifts in demand between sectors or regions of the economy, thus stifling the free working of the labour market to allocate resources efficiently. Also, it locks negotiators into fixed periods for pay settlements when the economy might be better served by greater flexibility.

In the corporatist economies of Scandinavia negotiations often cover a number of other factors in addition to wages. One result is that unions may accept moderate wage rises in exchange for other benefits such as tax reductions, expansionary macroeconomic policies which stimulate employment growth or increased power in other areas of the labour market. Bargaining between labour and employer confederations, with government representation also present, overcomes many of the informational difficulties associated with wage setting. By stressing the output and employment consequences if labour should gain an increased share in income (for example, by pressing high wage demands in the face of shocks to output), this approach encourages unions to offer a wage response which is consistent with maintaining current levels of employment. In fact, this has happened in the highly corporatist Scandinavian economies, especially in Sweden, where the labour organization agreed to the pay norm that labour should maintain a constant share of income in the tradables sector.

The effect of synchronizing pay negotiations should be to ensure that wage settlements are realistic in relation to the available spending power in the economy. In terms of our model the effect should be to reduce the intercept on the wage equation.

The tradition in the UK of decentralized wage bargaining, often between shop stewards and managers at plant level, is long established and might well be difficult to break. Rank and file ratification of nationally negotiated agreements seems to be part of the democratic tradition of British unionism. Radical legislation to change the structure of bargaining could encounter intense opposition from unions, and might attract the sympathy and backing of a substantial proportion of the population. However, it is clear that the rewards to a move in the direction of a national pay strategy and co-ordinated wage bargaining, in terms of lower inflation and higher employment levels, could be substantial.

8.9.4 Duration of pay agreements

The duration of agreements relating to rates of pay may affect the degree of effective short-term indexation, either explicit or implicit, of nominal wages to prices. If nominal wages respond fully in the short term to price increases originating elsewhere, say from a shock to the sterling price of primary commodities, then it is clear from our model that, given the inflation indexation of price-setting in the goods market, these wage increases will be transmitted into price rises next period and will therefore lead to a sustained increase in the rate of inflation.

In the UK economy, pay agreements are typically of short duration (1 year) and the evidence (Chapter 3) suggests that each annual settlement takes full account of the published rise in retail prices since the previous settlement was agreed. In contrast the US and Canada often have labour contracts of two to three years in duration, with little explicit indexation to the outturn on price inflation (Bruno and Sachs 1985 have a convenient summary). As a result there is a less immediate sensitivity of wage rises to price shocks in North America than in the UK. We would expect to find that the specification of the wage equation for the US would involve longer lags than those in our model of the UK. This would mean that a rising rate of price inflation following, for example, a real rise in basic commodity prices will automatically reduce the real wage rather than being reflected in higher nominal wage rises. This will act as a brake on the inertia of the wage–price spiral, which is so important to some of the results in Chapters 5 and 6.

In addition to this automatic short-term adjustment of real wages in the face of an adverse price shock in North America, the somewhat sluggish response of wages to unexpected price increases enables the authorities to follow a mildly expansionary monetary or fiscal policy from time to time. For example, this can prevent the painful recessionary effects of a terms of trade deterioration from influencing the economy, without risking too much of a rise in inflation. This was the policy chosen by the US following the 1979 oil price rise, and the result was that unemployment returned to its earlier level long before European employment did, with no apparent continuing deleterious effect on inflation.

8.10 INCOMES POLICIES

8.10.1 Introduction

The UK had a long and rich tradition of prices and incomes policies throughout the 1960s and 1970s, under both Labour and Conservative governments. These periods provide valuable testimony for the potential, or otherwise, of incomes policy as an effective anti-inflation instrument. This suggests that, in general, governments experience difficulty in implementing incomes polices for long periods of time. Further, the termination of an incomes policy tends to be characterized by a return to collective bargaining with unions attempting to make up for the real wage loss incurred during the period of nominal wage rise restrictions.

8.10.2 Empirical evidence

The evidence on the effectiveness of incomes policies, presented in Chapters 3 and 7, suggests that an incomes policy that lasts one year (one wage round) is of little use because the catch-up at the end, which brings the real wage back to where it would otherwise have been, cancels out the entire beneficial effect of the restraint (Figure 7.10). On the other hand, this evidence also implies that an incomes policy that lasts longer, say the three years of labour's 'social contract', can have an effect on inflation that persists for some time after the policy has ended due to the inertia of the inflation spiral (Figures 7.9 and 7.10, and Table 7.4).

Thus, according to the model, and conditional on the validity of the estimated values of the various coefficients, the shorter period of incomes policy had an effect on inflation which was merely temporary with the subsequent catch-up almost exactly reversing the effect on inflation. The only incomes policy in the UK during the period covered which seems to have had a substantial and sustained effect on the level of wage inflation was the three year voluntary incomes policy implemented in four separate phases by the Labour government, starting in August 1975. Of course, the breakdown of the policy in late 1978 was met with an upsurge in wage demands (and, indeed, the defeat of the government the following year after the 'winter of discontent'). Our estimates suggest, however, that given other factors such as the second sharp rise in real oil prices the wage rise that took place in the following round left intact most of the cumulative gains achieved in the previous three years. The subsequent decline in influence shown in Figure 7.10 indicates the effect of the deviation from full domestic inflation indexation in the inflation spiral.

8.10.3 The theory of incomes policy

An incomes policy aims to restrict the **nominal** rise in wages to a given level. Given that price rises are spread throughout the year, reductions in price rises follow the lower wage rise for any given group of employees with a lag. This lag means that, until all the price effects of some wage round affected by incomes policy have fed through, there is a reduction in the level of the real wage below the level it would have taken in the absence of the policy.

The algebra of an incomes policy works in the following way. Start from the Expectations Augmented Phillips Curve, a convenient exemplification of a wage equation for this purpose:

$$\Delta w = \Delta p^e - \alpha(U - \overline{U})$$

and assume that Δp^e is replaced by $\eta \Delta p^e + (1 - \eta)\text{pol}$ where pol represents the wage 'norm' and is related to the expected price rise by:

$$\text{pol} = \Delta p^e - \delta$$

If price expectations are extrapolative, $\Delta p^e = \Delta p_{-1}$, and if price rises are determined solely by wage rises, $\Delta p = \Delta w$, then:

$$\Delta w = \Delta p^e - (1 - \eta)\delta - \alpha(U - \overline{U})$$
$$= \Delta w_{-1} - (1 - \eta)\delta - \alpha(U - \overline{U})$$

or

$$\Delta(\Delta w) = - (1 - \eta)\delta - \alpha(U - \overline{U})$$

In this case, wage rises are decreased by $(1 - \eta)\delta$ in each wage round, even if unemployment is at the NAIRU. The cost is a reduction in the real wage (and an offsetting rise in profits) while the policy is operating, rather than a rise in unemployment and, possibly, damage to the fabric of the economy.

The initial cut in the wage rise at the start of the policy leads to a fall in the real wage and, other things being equal, to an offsetting rise in profits: it causes a shift in real income from wage earners to shareholders. This real wage reduction persists (other things being equal) for the duration of the policy, with nominal wage rises restrained to lower levels in each successive wage round. At the end of the period of wage constraint, when the policy is lifted, the rebound takes the real wage back up to the level it would otherwise have taken (with share-holders suffering a corresponding loss) and thereby gives a small boost to inflation. Typically, because this is equal to the downward bias in the real wage it will be approximately equivalent to one year's cut in inflation due to the incomes policy.

Suppose, therefore, that the policy lasts four years, and that it cuts 3 per cent off nominal wage rises in each year compared to what would otherwise have been the case. The real wage will typically be reduced by about half of this (1.5 per cent) on average throughout the four year period.[16] The rate of inflation at the end of the policy will have been reduced by 12 per cent (other things being equal) and one year later will have risen by 3 per cent due to the bounce-back effect leaving a net benefit of 9 per cent off inflation.

One disadvantage of a successful incomes policy is, of course, the temporary failure to allow movements in relative wages to give correct signals relating to individual sectors of the labour market.

8.10.4 Incomes policy and institutional structure

The difficulty of sustaining an incomes policy in the UK for an effective length of time is not surprising given the decentralized institutional framework of the UK wage bargaining process. Union leaders have, on occasion, appeared to be willing supporters of the principle of incomes policy, realizing that the result of free bargaining can simply be higher inflation with all its associated costs, and no aggregate increase in real wages. However, the natural objective of each union is to ensure that its members do not lose out and, indeed, that they achieve a greater increase in nominal wages than is obtained by others, thereby securing real wage gains. The result of a large number of unions pursuing these tactics will, of course, be leapfrogging and increased price inflation.

Incomes policies in the decentralized bargaining framework in the UK thus have an inherent instability and tend to deteriorate before sufficient time has passed to allow them to have more than a passing effect on inflation. It may be only when the bargaining process is highly centralized or co-ordinated that the authorities can sustain the policy long enough for its effects to cumulate and feed into the inflation spiral without being neutralized by catch-up effects.

8.10.5 A tax based incomes policy

The difficulties involved in maintaining incomes policies for long enough to have a net beneficial effect in the longer term have led to the proposal for a tax based incomes policy (as set out in Layard and Nickell 1986).

This would involve an annual economic assessment of the expected growth in labour productivity and other relevant factors, probably held in the months before the Budget. As a result of this a wage 'norm' would need to be agreed by consensus among the 'social partners', the TUC, the CBI and the government. Thereafter, any firm that allowed earnings to rise by more than the 'norm' would have to pay the Inland Revenue a sum related to the excess on its wage bill.

This puts an increased emphasis on the 'norm' emerging from the annual assessment, in comparison with the co-ordinated wage bargaining idea described in section 8.9.3. It also adds the possibly unnecessary incentive of a tax on firms that exceed it. Nevertheless, this is an additional instrument that could be utilized if the institution of a national economic assessment with co-ordinated wage bargaining were implemented.

8.10.6 Indexation of wages

It has been suggested by some that indexation of wage settlements to price rises could be used to moderate the impact of inflationary expectations since, in an indexed pay deal, wage settlements will respond to the actual rate of price inflation rather than to its expected rate plus a margin for expected productivity growth.

However, this presents two problems. First, the indexed rise tends to act as a floor, with many employees finding good reasons for a larger rise than that permitted. Second, price rises reflect the perceived increase in total unit costs, albeit with a mark-up that varies with the level of activity and with competitors' prices. Substantial falls in the rate of price inflation are generally **preceded** by a fall in either the rate of nominal wage growth or the rate at which import prices in domestic currency are rising. It is rare for a decline in inflation to be triggered by a contraction in the goods market since the effect of activity on price setting seems to be relatively slight, compared to that on wage setting. A policy to index wages would only be useful if price inflation responded to deflationary policy more quickly or more strongly than wage inflation.

Indeed, there is a sense in which wage–price indexation is an inherently inflationary device; for it reinforces the wage–price–wage cycle. Table 7.2 indicates the extent to which this means that last year's inflation causes inflation in the current year.

8.10.7 Conclusions on incomes policies

Some form of institutional restructuring of the wage bargaining system, probably a 'national economic concensus' or a system of co-ordinated bargaining rather than an incomes policy, is potentially a highly useful and direct method of moderating nominal wage increases and so reducing the tendency to high inflation. Further-more, by agreeing to a reducing norm, this could potentially be a powerful way of reducing inflation once it has got out of hand. However, the potential of this approach to have a lasting effect on the domestic inflation rate depends upon the duration of the policy being long enough to prevent the catch-up that follows the end of the policy from eroding the entire effect of the nominal wage moderations achieved.

The main economic disadvantage of incomes policy relates to its potential for distorting relative wages and preventing market forces leading to an efficient allocation of resources in the labour market. Politically it is extremely unpopular. The experience of the late 1970s is seen as demonstrating that incomes policies have been tried and failed, with the effect of the oil price rise on price inflation (and on the whole economy budget constraint, section 3.2) allocated to the catch-up after the policy. Incomes policy is seen as an election loser. Nevertheless, it may, in fact, be less painful and damaging politically than a government induced recession.

Incomes policies clearly have a potential role to play, not just as an independent instrument, but also as a complement to and in support of a macroeconomic policy to reduce inflation. Here their effect would be to dampen inflationary expectations and enhance the effect of a contractionary monetary or fiscal policy, rather than to reduce wage settlements directly.

8.11 THE GOODS MARKET

8.11.1 Introduction

We have seen from the results in Chapters 6 and 7 that the scope for changes in inflation originating in the domestic goods and services market seems to have been comparatively small. Indeed, this came as no surprise since the role of price-setting had already been identified as being arguably more relevant to the real wage than to inflation (in section 3.2.3).

Nevertheless, by increasing the scope for competition within the goods market the authorities may not only prevent managers in a monopolistic position, or involved in some implicit cartel, from permitting increases in prices that would not have taken place in a competitive industry, they may also prevent them from allowing unnecessary increases in labour costs and passing the effect of these on to the consumer in the form of higher prices. Wage rises are determined through negotiation between firms and unions. If a firm in an industry that contains an element of cartel can pass on increases in labour costs in the form of higher prices, then introducing a greater degree of competition into the goods market may have a significant effect on the outcome of the wage bargain. Thus, it may be possible to reduce inflationary pressure in the labour market indirectly, by means of structural changes to the goods market.

8.11.2 Enhancing competition in goods markets

If firms operate in a highly competitive market they are, to a considerable extent, price takers, and they have little influence on the price they charge: if they exceed the 'going' price they will sell less of their product and may be unable to survive. As a result, competitive firms are unable to be complacent; they have a continual incentive to drive down their own costs relative to those of their competitors while at the same time facing an imperative to maintain the quality of their product.

However, most large industrial firms do not trade in highly competitive markets, rather they operate as oligopolists or monopolists. As such, and within limits, they can dictate the prices at which they sell their goods at least in the short term. These firms have less incentive to take a hard stance in wage bargaining than firms in more competitive industries; they are secure in the knowledge that they can raise their prices by more than their limited number of relatively distant rivals without too drastic an effect on their market share. Thus, the greater the market power that a firm is able to achieve, the less the cost (in terms of lost revenue and market share) it will incur from conceding to wage demands above those that can be justified in terms of the fundamentals. And unnecessarily large wage rises have knock-on effects: for price rises in the firm concerned, for wage bargaining in other industries, and so for price rises elsewhere and for inflation generally.

The case of a cartel is worse. Continual agreement between the decision takers in one industry to raise their prices by more than can reasonably be justified, often in a sector with a very low price elasticity for the demand for its output, will result in a persisting upward pressure on inflation, that is, a non-zero intercept on the price inflation equation.

One policy initiative which could increase competition (and efficiency) in domestic markets would be simply to intensify the attack on cartels. It would involve a substantial increase in the penalties imposed by the Office of Fair Trading on those who make agreements that contravene the Restrictive Trade Practices Act, along with an increase in the OFT's power to seek evidence. The law is far stricter in both the US and the EC than in the UK. In the US companies can be fined up to $10 million if they are judged to have been cheating the public. In EC law (which applies only to international trade) penalties can amount to 10 per cent of turnover. Further, in the EC dawn raids can be made on the offices of suspects to seek evidence, whereas under domestic UK legislation companies are merely requested to submit material to the OFT.

Legislation of this sort would have little effect on the structure of industry, in that it would be unlikely to lead to the breaking up of large conglomerates or to a reduction in concentration (these are determined largely by technology and the optimal size of firms in different industries). It could, however, provide a step in the right direction through the introduction of stricter rules against anti-competitive practices and by doing so reduce the continuing upward pressure on inflation which operates through the wage equation but originates with firms' behaviour.

8.11.3 Price controls

(a) Price caps for individual industries

A form of price regulation that smacks of central planning when applied in the private sector was suggested by Tylecote as early as 1981.[17] It is effectively the same as the '$RPI - X + Y$' of the regulated privatized monopolies. Tylecote argued that the authorities should attempt to operate price controls which mimic the competitive market. Large firms, leaders in their sectors, would have constraints placed on the rate at which they were allowed to increase their prices according to criteria regarding the estimated potential for productivity growth and differential wage norms (the 'X' factor of price regulation). Increases in external costs such as raw materials, which are outside the control of individual firms and have the effect of raising marginal production costs of all the enterprises in an industry, would be passed on to the consumer in the form of higher prices, as is the case in the competitive market (the 'Y' factor). Thus, firms would be prevented from passing on excessive increases in internal costs, which are essentially within its control including, in particular, unjustifiable increases in unit labour costs.

This scheme would involve centrally determined norms for productivity growth. Firms would bargain about wage rises as usual, but their bargaining stance would be drastically altered. Whereas previously they enjoyed the protection of their oligopolistic or monopolistic market and could afford to pass on any premium on the agreed wage rise to the consumer in the form of price increases, awarding pay increases above the norm would now mean an erosion of their profits and could even result in bankruptcy. Their resolution to become tough negotiators would be strengthened. In addition, managers would become more concerned with the efficiency of production and the reduction of costs, for this would be the way in which an increase in profits could be achieved.

There are, of course, a number of objections to a scheme of this nature. One relates to the degree of administrative complexity required to implement and run it. A second is that the level of the constraint (the value of 'X') will always be 'wrong' and subject to dispute. A third objection concerns the way in which this method of price control obscures the working of markets to indicate the relative values placed by society on different goods and services and allocate resources efficiently.

(b) Prices policies

Serious economic distortions can also arise if general price controls, such as might accompany an incomes policy, prevent the realignment of relative prices. For if relative prices cease to reflect the market fundamentals, prices will no longer be useful in conveying information to producers on the value consumers place on their goods. As this occurs, the cost of the intervention, in the form of reduced economic efficiency in the allocation of resources, could outweigh any gains in terms of efficiency or lower inflation from the incentive effects of this form of price control; the policy would then become counterproductive. The enormous burden of efficiency costs which can arise in the long term if distortions such as these are not corrected is graphically illustrated by the Eastern European centrally planned economies where products are regularly in short supply.

Further, even if this type of price control were justifiable in terms of economics, it may be unacceptable politically. To the extent that price controls of this sort exist at present, they are limited to the newly privatized state monopolies. Increasing their scope would be likely to create public mistrust as to how far the state intended to extend its control over industry.

8.12 INFLATION AND THE RETAIL PRICES INDEX

The Retail Prices Index (RPI), the principal domestic index of consumer price inflation, contains a number of elements that are not really appropriate to an indicator of the rate of inflation; they pertain to the RPI's other role, that of indicating the cost of living. Thus the RPI includes the effect of mortgage interest rates, as well as 'administered' prices such as local authority rents. The inclusion of these means that the index does not give, indeed is not intended to give, a picture of the underlying trend in the movements of market-based prices. Instead it is sensitive to changes in policy. In particular, the index picks up an upward shift whenever the government uses interest rates as an instrument with which to control inflation and a compensating downward shift when this policy is reversed (Figures 7.11 and 7A.3).

The effect of these is more than merely inconvenient. Because changes in the RPI are widely used as the basis for the negotiation of pay awards, an increase in interest rates which in no way reflects the trend in market prices for consumers, will feed through on to wages and, through the effect on costs, have an inflationary impact on the Producer Output Price Index. Its effect will then continue to pass around the inflation spiral until it is unwound by a lowering of interest rates.

Omitting mortgage interest rates from the RPI would mean an end to the policy induced **upward** effect on the wage–price spiral that occurs whenever the authorities raise interest rates with the intention of putting **downward** pressure on inflation. Although this would have no permanent effect on the level of inflation, it would reduce the amplitude of the oscillations in inflation that occur, and therefore reduce the uncertainty associated with the path of inflation. Further, to the extent that there is partial price indexation in areas such as pensions, there may be a lasting benefit in reducing the volatility of the inflation rate.

A more profound effect on inflation would be achieved if the role of the RPI could be filled by an indicator of the price rise consistent with full employment, or, in the case of the ERM, with a Europe-wide inflation indicator.

8.13 CHANGES IN REAL COMMODITY PRICES

8.13.1 Introduction

It is clear from the analysis in Chapter 7 that changes in real commodity prices have had a substantial influence on inflation rates in the developed world in recent years. Here there are two issues that need to be addressed: real commodity price volatility, and trend changes in real commodity prices. There is little that one country acting on its own can do about these, and our model has little relevance to these issues.

8.13.2 Commodity price volatility

It is often the case that rapid rises in the prices of primary commodities, putting upward pressure on inflation rates throughout the developed world, are caused by a temporary rise in demand or a temporary supply side shortage. If this is the case, then when the cause ceases to operate the commodity prices will fall back in real terms to the level that operated previously (other things being equal), and this will take developed countries' inflation rates back to the level they would otherwise have been (once the lags have fed through). One policy option would therefore be to tolerate a rise in inflation from such a source until such time as it reverses itself.[18]

However, some argue that the volatility of the market for primary commodities is suboptimal.[19] The benefits of commodity price stability, which include the avoidance of the costs associated with macroeconomic policies to cut inflation, are social benefits not realized by those who hold stocks of storable commodities. They will therefore hold less than would be optimal to prevent volatility. It appears, therefore, that there may be some theoretical justification for government intervention in commodity markets to stabilize price fluctuations.

One way in which price stabilization might be achieved would be through the management of stockpiles of storable primary commodities, 'buffer stocks', by an international agency. The stockpile would be run down or built up in such a way as to equilibrate world demand and supply and hold the price within an acceptable range. This requires a substantial initial outlay of capital to buy the commodities to be held in buffer stocks and, clearly, it can only apply to commodities that are homogenous in nature, non-deteriorating and easy to store.

The most fundamental problem in implementing such a scheme is the difficulty in distinguishing between longer term trends in demand and supply, which generate useful price signals, and movements which simply represent short-term cycles. For example, a buffer stock may be depleted to prevent price increases in what is seen as a temporary period of decreased supply (increase in demand). However, this may mean that larger and more rapid increases in price are required at a later stage when the buffer stock is exhausted and it is realized that, in fact, the supply reduction (demand increase) is sustained. The price change that was damped by intervention may turn out to have been a market signal needed for the stability of the market in the future. The collapse of the tin agreement is good example of this.

8.13.3 Trend changes in real commodity prices

There has been a trend downward effect on inflation in developed countries from primary commodity prices during the last few decades. This is because the cost of production and extraction declines with new technological developments, among other things. However, this will not necessarily be the case in the future. Indeed, there are two reasons why the prices of these goods may create a tendency for upward pressure on finished goods' price-setting in the future. First, as exhaustible resources become scarcer, both the cost of extraction and the rent associated with them (any price premium associated with the increasing scarcity) are likely to rise. Second, the distribution of income between the developed world and the third world may change (as, indeed, it has in regard to oil producing economies). In each of these circumstances there would be a net upward pressure on inflation originating in the markets for primary commodities. This, according to our model, could be of great importance to the determination of the inflation climate in the developed world.

The solution, according to our model, would be for workers in developed countries to accommodate the change in the terms of trade by modifying their real wage expectations. These are implicit in the wage setting process in labour markets of the developed countries according to our model. As real commodity prices rise real labour costs in developed economies need to fall to accommodate the change in terms of trade (the postulated change in income distribution between the developed world and the third world). If this were to take place, the upward and downward pressures on inflation would cancel. However, it is far from clear how this could be achieved.

8.14 CONCLUSIONS

We have reached the following broad conclusions on policy.

The foreign exchange market can only be used temporarily as a direct instrument for controlling inflation. Its longer term potential depends on effects that operate through other markets. Further the data suggest that expectations have little effect on inflation. Given these, any policy to control inflation must be targeted on either the goods and services market (price-setting) or the labour market (wage-setting).

We take the view that, of these, the labour market is the preferable policy target. This is for two reasons. First, the labour market seems to be more responsive to external pressures (Figures 7.9 and 7.11 show the effect of the policy measures in the early 1980s on the two markets). It is very difficult to assess what the equilibrium price of any given type of labour should be at a given time, and this may explain why relatively large shifts in real wages are accommodated in the labour market from time to time. In the goods market, however, given the desire to maximize profits and given knowledge of costs, it is far clearer what the price of a good should be in a balanced market. As a result it seems to be easier to shift wages away from the level a freely operating market would set in equilibrium than it is to shift prices away from the level the firm would choose in normal market conditions.

Second, it seems likely that the damage caused by downward pressure in the labour market is less lastingly harmful than that caused by downward pressure in the goods market. In the labour market there might, perhaps, be a temporary loss of real earnings for most workers along with some temporary distortions in relative earnings from those implied by the interaction of demand and supply in the market. In the goods and services market such downward pressure might lead to the scrapping of economically viable machinery, that is, to the permanent wastage of economic resources.

A choice remains. So long as there is an adequate 'levels' effect, inflation can be squeezed out of the system by creating high unemployment (excess supply in the labour market) and holding unemployment high while inflation falls. This is the procedure that is implied by the 'once-removed' type of anti-inflationary strategy that targets money supply growth or nominal exchange rate stability and then uses fiscal and monetary policy to ensure that targets are met.

Alternatively, inflation can be attacked more directly. Wage bargainers could be encouraged to use a 'full employment' inflation indicator in place of the RPI. Alternatively, an incomes policy will put a direct downward pressure on nominal wage settlements. Throughout the period during which the incomes policy operates, when inflation is falling progressively further below the level it would otherwise have taken, the real wage is likely to be lower than it would otherwise have been (and profits higher). This will only be effective if sufficient cooperation can be coaxed from those concerned.

Which of these is most likely to succeed? Which is least costly? Both of these questions involve judgements that are beyond the scope of this book.

REFERENCES

Alesina, A. and Summers, L. (1991) Central bank independence and macroeconomic performance: some comparative evidence, Harvard Institute of Economic Research Discussion Paper No. 1496.

Barrell, R. (1990) Has the EMS changed wage and price behaviour in Europe? *National Institute Economic Review*, 117, 64–72.

Baumol, W. J. and Quandt, R. E. (1964) Rules of thumb and optimally imperfect decisions, *The American Economic Review*, 54, 23–46.

Beckerman, W. and Jenkinson, T. (1986) What stopped the inflation? Unemployment or commodity prices? *The Economic Journal*, 96, 39–54.

Bird, P. J. W. N. (1983) Tests for a threshold effect in the price–cost relationship, *Cambridge Journal of Economics*, 7, 37–53.

Blanchard, O. L. and Summers, L. H. (1986) Hysteresis and the European unemployment problem, *National Bureau of Economic Research Working Paper No. 1950*.

Bosworth, B. P. and Lawrence, R. Z. (1982) *Commodity Prices and the New Inflation*, Brookings Institution, Washington, DC.

Bruno, M. and Sachs, J. (1985) *Economics of Worldwide Stagflation*, Basil Blackwell, Oxford.

Foster, N., Henry, S. G. B. and Trinder, C. (1984) Public and private sector pay: a partly disaggregated study, *National Institute Economic Review*, 107, 63–73.

Friedman, M. (1968) The role of monetary policy, *The American Economic Review*, 58, 1–17.

Gardner, N. (1990) *In the ERM; Achieving Full Employment in the 90's*, Campaign for Work, Research Report, Vol. 2, No. 7.

Gordon, R. J. (1985) Understanding inflation in the 1980s, *Brookings Papers on Economic Activity*, 1, 263–99.

Hirsch, F. and Goldthorpe, J. H. (1978) *The Political Economy of Inflation*, Martin Robertson, Oxford.

Layard, P. R. G., Baevi, G., Blanchard, O., Buiter, W. H. and Dornbusch, R. (1984) Europe: the case for unsustainable growth, Centre for European Policy Studies, Paper 8/9.

Layard, R. and Nickell, S. (1986) *An Incomes Policy to Help the Unemployed*, Employment Institute, London.

Muth, J. F. (1961) Rational expectations and the theory of price movements, *Econometrica*, 29, 315–35.

Okun, A. M. (1978) Effective disinflationary policies, *American Economic Review*, 68, 348–52.

Phelps, E. S. (1967) Phillips curves, expectations of inflation and optimal unemployment over time, *Economica*, 34, 254–81.

Shiller, R. J. (1978) Rational expectations and the dynamic structure of macroeconomic models, *Journal of Monetary Economics*, 4, 1–44.

Smith, J. G. (1990) *Pay Strategy for the 1990s: Inflation, Jobs and the ERM*, Institute for Public Policy Research, Economic Study No. 8.

Tylecote, A. (1981) *The Causes of the Present Inflation*, The Macmillan Press, London and Basingstoke.

Wallis, K. F. (ed.) (1987) *Models of the UK Economy*, Oxford University Press, Oxford.

ENDNOTES

1. The papers in Hirsch and Goldthorpe (1978), for example, as well as Beckerman and Jenkinson (1986), Gordon (1985) and others.
2. Chapter 3, note 5.
3. Blanchard and Summers (1986).
4. It has often been the case that a sustained rise in unemployment is not associated with a decline in inflation. A recent example concerns the effect on inflation in France and Italy of the rise in unemployment associated with complying with the ERM during the period since 1983. Economists have tended to explain this type of outcome in terms of a rise in the NAIRU (e.g., Layard *et al.*, 1984).
5. The president of the Bundesbank is appointed by government for an eight year period.
6. E.g., Alesina and Summers (1991).
7. Barrell (1990).
8. There is not yet any sign of the inward shift in the short-term unemployment–inflation trade-off predicted by the EAPC.
9. This can be seen by writing the adaptive expectations hypothesis for today's expectations $(\Delta_t p_{t+1}^e)$ of future price rises (Δp_{t+1}) in the form:

$$\Delta_t p_{t+1}^e = \Delta_{t-1} p_t^e + \mu(\Delta p_t - \Delta_{t-1} p_t^e) + u_t$$

where $1 > \mu > 0$ and u_t is a normally distributed random residual. This can be expressed as:

$$[1 - (1-\mu)L]\Delta_t p_{t+1}^e = \mu \Delta p_t + u_t$$

(where L is the lag operator) and rewritten in the form:

$$\Delta_t p_{t+1}^e = \mu \sum_{i=0}^{\infty} (1-\mu)^i L^i \Delta p_t + \sum_{i=0}^{\infty} (1-\mu)^i L^i u_t$$

10. E.g., Phelps (1967), and Friedman (1968).
11. Muth (1961) has an early exposition of the idea, and Shiller (1978) a helpful summary.
12. A switch from income tax to VAT or *vice versa* will obviously have a temporary effect on measured price inflation. However, the effect of the retention ratio on wage settlements should mean that lower rises in labour costs offset the effect of the VAT rise on final goods' prices in the long term (apart from any remaining money illusion).
13. A dummy variable included in the wage equation to pick up the effect of this on the magnitude of the intercept to the equation is found to vary in sign and significance depending on the precise timing with which it is specified.
14. Bruno and Sachs (1985) give an excellent empirical description of the effect of corporatism on OECD wage setting.
15. There are suggestions along these lines in Smith (1990) and in the papers in Gardner (1990).
16. Prices will rise by less as a result of the lower increase in nominal wages. Indeed, price increases will be moderated sufficiently to bring the real wage back into line with the 'fundamentals'. By the year's end, therefore, the real wage will have returned to the value it would have taken in the absence of the policy. The loss of real wage growth is therefore roughly equal to half of the reduction in nominal wage growth at the time of the wage settlement.
17. Tylecote (1981).
18. There is some evidence supporting an asymmetric effect on price inflation from commodity markets (Bird 1983).
19. E.g., Bosworth and Lawrence (1982).

9

Summary and conclusion

9.1 INTRODUCTION

The purpose of this chapter is to draw together and summarize the most important results and conclusions.

9.2 THE WORKING OF THE INFLATION SPIRAL

Our main objective has been to describe the way the inflation spiral in the UK works. In this task we start from the proposition that inflation results from the interaction of markets over time. Increases in prices cause increases in wages which, in their turn, cause further increases in prices. Increases in domestic prices put downward pressure on the exchange rate. A fall in the exchange rate produces increases in the prices of imported goods and so leads to further increases in domestic prices. These feed-backs are modelled in Chapters 2, 3 and 4.

We have found that, if there is no money illusion in any of these markets so each of these feed-backs automatically has full inflation indexation, then any temporary domestic pressure that leads to faster price rises produces an enduring rise in inflation. Any temporary disinflationary pressure, in the same way, produces an enduring fall in inflation (Chapter 5). Furthermore, a continuing (net) inflationary pressure, such as might arise from persistent real wage pressure in the labour market, will lead to accelerating inflation, other things being equal. Eventually this would result in extreme price instability or hyperinflation (Chapters 5 and 6). The control of inflation is therefore a serious issue.

There is no direct role for money growth in any of the structural equations for price setting derived in Chapters 2, 3 and 4. There remains a possibility that money growth affects the price expectations of those who negotiate in the labour market, or of speculators in the foreign exchange market, and that these influence the inflation outcome. But even if the *a priori* case for such a role for the money supply were not so unconvincing, and were supported by the casual empiricism of hearsay and newspaper reports, the data currently available suggest that price expectations have little influence on inflation. It seems that it is mainly the published RPI figures that affect wage settlements, not price expectations, and there is no empirical support for a price expectations effect on the exchange rate. An indirect role for monetary policy certainly exists, since this will influence all the aspects of activity that impinge upon the spiral.

In normal circumstances an increase in domestic demand, that is, an outward movement of the demand schedule, will lead to a greater rise (or a smaller fall) in both output and prices than would otherwise have been the case. A fall in demand, an inward shift in the demand schedule, will have the opposite effect and lead to a decrease in both output and prices (or a smaller increase than would otherwise have taken place). It follows that the underlying level of inflation is not necessarily affected by fluctuations in the level of demand as any upward pressure in an upswing will be broadly offset by downward pressure in a downswing. However, overheating, an increase in demand which leads to bottlenecks, will result in a disproportionate rise in prices. This will produce a ratchet effect, with the exaggerated increase in inflation which takes place every time overheating occurs not offset by a symmetric decrease when demand returns to normal levels (Figure 2.2).

It would be difficult to avoid implementing a macroeconomic policy that had a risk of this occurring from time to time. It is therefore essential to have a policy for dealing with the high rates of inflation that come about as a result of such policy hiccoughs.

One way of preventing the full inflationary effect of a bout of domestic inflationary pressure from being seen in the actual inflation rate is to hold the exchange rate up by raising domestic interest rates relative to those abroad. Besides the automatic downward pressure in the domestic goods market engendered by this policy, it will prevent the rise in import prices in domestic currency that would result if the exchange rate moved to maintain purchasing power parity. If this is done, the feed-through of domestic inflation from one period to the next will be less than complete, and the rise in inflation following a phase of upward pressure will die away instead of persisting. Lower inflation will, effectively, have been imported from abroad (Chapter 5).

Unless a countervailing domestic disinflationary pressure deals with the original problem at source, the result of this policy will be a loss of international competitiveness that will increase the current account deficit (or reduce the surplus). This means that there will be a larger inflow of funds on capital account than would otherwise have been the case, attracted by the high expected return. This continuing inward investment by foreigners will lead to a gradually increasing outflow of interest, profits and dividends and, in the longer term, this will need to be financed by a trade account surplus. At some point the increasing disequilibrium in asset allocation implied by this strategy will need to cease. For this reason, unless relative prices adjust, the exchange rate will eventually need to fall to reinstate competitiveness. Indeed, the exchange rate may need to be below the *ex ante* market clearing level for a period, so the current account and capital account disequilibria will be such as to unwind the net balances held by foreigners (Chapter 4).

This situation is analogous to preventing the flow of water down a hill by building a dam. The water (potential price rises) builds up behind the dam (a high exchange rate). While the dam is holding back an increasing volume of water the flow down the hill (the price rises) will be less than would otherwise have been the case. However, the build up behind the dam (the foreigners' balances) cannot continue for ever. At some point the lake must stop increasing in depth (there must be a return to purchasing power parity). Further, at some point the level of the lake must return to an equilibrium level (the balances must fall again). When that happens, if the level of the water has not been reduced by other means (eg. disinflationary domestic measures, enhanced by the effect of the high exchange rate), the delayed flow down the hill (price rises) will take place.

9.3 THE LIKELY CAUSE OF A RISE IN INFLATION

9.3.1 Introduction

The next question addressed concerns the likely cause of a rise in domestic inflation. The theoretical analysis (Chapter 5) implies that if the domestic economy is in equilibrium its inflation rate follows that of the countries with which it trades reflecting, in particular, the effect of any upward pressure in the world market for primary commodities (Figure 7.5). Any enduring variation from this is caused by the cumulated effect of upward and downward pressures on price margins either in the domestic goods and services market or in the domestic labour market. Deviations from the *ex ante* market clearing level of the domestic exchange rate will produce effects on inflation which, though necessarily reversed in the very long term, can persist for considerable lengths of time.

9.3.2 The domestic market in goods and services

Apart from the important exception of overheating, the domestic market in goods and services seems to have somewhat less potential for generating inflationary pressures than the labour market (sections 3.2.3 and 2.6, and Chapter 7). Thus, activity variables, and the other pressures on margins in these markets, appear generally to have had a larger impact on inflation when they operate through the labour market rather than through the market in goods and services (Figures 7.9 and 7.11). Indeed, the analysis in Chapter 7 suggests that, apart from the incident in 1980/81, the activity effects in the goods market had a relatively small influence on the rate of inflation during the fifteen years examined.

This may reflect the fundamental nature of the two markets, or it may be the result of policy initiatives during the period. It may be that imposing a temporary squeeze on profit margins is more likely to inflict serious long-term damage to the productive potential of the economy than a squeeze on real wages. According to our model (Chapters 2 and 3), the level of activity at which inflation 'takes off' is determined partly by the productive capacity of the economy (through the capacity term in the price equation) as well being influenced by excess demand in the labour market. Thus, each time a recession is so sharp that it causes potentially viable productive capacity in the economy to be written off, there is a danger that in the next upturn bottlenecks are reached at a lower level of activity. This possibility may have influenced the design of anti-inflation policies, leading to a greater pressure being put on the real wage than on profit margins whenever there has been an attempt to squeeze inflation out of the system.

An obvious effect of damaging the productive potential of the economy is that inflation would begin to ratchet up at a higher level of unemployment after each cycle. This could be interpreted as signalling that there has been a rise in the NAIRU which requires adjustments to the labour market, when in fact the cause is a lack of productive capacity in the goods market.

9.3.3 The domestic labour market

Chapter 7 suggests there may generally be more potential for inflationary pressure to originate in the labour market than in the goods market. Pressure in the labour market can have a number of causes. The conventional wisdom (the Phillips curve) that suggests that it is always related to excess demand (the deviation of unemployment from its market clearing level) is an over-simplification. Anything that holds the *ex ante* real wage above the level warranted by labour productivity, taxes and the terms of trade will give an upward boost to inflation: prices will respond to the increase in costs implied by an unrealistic nominal wage rise by rising by more than they otherwise would have done and the effect will continue round the spiral.

We have seen (Chapter 3) that the likely causes of a high *ex ante* real wage include a wide range of market imperfections. Excessive union bargaining power is the most obvious. A wage bargaining structure that encourages leapfrogging is another. Others include the monopoly (or cartel-based) power of firms to pass on the cost of a wage rise to consumers, and anything that provides a firm with an incentive to pay more than its rivals in order to keep its personnel.

9.3.4 World markets in primary commodities

Chapter 7 indicates the important role world markets in primary commodities play in generating inflation in developed economies. The causes of inflation escalation which originate in the markets for primary commodities include mismatches of demand and supply and increases in the cost of supply. An excess demand may arise from a conjunction of business cycles in the developed world (as in the early 1970s), from an institutional change in the provision of the supply (the establishment of OPEC) or from some supply side disaster (a poor harvest, for example).

9.3.5 Conclusion

The most likely causes of inflation seem generally to be: an increase in primary commodity prices feeding in from world markets; the effect of a number of different factors that operate in the domestic labour market; and the effect of overheating (bottlenecks) on price-setting in the domestic goods and services market. In the UK during the period studied, 1970 to 1985, the main causes seem to have been commodity price volatility and real wage aspirations in the labour market.

9.4 POLICY SUGGESTIONS

9.4.1 Avoiding high inflation

Next we consider what policies the model suggests are necessary to maintain inflation at an acceptably low level. Given the analysis of Chapter 7 the clear starting point is to try to ensure that the labour market is not structured in such a way as to encourage or permit nominal wage settlements in excess of the rate implied by the whole economy productivity growth, the terms of trade and the level of taxes (section 8.9). One way of doing this might be to encourage wage negotiations to centre around an inflation index consistent with full employment, such as a Europe-wide price index, instead of the RPI.

Second, in order to prevent the domestic inflation rate from becoming unacceptably high, it is clearly important that the government avoid over-heating the economy (section 8.3).

Third, if it becomes necessary to induce a recession in order to cure a bout of domestic inflation then, in order to avoid a tendency to high inflation in the future, it is important that it should not be too violent or too deep, so that the fabric of the economy, its productive potential, is not damaged. Too stringent a recession may reduce the capacity of the economy to produce at full employment in the future without reaching bottlenecks and creating upward pressure on inflation. Thus, too powerful an anti-inflation policy today may be part of the 'cause' of tomorrow's bout of inflationary pressure (section 8.2.4).

Fourth, it is clearly important not to allow inflation to get so far out of line with that of the trading partners that foreign exchange market operators come to expect inflation indexation of the exchange rate. If this occurs, any inflationary pressure in the domestic economy will run straight through into price rises creating a volatile inflation rate. Further, any increase in inflation will remain in the system until offset by a painful countervailing downward pressure (sections 6.4 and 8.5.4).

9.4.2 To cure high inflation

Finally there is the question of how best to reduce the rate of inflation when it has got out of control. We have seen that policies that operate solely through the foreign exchange market, and have no labour or goods market effects, can have only a temporary effect; and that there is little evidence of an effect of expectations on inflation, so policies that rely on influencing expectations are unlikely to be successful. We are left with policies that operate primarily through the goods and services and/or the labour market.

The potential for successful downward pressure on price-setting in the goods market appears to be limited. This would either involve implementing a prices policy: restricting price rises to create lower real profits (the goods market counterpart of an incomes policy, in which nominal wage increases are restricted to create lower real wages); or, it would mean establishing a situation (a high real exchange rate, for example, or a recession) in which profits were automatically squeezed.

A prices policy might lead to serious distortions: it would prevent relative prices from moving to reflect the changing tastes of consumers and so could bankrupt firms that are economically efficient and would be viable and provide employment in normal circumstances. It could damage the fabric of the economy.

A policy which creates an effective squeeze on profits without damaging the productive potential is not easy to implement. First, either a recession or a high exchange rate will squeeze margins to some extent, but our model suggests that in each case the main part of the effect on inflation is reversible and will be cancelled by the effect of expanding margins when the policy initiating the squeeze ceases. Second, too stringent a squeeze on profit margins will again damage the productive capacity in the economy, so that inflation is likely to take off again, and at a lower level of activity, when the downward pressure is released.

Virtually the only way, therefore, for the authorities to create a long term reduction in domestic inflation is to persuade the labour market to accept, for a period of some years, an *ex ante* real wage that is lower than would otherwise have been the case given labour productivity, the level of taxes and the terms of trade. Indeed, it can be argued that a main aim of any fiscal or monetary contractionary policy is to squeeze inflation out of the system by creating a situation in which employees are prepared to accept nominal wage rises low enough to result in a fall in the real wage. This being so, the remaining question is how best to achieve a temporary reduction in the real wage.

(a) Deflating the economy may not work and inflicts pain

We have seen (section 8.2.3) that it is the precise form of the dependence of wage-setting (and price-setting) on the level of excess demand that determines whether deflation cures inflation or merely creates a temporary respite. If the **change** in the real wage depends on the **level** of excess demand, then inflation will be falling all the time demand is held (by the authorities) below the equilibrium level. When demand is allowed to rise again to the market clearing level there will be a small increase in the rate of inflation (other things being equal) but this will only cancel the fall associated with the original decrease in demand; the fall in inflation that took place while demand was held low will persist.

On the other hand, if the **change** in the real wage depends on the **change** in demand, then inflation will remain constant while a recession is in operation (apart from the feed-through of lags): any reduction in inflation observed during the onset of the recession will be reversed during the period of expansion at the end of the recession.

Both theory and data fail to distinguish clearly between these two hypotheses (Chapter 3). This means that the pain we suffer as government after government deflates the economy and creates a recession to squeeze inflation out of the system, possibly by holding the nominal exchange rate constant, may be suffered in vain. Further, the damage caused to the fabric of the economy during these recessions may make it inevitable that, in the future, inflationary bottlenecks are reached before unemployment is reduced to an acceptable level.

(b) A counter-inflationary macroeconomic framework

There have been many attempts to create a macroeconomic framework that will put automatic downward pressure on both price-setting and nominal wage settlements. One of the characteristics of the monetarism of the early 1980s was the authorities' belief that an announcement concerning the target growth of the money supply would influence the inflation expectations of wage bargainers. This lost credibility as the money supply failed to conform to Treasury and other forecasts. Further, econometric analysis supports the view that wage negotiations have continued to be based on the latest published figures for the RPI (Chapter 3).

One of the stated purposes of entry into the ERM is, again, to put downward pressure on wage settlements. As manufacturers of tradable goods find their product is becoming uncompetitive in domestic and world markets, their margins will be squeezed and they will increasingly exert downward pressure on their costs. This will feed beneficial influences into the domestic labour market. But such firms will have increasing difficulty in hiring high quality personnel, and this may be reflected in a decline in the relative quality of domestic traded goods in the longer term (section 8.4.3).

(c) Incomes policy may be better, more effective and less painful

We have argued that every viable anti-inflation policy operates, in the main, either directly or indirectly, through downward pressure in the labour market. This being so, it seems reasonable to ask whether the objective of temporary lower real wages might be achieved with less pain if it were approached directly: by replacing the role of the RPI in wage bargaining by an agreed 'norm' or by an indicator of other countries' inflation rates.

If the labour market could be restructured in such a way as to minimize the potential for the leapfrogging effect – if it enabled a nationally agreed 'norm' to be agreed, an inflation tax to be imposed if necessary and, indeed, an incomes policy to be used as a last resort – then the UK might find itself in a situation in which it had some control over its inflation rate.

9.4.3 Conclusion

We have reached two main conclusions regarding anti-inflation policy: we believe such a policy would still be needed if the UK were to enter a single currency Europe.

- First, the policy of reducing high inflation by creating a recession needs careful review. The evidence suggests that much, maybe all, of its effect on the inflation rate is merely temporary, reversed when activity expands. Further, this policy may make higher inflation more likely; it might reduce the productive capital in the economy so that full employment cannot then be achieved in the shorter term without inflation accelerating.
- Second, virtually all policies to reduce inflation operate through a temporary reduction in the real wage. This objective could be addressed more directly if the wage bargaining machinery was restructured to allow for the possibility of intervention by the authorities or if wage bargaining centred around a European inflation measure instead of the RPI.

If, in addition to fiscal policy and monetary policy, the government could influence the broad level of wage settlements, it could then manage all aspects of the macroeconomy effectively.

Index